State Level Public Enterprises in India

Published by
ACADEMIC FOUNDATION
in association with

Institute of Public Enterprise

R.K. Mishra, Sr. Professor and Director, Institute of Public Enterprise (IPE), Hyderabad, India, is a graduate of International Management Program, SDA Boccioni, Milan. He has been a Fellow of British Council and Commonwealth Secretariat and a Task Force Member on Memorandum of Understanding (MoU) by Department of Public Enterprises (DPE) for Corporate Social Responsibility (CSR) and Sustainable Development. He is a member of the UN Task Force on International Task Force on Standards of Excellence in Public Administration and Education and is associated with the United Nations Development Programme (UNDP) project on 'Macro-Economics of Poverty Reduction' carried out by RBI's Indira Gandhi Institute of Development Research (IGIDR). He has handled assignments for the Union Ministries of Finance, Power, Heavy Industries, Trade and Commerce, Heavy Industry and Public Enterprises, and Disinvestment. He has prolifically published many articles and books and conducted several training programmes in this area.

Ch. Lakshmi Kumari is Assistant Professor in the area of Economics at IPE, Hyderabad. She is a resource faculty to various MBA programmes. She is presently working on the database on State Level Public Enterprises. She has been associated with various research projects in the area of public enterprises and has organised a number of training programmes.

K. Srinivas is an assistant professor at IPE, Hyderabad. He has published more than 20 research papers in national and international journals of repute. He is Post Graduate in Economics from Andhra University and summer course in economics at CERGE–EL, Charles University, Czech Republic. His areas of interest include applied economics with special reference to social and economic development, technology management and innovations, public enterprises, issues in development economics and public policy.

State Level Public Enterprises in India

Performance and Prospects

R.K. Mishra,
Ch. Lakshmi Kumari
and K. Srinivas

ACADEMIC FOUNDATION
NEW DELHI

www.academicfoundation.com

First published in 2014
by

ACADEMIC FOUNDATION
4772-73 / 23 Bharat Ram Road, (23 Ansari Road),
Darya Ganj, New Delhi - 110 002 (India).
Phones : 23245001 / 02 / 03 / 04.
Fax : +91-11-23245005.
E-mail : books@academicfoundation.com
www.academicfoundation.com

in association with
Institute of Public Enterprise, Hyderabad

Disclaimer:
The findings/views/opinions expressed in this book are solely those of the authors and do not necessarily reflect the views of the publisher.

Cataloging in Publication Data--DK
Courtesy: D.K. Agencies (P) Ltd. <docinfo@dkagencies.com>

Mishra, R. K., 1948-
State level public enterprises in India : performance and prospects / R.K. Mishra, Ch. Lakshmi Kumari and K. Srinivas.
p. cm.
Includes bibliographical references (p.).
ISBN 9789332701564

1. Government business enterprises--India--States. I. Title.

DDC 338.620954 23

Typeset by Italics India, New Delhi.

Printed and bound by The Book Mint, New Delhi.
www.thebookmint.in

Contents

Part II

State-wise Scenario: Performance of State Level Public Enterprises

List of Tables and Figures

Tables

Figures

Preface

The state level public sector enterprises (SLPEs) are fascinating entities. These institutions are set up for the development of infrastructure in different states and union territories (UTs). Their role in social and economic development has been discussed in many forums. Their contribution in bringing about economic improvement and social welfare has been analysed by various researchers, academicians and economists. In India, there are about 853 working SLPEs, which extent their contribution to national growth. These enterprises had registered a phenomenal growth during the period 1961-1985. There have been both economic and social objectives behind the establishment of SLPEs. The SLPEs have been set up by different states to provide direct and indirect employment to people, leading to development of a particular region, and create wealth for the nation in general.

The broad structure of the book is as follows: Part I discusses the "macro view" which contains information on the growth and performance of SLPEs in various states and UTs covering their objectives, form of organisation, functional classification, investment, employment, profitability, grants/subsidies received by the SLPEs at the all-India and at the aggregate (state) levels, and dimensions of performance. Part II on 'State-wise Scenario of SLPEs' offers a discussion on the growth and development of SLPEs state wise, and contains analysis of basic financial data, top profit and loss making institutions, employment, budgetary support received by SLPEs and their contribution to state's gross domestic product (GDP). The performance of these enterprises varies from state to state based on the socioeconomic and political philosophy of each state and also the degree of professionalisation of their managerial personnel.

The book reveals that a large number of SLPEs were established for important tasks of social and economic development. But their performance has been far below expectations. The book highlights the gap between expectations and achievements and suggests that more information on SLPEs should be generated and research should be focused to develop greater understanding of their potential, problems and prospects.

The book will be highly useful to policy makers, civil servants, financial institutions, financial advisors, academicians and researchers in management, economics, commerce, public administration and law. It will also be useful to the masters and doctoral research students.

— R.K. Mishra

Introduction

The state level public enterprises (SLPEs) were set up specially to meet the gaps in the social and economic development, such as industrial growth, employment creation, health, education and provision of amenities. Services like electricity, medical care, transportation, irrigation, tourism, warehousing and water facilities reached people in far-off places due to public enterprises. Over the years the central enterprises have been the subject of study and discussion, the SLPEs however have remained unexplored.

The SLPEs in India owe their origin to features like inheritance from the princely states, the practice of utilising local resources for local needs and to fulfill the states' responsibilities towards the people. A number of enterprises were incorporated under different Five Year Plans. During the First and the Second Five Year Plan periods, on an average, six enterprises were established per year. The highest number of enterprises were set up during the Fourth and Fifth Five Year Plan periods.

These enterprises are classified into five categories, such as financial, manufacturing, promotional, utility and welfare enterprises. As on March 31, 2008, there were around 853 working SLPEs in India, as per the information from the Comptroller and Auditor General (CAG) of India. Kerala occupies first place in terms of the number of working SLPEs in the country. West Bengal and Karnataka occupies the second and third places respectively. About 34 per cent of the SLPEs are from the promotional sector followed by 29 per cent and 23 per cent in the manufacturing and the utilities sectors respectively. Of the 853 SLPEs, 47 per cent were profit-making enterprises and 42 per cent incurred losses. Accounts of about 11 per cent of SLPEs were not finalised and a few even did not initiate the process of finalising their accounts. Their contribution to GDP (ratio of turnover to GDP) was estimated at about 7.11 per cent in 2007-08.

The total investment in these enterprises stood at ₹ 3,13,268.89 crore in 2007-08 with a major contribution of 60.13 per cent coming from the long-term loans and 39.87 per cent from the paid-up capital. The major portion of the total investment is shared by Karnataka, Gujarat, Uttar Pradesh and Maharashtra. The numbers of employees in SLPEs increased from 18 lakh in 2006-07 to 19.2 lakh in 2007-08. Andhra Pradesh stood first in terms of having highest manpower in the SLPEs and was also ranked first in turnover and third in investment in the SLPEs.

The enterprises in Gujarat, Karnataka and Orissa are among the top profit-making enterprises. The states of Karnataka, Kerala and Tamil Nadu have the highest number of enterprises which make profits and were ranked first, second and third respectively in 2007-08. Kerala, West Bengal and Assam had the highest number of loss making state enterprises in India. Karnataka, Kerala, Tamil Nadu, etc., have adopted various policy measures to strengthen the SLPEs. Karnataka is assisting the enterprises in upgrading the technologies and restructuring the enterprises. Similarly, Kerala has adopted a 'Ten Point's Success Formula' for restructuring the enterprises. Therefore, it is suggestible that the successful models can be replicated in other states to make the SLPEs more efficient and productive.

Research Methodology and Data Variables

Both primary as well as secondary data sources were used for the study. Primary method involves collection of data through a standard questionnaire. The questionnaire has been circulated to all the SLPEs in view of collecting the information on their performance over the last three years. The parameters for analysis considered for this study include: total investment, capital employed, turnover, net profit/loss, accumulated profit/loss, number of employees, total return on capital employed, percentage of total return on capital employed and subsidies/grants.

Part I

Macro View

1

State Level Public Enterprises in India

Development and Performance

Introduction

The state level public enterprises (SLPEs) constitute an important segment in the Indian public enterprise system (Sankar *et al.*, 1990). These enterprises were set up within the ambit of the states of the union. As envisaged in Article 246 of the Constitution of India, the states started to set up public enterprises as an instrument of public policy to fulfill their socioeconomic objectives. The diverse activities that these enterprises undertook ranged from manufacturing, promotional, financial and utilities to welfare-oriented. The SLPEs were set up specially to meet the gaps in the social and economic development, such as industrial growth, employment creation, health, education and provision of amenities. Services like electricity, medical care, transportation, irrigation, tourism, warehousing and water facilities reached people in far-off places due to public enterprises. The policy of mixed economy led to the creation of a large number of SLPEs. A number of SLPEs were incorporated during different Five Year Plans under the Companies Act, 1956, Societies Act, 1912, through the acts passed in the state legislatures.

The SLPEs are numerous and engaged in activities which have closer impact on the lives of people. They differ with the central enterprises in terms of size of investment and turnover (Maheshwari, 1981). Over the years, the central enterprises have been the subject of study and discussion, whereas the SLPEs have remained unexplored (*Eleventh Five Year Plan 2007-2012*, Planning Commission, Government of India). The purpose of this volume is to study the development and performance of these enterprises. This chapter makes an attempt to discuss some of the salient issues like the classification, strategy, structure and performance. In order to achieve the objectives set out, the SLPEs have been classified into certain broad categories. The data and information used in this chapter has been obtained from the Comptroller & Auditor General (CAG) (Commercial) India, Department of Public Enterprise, GoI, and various state development reports by the Planning Commission and the valuable database on State Level Public Enterprises at the Institute of Public Enterprise, Hyderabad.

The structure of the chapter is as follows. Section I discusses the origin, objectives and overview of SLPEs in India. Sections II and III provide brief description of data and analysis of SLPEs in various states. Section IV ends the chapter with some concluding remarks.

I

Origin, Objectives and Overview of SLPEs

Mishra (2006) described that the growth of SLPEs is attributed to historical factors rather than ideological considerations. The SLPEs in India owe their origin to features like inheritance from the princely states, the practice of utilising local resources to meet local needs and to fulfill the responsibility of the states towards its citizens. Mishra (2006) also averred that some of the enterprises have started with a view to utilise the locally available raw materials like lime stone for cement or silica for glass works, clay for ceramics, bamboo for paper, etc.

The basic objectives of setting up of SLPEs are described by Sankar *et al.* (1989). According to them: (i) large number of SLPEs were set up as public organisations to take advantage of long-term institutional funding from financial institutions and development banks; (ii) many SLPEs were set up, in pursuance of the enactments by the central government to make the states as the partners; (iii) a considerable chunk of the SLPEs have seen the light of the day on account of the decisions of the various state governments to assume the entrepreneurial responsibilities in controlling inflation, equitable distribution of scarce commodities, mopping up of monopoly profits, and to create job opportunities, and to exploit local resources.

Figure 1.1

Plan-wise Growth of SLPEs

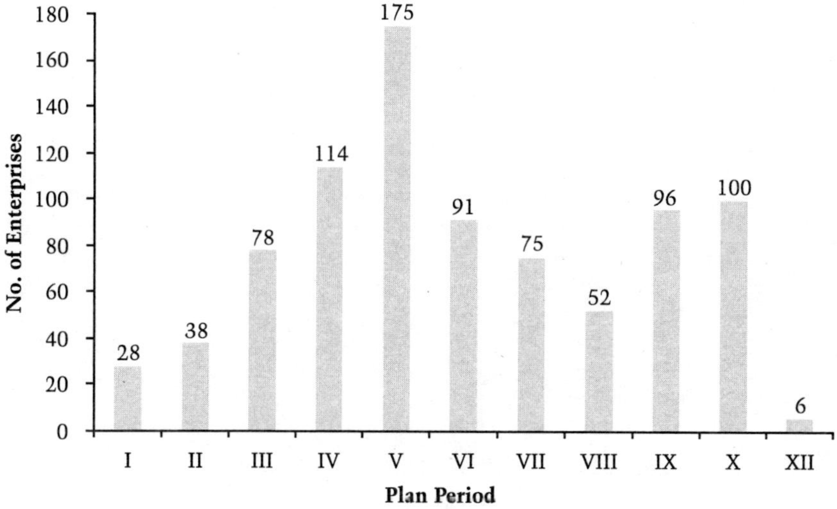

Source: CAG (Commercial) India, 2007-08.

A number of enterprises were incorporated under different Five Year Plans (Figure 1.1). During the First and the Second Five Year Plan periods, on an average, six enterprises were established per year. The highest number of enterprises were set up during the Fourth and Fifth Plan periods. Nearly 20 per cent of the enterprises were set up during the Fifth Plan in Kerala (23), Uttar Pradesh (21) and Tamil Nadu (16). Figure 1.2 shows the plan-wise growth of SLPEs in India. During 1961-1980, the SLPEs got expanded substantially in Andhra Pradesh, Gujarat, Haryana, Himachal Pradesh, Kerala, Maharashtra, Orissa, Punjab, Bihar, Uttar Pradesh and Rajasthan. On the other hand, in the states like Assam, Nagaland, Mizoram, Manipur, Tripura and Arunachal Pradesh, the growth of SLPEs started after 1980s (Sankar *et al.*, 1989).

Figure 1.2

Top 10 States in Terms of Working SLPEs

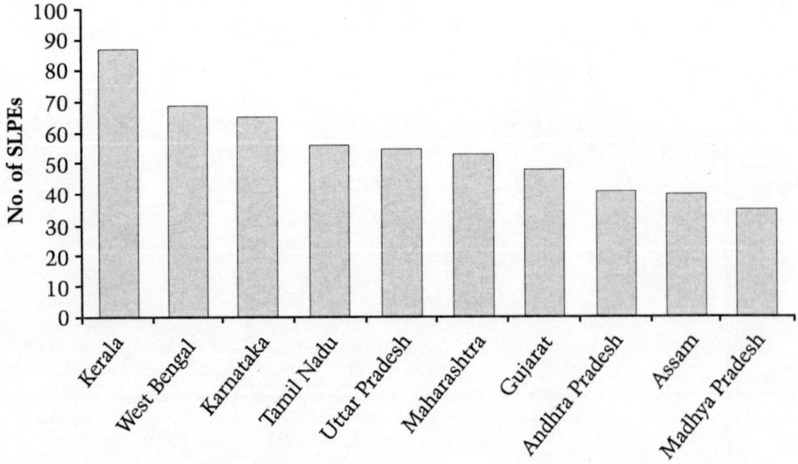

Source: CAG (Commercial) India, 2007-08.

There is no regular survey carried out for SLPEs (*Eleventh Five Year Plan 2007-12*, Planning Commission, GoI). As on March 31, 2008, there were around 853 working SLPEs in India, as per the information from the CAG, India. Kerala occupies the first place in terms of the number of working SLPEs in the country. West Bengal and Karnataka occupy the second and third places respectively. Out of the total working SLPEs, 398 were profit-making units and 354 were incurring losses. The SLPEs' contribution to the country's GDP stood at 7.11 per cent in 2007-08. The total investment in SLPEs was ₹ 3,13,268.89 crore in 2007-08, a major contribution of 60.13 per cent from the long-term loans and 39.87 per cent from the paid-up capital. The number of employees in these SLPEs was 19.2 lakh in 2007-08.

Categorisation of SLPEs

These enterprises are classified into five categories: financial, manufacturing, promotional, utility and welfare enterprises. Table 1.1 depicts the main aim behind starting the enterprises in the respective categories and the states having highest number of enterprises.

Table 1.1

Typology of SLPEs

Type of Sector	*Major Aim*	*States with Highest Nos.*
Manufacturing	The manufacturing enterprises dominated the scenario because various state governments emulated the central government in giving a fillip to industrialisation.	Andhra Pradesh, Assam, Gujarat, Karnataka, Kerala, Maharashtra, Tamil Nadu, Uttar Pradesh and West Bengal
Financial	The financial enterprises received an encouragement to provide financial thrust and create a suitable infrastructure at the state level.	Andhra Pradesh, Assam, Gujarat, Karnataka, Kerala, Maharashtra, Tamil Nadu, Uttar Pradesh and West Bengal
Promotional	The promotional enterprises were set up to orient social activities with an economic tinge at the state level.	Andhra Pradesh, Assam, Gujarat, Karnataka, Kerala, Maharashtra, Tamil Nadu, Uttar Pradesh and West Bengal
Utility	The utility enterprises comprised the state road transport corporation and the unbundled power sector enterprises.	Andhra Pradesh, Delhi, Karnataka, Orissa, Tamil Nadu and West Bengal
Welfare	The welfare corporations were started with the explicit objective of helping a particular segment of society which could not have obtained help under the normal market conditions.	Maharashtra, Kerala and Uttar Pradesh

Source: Mishra and Lakshmi (2006).

The number of enterprises functioning under each category is shown in Figure 1.3. Nearly 34 per cent of the SLPEs are from the promotional sector followed by 29 per cent and 23 per cent in the manufacturing and utilities sectors respectively. A small number of enterprises are functioning under the financial and welfare sectors.

Status of SLPEs in India

Of the 853 SLPEs, 47 per cent were profit-making enterprises and 42 per cent incurred losses (Figure 1.4). About 11 per cent of SLPEs accounts were not finalised and a few have not initiated their operations. Among the profit-earning enterprises, about 46 per cent of the enterprises are concentrated in Karnataka, Kerala, Tamil Nadu, Gujarat and Uttar Pradesh. Governments in these states are initiating protective measures for the survival of the SLPEs in a world of changing technology and productivity of inputs.

Figure 1.3

Categorisation of SLPEs

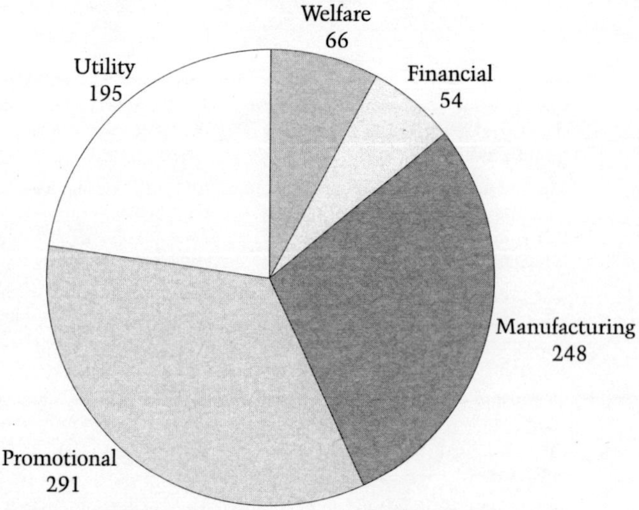

Source: CAG (Commercial) India, 2007-08.

Figure 1.4

Status of SLPEs in India

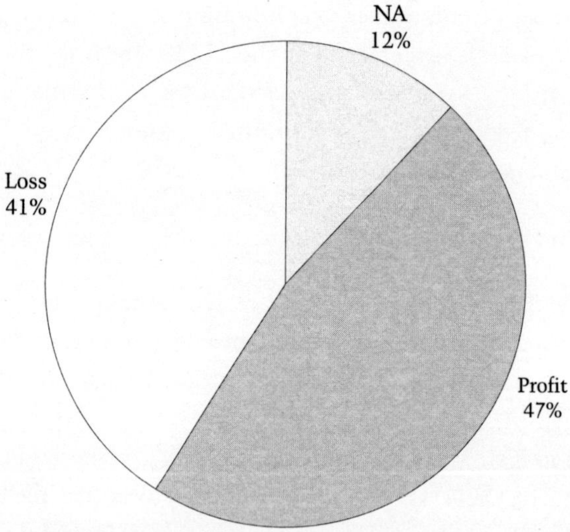

Note: NA: Accounts not finalised.

Source: CAG (Commercial) India, 2007-08.

II

Financial Performance

Performance improvement of an enterprise depends upon the decisions of the respective boards. It is felt that every enterprise should achieve turnaround within a span of every five years. The turnaround strategies for sick enterprises are different from those that are functioning smoothly. In case of the latter, turnaround can be called 'healthy turnaround.' Today, several enterprises in the country continue to run efficiently due to the opening up of the economy and active involvement and leadership of the respective state governments. No doubt, the private competition has increased over the years, but with support from the state and in the light of the new economic reforms of corporate governance,[1] public enterprises could achieve efficiency and also welfare.

The total investment of SLPEs comprises sum of total of the investments in the form of equity and debt capital by state government and others including the central government, holding companies and other financial institutions (Sankar *et al.*, 1989; 1991; Mishra, 2006). The total investment in these enterprises stood at ₹ 3,13,268.89 crore in 2007-08 with a major contribution of 60.13 per cent coming from long-term loans and 39.87 per cent from paid-up capital. The major portion of the total investment is shared by Karnataka, Gujarat, Uttar Pradesh, Maharashtra, etc. (please see Annexure Table A-1.1).

---

1. Temasek, Singapore: one of the largest state investment agencies owned by the state of Singapore; Baosteel, China: one of the largest steel producing company in the world owned by the state of China (PRC); EdF, France: one of the largest power generating-cum-distributing company in France owned by the state—which is also one of the largest power generating companies in the world; ENI Italy: one of the largest energy groups in the world, owned by the State of Italy; also Oil & Natural Gas Corporation of India, which figures as the largest Indian company in FT 500, which is also owned by the state. These are not the only examples of state-owned enterprises (SOEs) which are also called the public enterprises—which are managing huge operations with great efficiency in various developed and developing countries of the world. Volkswagen in Germany, Pohang Steel in South Korea, Pertamina in Indonesia, Khazana in Malaysia—we can go on adding similar public enterprises in other countries to the list. Indeed, even in India where several public enterprises are rightly under attack for their less than satisfactory performance—some of the largest and best run corporate enterprises like ONGC, Indian Oil, National Aluminum, Steel Authority of India, etc., are SOEs (Basu, 2008).

Top 10 States in Terms of Investment

Investments in SLPEs are constituted from the paid-up capital and long-term loans. The top 10 states with highest total investments in 2007-08 are shown in Table 1.2. Karnataka tops the list with 15.3 per cent of total investments in SLPEs in India, followed by Gujarat (14.8%), Uttar Pradesh (9.1%), and Maharashtra (9%).

Table 1.2

Top 10 States in Terms of Investments in SLPEs

S. No	*States*	*Total Investment (in crore)*	*% of Total Investment in SLPEs*
1	Karnataka	47813.29	15.3
2	Gujarat	46506.81	14.8
3	Uttar Pradesh	28399.42	9.1
4	Maharashtra	28297.41	9.0
5	Rajasthan	22811.41	7.3
6	Tamil Nadu	18719.70	6.0
7	Haryana	17449.66	5.6
8	Madhya Pradesh	14711.07	4.7
9	Punjab	14045.04	4.5
10	Delhi	13680.18	4.4

Source: CAG (Commercial) India, 2007-08.

By adopting progressive policies, Karnataka is building a strong and vibrant industrial base and strengthening the SLPEs. The policies that the state adopted for strengthening the SLPEs are: (i) assisting the enterprises to upgrade their technologies, (ii) assisting the SLPEs to face the increasing competition and (iii) radical restructuring of the SLPEs as well as government infrastructure agencies to stay ahead in the competition.

Turnover and Capital Employed

Capital employed is the value of the assets that represents the company's ability to generate revenue. Turnover embodies how quickly the inventory is sold. A high turnover means that goods are sold quickly, while a low turnover means that goods are sold more slowly. Figures 1.5 and 1.6 show the capital employed and the turnover in the SLPEs. As per the figures, Gujarat stands first in capital employed, whereas it occupies

Figure 1.5

Top 10 States in Terms of Turnover

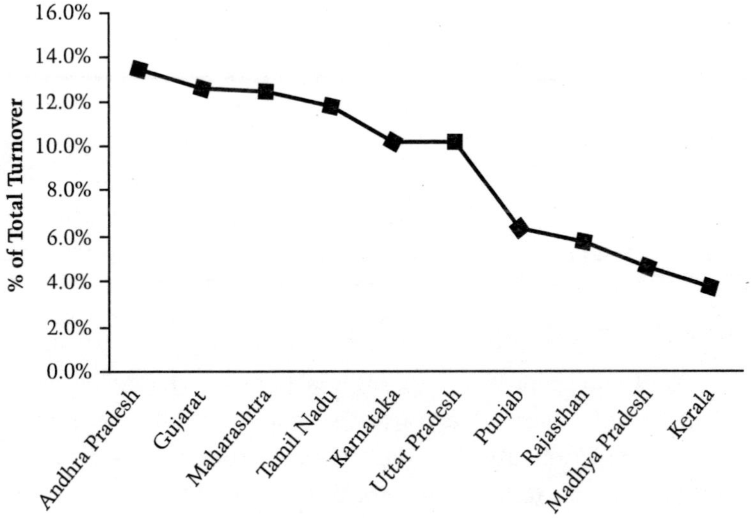

Source: CAG (Commercial) India, 2007-08.

Figure 1.6

Top 10 States in Terms of Capital Employed

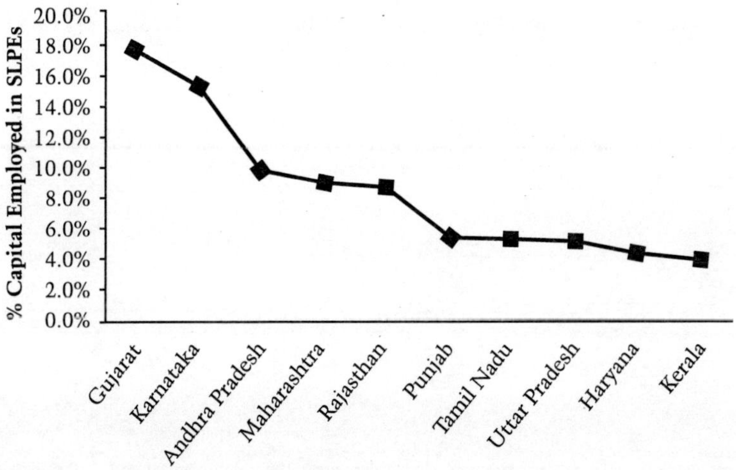

Source: CAG (Commercial) India, 2007-08.

second place in terms of revenue generation. It indicates that though the investment in these enterprises is high, there is a need for improving the sales. At the same time, the capital employed in Andhra Pradesh is 9.9 per cent and it has generated revenue of 13.4 per cent of the total capital employed and turnover in SLPEs. Haryana occupies ninth position among the top 10 states in terms of capital employed, but the SLPEs are incurring losses. Therefore, the SLPEs need to adopt strategies to promote sales, to increase productivity and adopt cost cutting measures. This would lead to an increase in turnover and enhance the contribution of SLPEs to the GDP of the state as well as the country.

SLPEs and Manpower

The SLPEs are, generally, huge organisations which employ large work force. The organisational structure is built around different divisions of marketing, production, finance and human resource management. The number of employees in SLPEs increased from 18 lakh in 2006-07 to 19.2 lakh in 2007-08. Table 1.3 provides information on the states with highest manpower in SLPEs and their share in total manpower employed in these enterprises. The increase in manpower has registered a growth rate of 6.7 per cent in 2007-08. Andhra Pradesh topped the list of 10 states in terms of manpower, ranked first in turnover and third in investment in the SLPEs. The top 10 states account for 84 per cent of the total manpower in SLPEs.

Table 1.3

Top 10 States in Terms of Manpower in SLPEs

States	*No. of Employees*	*% of Total Manpower in SLPEs*
Andhra Pradesh	262054	13.6
Tamil Nadu	255316	13.3
Maharashtra	218389	11.4
Jammu and Kashmir (J&K)	189661	9.9
Karnataka	168811	8.8
Uttar Pradesh	130077	6.8
West Bengal	121548	6.3
Rajasthan	91173	4.7
Punjab	87131	4.5
Kerala	86305	4.5

Source: CAG (Commercial) India, 2007-08.

III

SLPEs in States

The SLPEs have played a very important role in the overall development of the states. In this regard, most state governments have set up Bureau of Public Enterprises/Public Enterprises Departments for coordinating/management of SLPEs. In several states, these functions are performed by the Departments of Industries or Finance. The SLPEs thus fall under the administrative control of various ministries/departments in different states. The state-wise performance is discussed briefly in the following paragraphs and tables, which also provide information on top profit- and loss-making states/union territories (UTs).

Top 10 Profit-making and Loss-making States

The maximum number of profit-making and loss-incurring enterprises in different states are shown in Tables 1.4 and 1.5. Karnataka, Kerala and Tamil Nadu have the highest number of profit-making enterprises which are ranked first, second and third respectively. Kerala, West Bengal and Assam were having the highest number of loss-making SLPEs in India. The states like Karnataka, Kerala, Tamil Nadu, etc., have adopted various policy measures to strengthen the SLPEs. Karnataka is assisting the enterprises in upgrading technologies and restructuring them. Similarly, Kerala has adopted a 'Ten Point Success Formula' for restructuring the enterprises. Therefore, it is clear that successful models can be replicated in other states to make the SLPEs more efficient.

Table 1.4

Top 10 Profit-making States

S. No.	*State*	*No. of Profit-making Enterprises*
1	Karnataka	44
2	Kerala	40
3	Tamil Nadu	35
4	Gujarat	33
5	Uttar Pradesh	30
6	West Bengal	26
7	Maharashtra	26
8	Andhra Pradesh	21
9	Madhya Pradesh	20
10	Orissa	19

Source: CAG (Commercial) India (2007-08).

Table 1.5

Top 10 Loss-making States

S. No.	State	No. of Loss-making Enterprises
1	Kerala	40
2	West Bengal	34
3	Assam	31
4	Uttar Pradesh	25
5	Maharashtra	22
6	Tamil Nadu	18
7	Karnataka	13
8	Madhya Pradesh	13
9	Bihar	13
10	Uttarakhand	12

Source: CAG (Commercial) India (2007-08).

Top 10 Profit-making and Loss-making Enterprises

Tables 1.6 and 1.7 depict the top 10 profit- and loss-making enterprises in India. The enterprises in Gujarat, Karnataka and Orissa are among the top 10 profit-making enterprises. Most of the enterprises from the power sector come under the top 10 profit- and loss-making enterprises in India. A small number of enterprises from the power sector are gaining and incurring losses in few states.

Table 1.6

Top 10 Profit-making Enterprises in India

(₹ in crore)

S. No.	Name of the Enterprise	Profit
1	GRIDCO Limited	56605.07
2	Gujarat State Electricity Corporation Limited	50748.79
3	Gujarat Mineral Development Corporation Limited	40839.48
4	Orissa Mining Corporation Limited	39966.59
5	Jammu and Kashmir Bank Limited	36000.42
6	Gujarat State Petroleum Corporation Limited	30383.00
7	Chhattisgarh State Electricity Board	26884
8	Maharashtra State Power Generation Company	26406.34
9	Karnataka Power Corporation Limited	25022.67
10	Karnataka State Electricity Board	21742

Source: CAG (Commercial) India (2007-08).

Table 1.7

Top 10 Loss-making Enterprises in India

(₹ in crore)

S. No.	*Name of the Enterprise*	*Loss*
1	Punjab State Electricity Board	162638.62
2	Delhi Transport Corp	95482.32
3	Bihar State Electricity Board	85461.42
4	Madhya Pradesh Paschim Kshetra Vidyut Vitran	67980.32
5	Jammu & Kashmir State Power Development Corp.	64650.2
6	MP Purva Kshetra Vidyut Vitran	61377.7
7	Maharashtra State Electricity Distribution	60661
8	Dakshinanchal Vidyut Vitaran Nigam Limited	59144.06
9	MP Madhya Kshetra Vidyut Vitran	49422.36
10	Maharashtra State Electricity Board	42129.26

Source: CAG (Commercial) India (2007-08).

The reasons for the grave conditions of these enterprises may not totally be confined to the finance-related aspects like acute shortage of working capital, incurrence of cash losses, erosion of net worth, lack of internal resources and liquidity constraints leading to delayed/irregular payments. It might partly be attributable to the technical aspects such as outdated equipment, outdated technologies/products and recurring breakdowns, as well lack of customer orientation and quality problems.

IV

Concluding Remarks

The SLPEs are extended arms of the state governments in the task of the promotion of economic and social development by implementing the central government schemes in various states. Though these enterprises are important as policy tools in the hands of the states of the Indian Union, their performance on all fronts turned out to be below expectations in a few states. In addition, while performance of public enterprises varies from state to state, even in the states with better performance record, the overall picture is not so bright (Maheshwari, 1981).

Support by the central and the state governments in the form of subsidies and grants amounted to ₹ 30,846.59 crore in 2007-08. Despite such massive support, a large number of enterprises in various states do not seem to be efficient in terms of their productivity, financial and operational performance. Therefore, it is suggested that apart from providing budgetary support to these units, the central as well as state governments need to invest in research and development and adopt restructuring measures. With a view to reduce manpower in the SLPEs, the employees were offered compensation if they opted for early retirement and insurance and retraining facilities were also given (Eleventh Five Year Plan 2007-2012, Planning Commission, GoI).

The discussion above indicates that a large number of SLPEs were established for important tasks of social and economic development. But their performance has been far below expectations. IPE (Institute of Public Enterprise) Database on SLPEs (2009) highlights the gap between expectations and achievements and suggests that more information on SLPEs should be generated and research should be focused to develop greater understanding of their potential, problems and prospects.

Recommendations

Identifying the basic causes for the continued sickness of SLPEs, despite providing repeated doses of subsidies and restructuring packages, is an issue of utmost importance. Every SLPE should be healthy and should stand on its own strengths. Introduction of new management strategies/ techniques alone would not provide total solutions, unless the basic level problems are first identified and addressed. The modern management techniques and plethora of management jargon are mere gadgets which are propagated by some one, who is unfamiliar with the real problems and without the skills to operate them. This calls for candid deliberation on the part of all employees' right from the bottom to the top, as they are the true partners and know the ground realities. They are the ones to cooperate with the management to implement the turnaround exercises, even if they entail inconveniences and sacrifices. Therefore, the focus should be on the existing strengths of the manpower in each enterprise, who should be properly inspired with the alluring opportunities, coupled with the competitive environment of the 21st century.

The success stories of many enterprises in India and throughout the world, where the problems once were acute and seemed irredeemable, can exercise in 'looking back to look ahead.' In such situations, certain measures of stabilisation and reconstruction are called for. They can broadly be classified into financial restructuring, business restructuring and manpower restructuring. Before deciding on the remedial measures simply based on a few symptoms (i.e., like symptomatic diagnosis in serious cases of disease), it is essential to conduct an in-depth review of all the causes. These causes may be divided into 'internal and 'external.' The internal causes include incompetent management, complacency, lack of good direction and control, low morale, low motivation, excess manpower, lack of teamwork and lack of planning. The external causes involve competition with forced prices, government policies and resource constraints.

What is essential to realise is the fact that the internal causes are more predominant compared to external causes. The internal causes of sickness are powerful and decisive in bringing down the performance of these enterprises. But the external factors also occasionally play a major role in exceptional cases such as sickness in the entire industry or during global meltdowns. Divestment of non-core businesses, downsizing, reduction of overcapacity, avoiding duplication efforts and some structural changes etc., may be called for to realise the identified synergies.

Part II

State-wise Scenario: Performance of State Level Public Enterprises

2 Andhra Pradesh

Introduction

Andhra Pradesh (AP) is India's fourth largest state by area and fifth largest by population. The state is endowed with abundant natural and human resources with competitive socioeconomic advantages. The state has witnessed a vibrant growth over the years. During the period 2004-05 to 2008-09, Indian economy grew at an impressive rate of 8.49 per cent, whereas the performance of the state economy was even more impressive as it registered an average growth of 9.07 per cent during the same period. This notable achievement of the state economy was backed by the remarkable progress registered by all the three sectors of the economy. The sectoral composition of the gross state domestic product (GSDP) in 2008-09 at constant prices is shown in Figure 2.1. The GSDP in 2008-09 at constant prices (1999-2000) is estimated at ₹ 2,51,431 crore as against ₹ 2,39,372 crore in the year 2007-08. The per capita income at constant (1999-2000) prices has gone up from ₹ 26,229 in 2007-08 to ₹ 27,362 in 2008-09, registering a growth of 4.32 per cent.

Overview of Industrial Sector

In AP, the industrial sector has gained in strength in many ways. It has become possible due to proactive role of state government *viz.*, effective policy implementation including single window clearance and incentives, establishing world-class infrastructure and, most importantly, making available power at the cheapest industrial tariff, thereby releasing entrepreneurial energies in private as well as public sector (*State Economic Survey 2009-10*, Government of AP). The state government established the Department of Industries in 1960 with the objective of establishing cottage and small-scale industries (SSI), industrial cooperatives and extending credit to artisans, block-level training-cum-production centres and rural artisan complexes. Guilds were also established for giving necessary

Figure 2.1

Sectoral Composition of GSDP at Constant (1999-2000) Prices in 2008-09

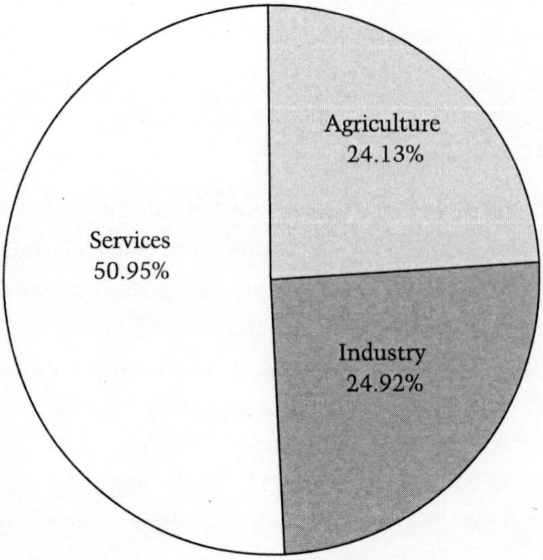

Source: *AP Economic Survey 2009-10*.

training to the artisans in rural areas. The government has taken up several initiatives to achieve the high growth rates in the industrial sector during the Eleventh Five Year Plan period.

Overview of SLPEs

The origin of SLPEs in Andhra Pradesh goes back to the period prior to the formation of the state in 1956. The erstwhile Nizam of Hyderabad sowed the seeds of industralisation in the state by setting up enterprises (Mishra and Lakshmi Kumari, 2006). Many enterprises like Hyderabad Allwyn, Hyderabad Chemicals and Fertilisers, Republic Forge Company, etc., still exist, which were started during the Nizam period. Considerable importance has been given to the SLPEs after the formation of the state. The major objectives of setting up of the SLPEs in the state are: capacity utilisation and marketing of services, identifying appropriate markets to supply commodities and services at appropriate price.

These enterprises were set up for the social purpose of serving all the people, including the weaker sections. There were 41 working SLPEs in AP as on March 31, 2008. About 24 per cent of them were set up during the Ninth Five Year Plan period. Nearly 51 per cent of the enterprises are making profits and 26 per cent are incurring losses. The total investment was ₹ 34,755.76 crore consisting of paid-up capital and long-term loans. The capital employed increased by 13.61 per cent in 2007-08. The total number of employees declined from 2.65 lakh in 2006-07 to 2.63 lakh in 2007-08. There is an increase in the turnover by 27.09 per cent with ₹ 31,835.06 crore in 2006-07 to ₹ 43,662.92 crore in 2007-08. The profits of the SLPEs in AP increased by 73 per cent i.e., from ₹ 95.30 crore in 2006-07 to ₹ 357.08 crore in 2007-08. The details are given in Table 2.1.

Table 2.1

Overview of SLPEs in Andhra Pradesh

(₹ in lakh)

Particulars	*2007-08*	*2006-07*	*2005-06*
Investment			
Paid-up capital			
State Govt.	617811.2	604684.6	603226.3
Central Govt.	94459.38	94840.08	94840.08
Others	1805.1	1803.94	1803.94
Total	714075.7	701328.7	699870.3
Long-term Loan			
Government	597677.5	378873.6	304468.8
Others	2163822	2239299	2166046
Total	2761500	2618173	2470514
Total Investment	3475576	3319502	3170385
Capital employed	3307728	2857697	2673329
Turnover	4366292	3183506	2901920
Net Profit/Loss	35708.15	9530.15	36060.71
Accumulated Profit/Loss	-276921	-22382.4	-237688
No. of Employees	262989	265063	271593
Total Return on Capital employed	208635.4	153106.7	146543.8
Percentage of Total Return on Capital Employed	327.16	361.16	465.72
Subsidies/Grants			
Central Govt.	44171.91	46120.38	32576.79
State Govt.	512485.8	445470.8	373186.1
Total	556528.1	491591.2	405762.9

Source: Comptroller and Auditor General (CAG) (Commercial) India, 2007-08.

Categorisation

The SLPEs are classified into five categories: financial, manufacturing, promotional, utility and welfare. The number of enterprises functioning under each category is shown in Figure 2.2. The promotional and manufacturing enterprises constitute the largest number. The increase in the number of profit-making SLPEs led to an increase in the total investment level. The investment was ₹ 33,195.02 crore in 2006-07 which increased to ₹ 34,755.76 crore in 2007-08. The investments are financed through the budgetary support from the state and central governments and other financial institutions.

Figure 2.2

Category-wise SLPEs in Andhra Pradesh

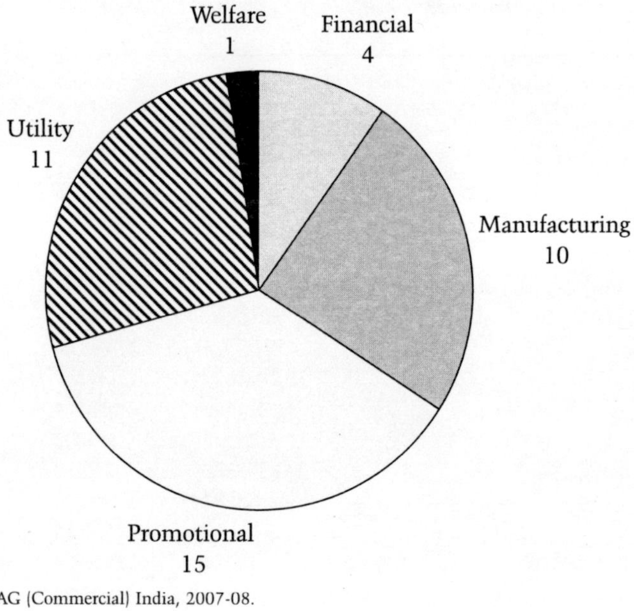

Source: CAG (Commercial) India, 2007-08.

Performance

In recent times, the performance of SLPEs in AP has improved drastically. The government has given serious attention to evaluate the performance of the SLPEs in the state. The Government of Andhra

Pradesh has evolved Public Enterprises Performance Index by incorporating the indicators like factor productivity indicators and total productivity indicators including total cost of production, expenses as a percentage of income, capital turnover capacity utilisation, working capital turnover, return on investment, return on capital utilisation, return on capital employed, profit on sales, etc.

Capital Employed and Turnover

The capital employed by all the 41 state level public enterprises was ₹ 33,07,728 lakh in 2007-08. It is estimated that the capital employed by the top five (AP GENCO, Singareni Colleries, AP TRANSCO, APSFC, etc.) SLPEs constitutes more than 70 per cent of the total capital employed by all the SLPEs in the state. The total turnover made by all the 41 public enterprises was ₹ 43,66,292 lakh in 2007-08.

Accumulated Profits and Losses

The accumulated losses of the SLPEs increased from ₹ 223.82 crore in 2006-07 to ₹ 2,769.21 crore in 2007-08 which in percentage terms is 92. Most of the enterprises in the promotional sector were incurring losses, increasing the accumulated losses. Though the enterprises in the manufacturing, utility and the financial sector were earning profits, but still there is no decline in the losses.

Table 2.2

Accumulated Profit and Loss of SLPEs

(₹ in lakh)

S. No.	*Particulars*	*2007-08*	*2006-07*	*2005-06*
1	Financial	-501.51	-9197.8	-11635
2	Manufacturing	-1834	-6191.3	-4072.5
3	Promotional	-156549	125319	-87575
4	Utility	-118036	-132313	-134406
5	Welfare	–	–	–
	Total	-276921	-22382	-237688

Source: CAG (Commercial) India, 2007-08.

Top Five Profit-making and Loss-making Units

Tables 2.3 and 2.4 present the top five profit- and loss-making units in AP. Andhra Pradesh Power Generation Corporation Limited, Singareni Collieries Company Limited and Andhra Pradesh State Financial Corporation are ranked first, second and third amongst the profit-making SLPEs in the state.

Table 2.3

Top Five Profit-making Units (2007-08)

(₹ in lakh)

S. No.	*Name of the Enterprise*	*Amount*
1	Andhra Pradesh Power Generation Corporation Limited	19763.59
2	Singareni Collieries Company Limited	17617.03
3	Andhra Pradesh State Financial Corporation	8951.31
4	Southern Power Distribution Company of AP Limited	8209.59
5	Andhra Pradesh Industrial Infrastructure Corp. Limited	5246.09

Source: CAG (Commercial) India, 2007-08.

Table 2.4

Top Five Loss-making Units (2007-08)

(₹ in lakh)

S. No.	*Name of the Enterprise*	*Amount*
1	Andhra Pradesh State Housing Corporation Limited	25173.25
2	Andhra Pradesh State Road Transport Corporation	11182.45
3	Andhra Pradesh State Irrigation Development Corp. Limited	325.62
4	Leather Industries Development Corporation of AP Limited	236.92
5	Andhra Pradesh State Minorities Finance Corp. Limited	133.34

Source: CAG (Commercial) India, 2007-08.

Andhra Pradesh State Housing Corporation Limited (APSHC), Andhra Pradesh State Road Transport Corporation (APSRTC) and Andhra Pradesh State Irrigation Development Corporation Limited (APSIDC) are the major loss-making enterprises. APSHC incurred loss owing to the lack of monitoring and inadequate control of the management leading to diversion and misappropriations of funds, malpractices and delay in completion of projects. APSRTC experienced loss due to inefficiency in the operation of services, increase in expenses due to procurement of new buses, software installation for the hospital management, etc., which increased the production cost. APSIDC incurred loss due to improper allocation of resources and implementation of schemes.

Budgetary Support

The grants and subsidies given by the state and central governments constitute the major share in the budget support followed by the equity. The details regarding budgetary provision towards equity, loans and grants/ subsidies for the period 2005-06 to 2007-08 are given in Table 2.5.

Table 2.5

Budgetary Support to SLPEs

(₹ in crore)

S. No.	*Particulars*	*2005-06*	*2006-07*	*2007-08*
1	Equity	27.44	14.42	131.4
2	Loans	287.74	817.04	21.67
3	Grants/subsidies	3730.36	4514.71	5124.86
4	Total	4045.54	5346.17	5277.93

Source: CAG (Commercial) India, 2007-08.

The budgetary support to the SLPEs has been varying over the years. The budgetary support increased from ₹ 4,045.54 crore in 2005-06 to ₹ 5,346.17 crore in 2007-08 i.e., by 24.33 per cent. There is a meager fall in the budgetary support in 2007-08. The government increased its grants and subsidies to the SLPEs especially in the power sector. The investments were made in the form of grants and equity by the government in 16 SLPEs in the state.

Contribution of SLPEs to State GDP

Of the 41 SLPEs functioning in the state, 21 enterprises are making profits and 11 are making losses. The SLPEs turnover to state GDP shows the extent of public enterprises activities in the state. Table 2.6 provides the details of SLPEs contribution to state GDP from 2005-06 to 2007-08.

Table 2.6

SLPEs Contribution to State GDP

(₹ in crore)

S. No.	*Particulars*	*2005-06*	*2006-07*	*2007-08*
1	Turnover	29019.2	31835.1	43662.9
2	State GDP	236034	269173	311752
3	Percentage of Turnover to State GDP	12.29	11.83	14.01

Source: CAG (Commercial) India, 2007-08.

The percentage of turnover to the state's GDP increased approximately by 2 per cent during 2006-2008. There is an increase in the turnover of the manufacturing, financial, promotional and the utility sectors, which led to an increase in the contribution to the state's GDP. Though there is an increase in the turnover by 27.09 per cent, its contribution to GDP increased by only 2.18 per cent. The losses of SLPEs are mainly attributable to deficiencies in financial management, planning, implementation of projects and inefficiency in running their own operations and monitoring.

Government Initiatives and Conclusions

The process of restructuring and divestiture of manufacturing enterprises was initiated in AP during mid-1980s. The Subramanyam Committee gave its recommendation with respect to 30 SLPEs in 1995. The public enterprise reforms started gaining momentum with the implementation of AP Economic Restructuring Project (APERP) funded by the World Bank. The APERP was implemented in two phases in AP and it took about four years to start implementation. Under the first phase, 19 enterprises were covered during the period 1999-2000, the enterprises restructured are 35, the enterprises closed are 24, the enterprises privatised are 12 and the enterprises disinvested are 9. In the second phase, around 61 enterprises were covered from 2002 to 2007, out of which 4 were privatised, 9 disinvested, 18 closed and 30 restructured. Although 90 enterprises were selected for the reforms, the reforms were completed in 80 enterprises; in case of 9 enterprises, reforms are underway and one enterprise is held up in the court.

The government initiated a number of policies in various fields like bio-technology, apparel industry, SSI, food processing industry, information and communication technology (ICT), infrastructure and others. The 'Industrial Investment Promotion Policy 2005-2010', provides a number of incentives to (i) SSI/tiny units, (ii) scheduled castes/scheduled tribes (SC/ST) entrepreneurs, (iii) women entrepreneurs, (iv) large- and medium-scale industries and (v) mega projects. To remove the existing barriers, create congenial and hassle-free investment climate and boost investor confidence, and provided better infrastructural facilities, and quality power in order to achieve balanced and sustainable economic growth.

Andhra Pradesh Industrial Infrastructure Corporation (APIICC) is entrusted with the responsibility of setting up industrial estates throughout the state by providing basic infrastructure such as sheds, internal roads, power, drainage, telephones, etc. Theme parks such as software park, apparel export park, biotech park and leather parks are set up on a priority basis so that specialised infrastructure, technology back-up and escort services can be accessed more easily. Research & development (R&D) is encouraged in order to promote new inventions from the laboratories to reach the industrial sector and increase productivity. The objective of the government is to make AP an attractive investment destination for foreign investment by improving infrastructure, technology upgradation, protecting intellectual property rights (IPRs), creating market-driven environment by encouraging competition with the private sector and implementing a regulatory mechanism for the entry and operation of firms. Restructuring of sick industrial enterprises is given special focus by the government.

3 Arunachal Pradesh

Overview of SLPEs

Arunachal Pradesh means "land of the dawn lit mountains." It is also known as "land of the rising sun." There were three working state level public enterprises in Arunachal Pradesh as on March 31, 2008. All the enterprises in the state are incurring losses. The total investment was ₹ 18.11 crore consisting of paid-up capital and long-term loans. The capital employed increased by 0.78 per cent in 2007-08. The total number of employees were 550 during 2007-08. There was a decline in the turnover by 3.99 per cent from ₹ 5.94 crore in 2006-07 to ₹ 5.71 crore in 2007-08. The loss of the SLPEs in Arunachal Pradesh was ₹ 4.77 crore in 2007-08. Thc dctails arc givcn in Tablc 3.1.

Table 3.1

Overview of SLPEs in Arunachal Pradesh

(₹ in lakh)

Particulars	*2007-08*	*2006-07*	*2005-06*
Investment			
Paid-up capital			
State Govt.	907.34	872.72	904.34
Central Govt.	0	0	0
Others	0	0	0
Total	907.34	872.72	904.34
Long-term Loan			
Government	713.55	713.55	0
Others	190.01	0	556.2
Total	903.56	713.55	556.2
Total Investment	1810.9	1586.27	1460.54
Capital employed	5003.48	4964.33	4925.53
Turnover	571.55	594.33	591.41
Net Profit/Loss	-477.27	-387.42	-496.55

contd...

...contd... *(₹ in lakh)*

Particulars	*2007-08*	*2006-07*	*2005-06*
Accumulated Profit/Loss	-287.35	3359.48	3294.39
No. of Employees	550	550	563
Total Return on Capital employed	-477.27	-387.42	-402.48
Percentage of Total Return on Capital Employed	0	0	0
Subsidies/Grants			
Central Govt.	20	0	0
State Govt.	0	40	0
Total	20	40	0

Source: Comptroller & Auditor General (CAG) (Commercial) India, 2007-08.

Categorisation

The SLPEs are classified into five categories: financial, manufacturing, promotional, utility and welfare enterprises. The number of enterprises functioning under each category is shown in Figure 3.1 below. There are no enterprises in the utility and welfare sector whereas, the other sectors have one enterprise each. The investment was ₹ 15.86 crore in 2006-07 which increased to ₹ 18.11 crore in 2007-08 i.e., 12.4 per cent. The investments are financed through the budgetary support from the state and central governments and other financial institutions.

Figure 3.1

Category-wise SLPEs in Arunachal Pradesh

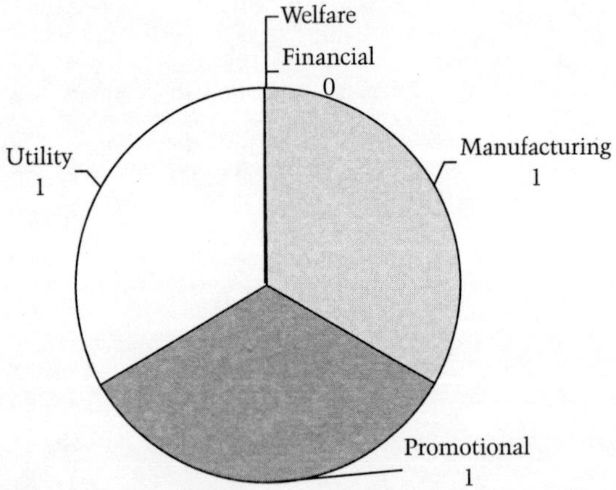

Source: CAG (Commercial) India 2007-08.

Accumulated Profits and Losses

The accumulated losses of the SLPEs increased from ₹ 1.3 crore in 2006-07 to ₹ 2.87 crore in 2007-08 by 54.77 per cent. The losses were incurred mostly in the financial sector. The enterprises in the promotional sector were earning profits, so there is a decline in the accumulated losses.

Table 3.2

Accumulated Profit and Loss of SLPEs

(₹ in lakh)

S. No.	*Particulars*	*2007-08*	*2006-07*	*2005-06*
1	Financial	-1902.1	-1744.7	-1679.6
2	Manufacturing	-24.8	-24.8	-24.8
3	Promotional	1639.56	1639.56	1639.56
	Total	-287.35	-129.96	-64.87

Source: CAG (Commercial) India 2007-08.

Top Loss-making Units

Arunachal Pradesh Forest Corporation Limited, Arunachal Pradesh Industrial Development and Finance Corporation and Arunachal Pradesh Mineral Development & Trading Corporation are the major loss-making units.

Table 3.3

Top Loss-making Units (2007-08)

(₹ in lakh)

S. No	*Name of the Enterprise*	*Amount*
1	Arunachal Pradesh Forest Corporation Limited	308.95
2	Arunachal Pradesh Industrial Deve. & Finance Corp.	155.66
3	Arunachal Pradesh Mineral Development & Trading Corp.	12.66

Source: CAG (Commercial) India 2007-08.

Performance and Government Incentives

Of the three SLPEs functioning in the state, all the enterprises are incurring losses. The losses of SLPEs are mainly attributable to deficiencies in financial management, planning, implementation of projects, running their operations and monitoring. The government is encouraging the establishment of industrial undertakings in the private and cooperative sectors for sustainable development of the state. The investors are encouraged to invest in textiles (handlooms and power looms) and handicrafts, electronics and knowledge-based industries, infrastructure, such as power and communications, tourism and industries based on the availability of resources in the region. To encourage the investors from outside the state, it is granting 100 per cent equity ownership for the entrepreneurs, for a period of 30 years by the end of which the equity will be reduced to 49 per cent. The priority is given to local population for employment opportunities and gainful self-employment in industrial and allied sectors.

4 Assam

Introduction

Assam was known as *Pragjyotisha* in the Mahabharata and Kamarupa in the 1st millennium. The state is endowed with petroleum, natural gas, coal, limestone and other minerals such as magnetic quartzite, kaolin, sillimanites, clay and feldspar. Assam is a major producer of crude oil and it accounts for about 15 per cent of India's crude output exploited by the Assam Oil Company Limited and natural gas in India. Asia's first successful mechanically drilled oil well was operational in Makum (Assam) way back in 1867. Assam's biggest contribution to the world is tea. Although having a poor overall industrial performance, several other industries have nevertheless been started, including a chemical fertiliser plant, paper mills, sugar mills, cement, cosmetics, jute mill, textile and yarn mills, silk mill, etc. Unfortunately many of these industries are facing losses and closure due to lack of infrastructure and improper management practices.

Despite its rich natural resources, and supply of 25 per cent of India's petroleum needs, the growth rate of Assam has not kept pace with that of India; differences increased rapidly since 1970s. Indian economy grew at 6 per cent per annum over the period of 1981-2000, whereas in Assam it was only 3.3 per cent. The contribution of the manufacturing sector to the state economy was 9.3 per cent only during 2008-09. The industrial scenario of the state is mainly confined with the growth of the employment-oriented small-scale sector. In the country's medium and large-scale industries, Assam's share is less than 2 per cent. However, the state government is taking measures for the implementation of various promotional schemes for sustainable growth and development of the industrial sector of the state.

Overview of SLPEs

The first SLPE in Assam was set up in 1954 and since then there is a steady growth in the number and scale of investment in public enterprises. There were 40 working SLPE in Assam as on March 31, 2008. About 23 per cent of them were set up during the Fifth Plan period. The total investment was ₹ 2,79,550.7 lakh consisting of paid-up capital and long-term loans. The capital employed increased by 55 per cent in 2007-08. The total number of employees was 38,805 which increased by 6 per cent in 2007-08. The turnover increased by 43 per cent from ₹ 1,15,721.4 lakh in 2006-07 to ₹ 2,03,856 lakh in 2007-08. The loss of the SLPEs in Assam is ₹ 25,918.8 lakh in 2007-08. The details are given in Table 4.1.

Table 4.1

Overview of SLPEs in Assam

(₹ in lakh)

Particulars	*2007-08*	*2006-07*	*2005-06*
Investment			
Paid-up capital			
State Govt.	124064.7	121812.5	118945.5
Central Govt.	2865.42	2865.42	2750.42
Others	1174.77	1121.99	1168.29
Total	128104.6	125799.6	122863.9
Long-term Loan			
Government	96832.94	75073.27	59124.03
Others	54613.13	60486.77	15418.8
Total	151446.1	135560	74542.83
Total Investment	279550.7	261359.7	197406.7
Capital employed	255982.8	140487.2	131978.2
Turnover	203856	115721.4	119271.5
Net Profit/Loss	-25918.8	-103327	-102970
Accumulated Profit/Loss	-102584	-642383	-641515
No. of Employees	38805	36307	23867
Total Return on Capital employed	-15232.6	-93575.2	-93605.9
Percentage of Total Return on Capital Employed	88.41	86.91	79.78
Subsidies/Grants			
Central Govt.	1476.75	3359.47	2365.16
State Govt.	30305.74	25537.77	56905.8

Source: Comptroller and Auditor General (CAG) (Commercial) India, 2007-08.

Categorisation

The SLPEs are classified into five categories: financial, manufacturing, promotional, utility and welfare. The number of enterprises functioning under each category is shown in Figure 4.1. The manufacturing, promotional and utility enterprises constitute the largest number. A multiplication in the number of SLPEs led to a rapid growth of investment in public enterprises. The investment increased from ₹ 1,97,406.7 lakh in 2005-06 to ₹ 2,79,550.7 lakh in 2007-08. The investments are financed through the budgetary support from the state and central governments and other financial institutions.

Figure 4.1

Categorisation of SLPEs in Assam

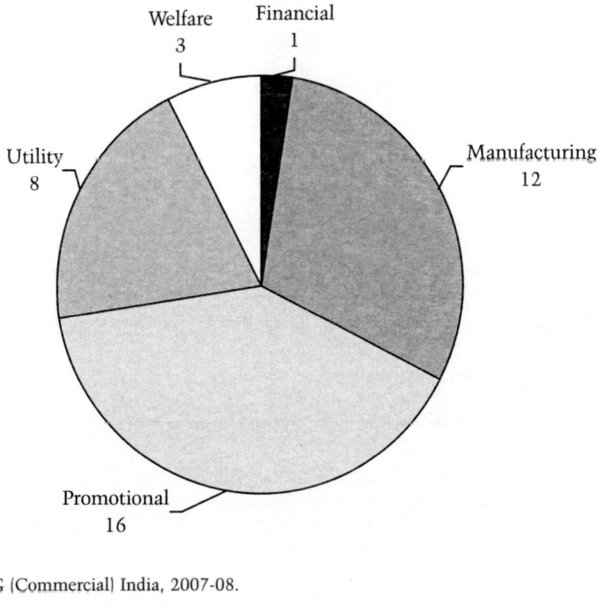

Source: CAG (Commercial) India, 2007-08.

Accumulated Profits and Losses

The accumulated losses of the SLPES declined from ₹ 6,42,383 in 2006-07 to ₹ 1,02,584 in 2007-08 by 84 per cent, incurred mostly in the utility and the promotional sector.

Table 4.2

Category-wise SLPEs Accumulated Profit and Loss

(₹ in lakh)

Category	2007-08	2006-07	2005-06
Financial	-8640.1	-6840.14	-6840.14
Manufacturing	-1497.2	-1774.59	-1685.83
Promotional	-23213.3	-20685.6	-19907.4
Utility	-68314.5	-612454	-612453
Welfare	-919.48	-629.15	-629.15
Total	-102584	-642383	-641515

Source: CAG (Commercial) India, 2007-08.

Top Five Profit-making and Loss-making Units

Tables 4.3 and 4.4 provide information on top five profit- and loss-making units in Assam. Assam Gas Company, Assam Petrochemicals Limited and Assam Tea Corporation are ranked first, second and third amongst the profit-making SLPEs.

Table 4.3

Top Five Profit-making Units (2007-08)

(₹ in lakh)

S. No.	Name of the Enterprise	Amount
1	Assam Gas Company Limited	2438.3
2	Assam Petrochemicals Limited	906.71
3	Assam Tea Corporation	278.56
4	Assam Police Housing Corp.	120.01
5	Assam Sate Text Book Production & Publication	91.25

Source: CAG (Commercial) India, 2007-08.

Assam State Electricity Board, Assam Power Generation Corporation and Lower Assam Electricity Distribution Company are the major loss-making units.

Table 4.4

Top Five Loss-making Units (2007-08)

(₹ *in lakh)*

S. No.	Name of the Enterprise	Amount
1	Assam State Electricity Board	13058.84
2	Assam Power Generation Corp.	4090.12
3	Lower Assam Electricity Distribution	2845.82
4	Upper Assam Electricity Distribution	2220.64
5	Assam State Transport Corporation	1673.4

Source: CAG (Commercial) India, 2007-08.

Budgetary Support

The grants and subsidies given by the state and central governments constitute the major share in the budget support followed by the equity. The details regarding budgetary outgo towards equity, loans and grants/subsidies for the period 2005-06 to 2007-08 are given in Table 4.5.

Table 4.5

Budget Support to SLPEs (2006-2008)

(₹ *in crore)*

S. No.	Particulars	2007-08	2006-07	2005-06
1	Equity	2.05	0.92	721.8
2	Loans	183.3	148.31	281.03
3	Grants/subsidies	303.08	255.38	592.74
4	Total	488.43	404.61	1595.57

Source: CAG (Commercial) India, 2007-08.

The budgetary support to SLPEs has been declining over the years. This could be one of the reasons for their dismal performance. Hence, the state government should initiate necessary measures for the revival and restructuring of the SLPEs in tune with the different successful models.

Performance

Of the 40 SLPEs functioning in the state, 31 enterprises are considered as loss-making units and only 6 units are making profits. SLPEs turnover to state GDP shows the extent of public enterprises activities in the state. Table 4.6 provides the detail of SLPEs contribution to state GDP from 2005-06 to 2007-08.

Table 4.6

SLPEs Contribution to State GDP

(₹ in crore)

S. No	*Particulars*	*2007-08*	*2006-07*	*2005-06*
1	Turnover	2038.56	1156.49	1190.99
2	GDP	72700	65033	57543
3	Percentage of Turnover to State GDP	2.8	1.8	2.1

Source: CAG (Commercial) India, 2007-08.

The percentage of turnover to the state GDP declined in 2006-07 due to the decline in turnover of promotional and manufacturing enterprises. But in 2007-08, there is 1 per cent increase in contribution to GDP owing to an increase in turnover from the SLPEs in manufacturing sector. According to the Department of Public Enterprises, Government of Assam, incompetence in management is one of the reasons for the poor performance of the SLPEs in the state. It is observed that each SLPE has its own obstructions, overstaffing is the one, which generally leads to poor financial performance. The other factors like ineffective management, inadequacy of capital, infrastructure constraints, etc., crippled some of the enterprises in the state.

5 Bihar

Introduction

Bihar is one of the fastest growing states in India. The economy of the state is largely service oriented, but it also has a significant agricultural base. The state also has a small industrial sector. The contribution of agriculture to gross state domestic product (GSDP) is 35 per cent in 2008 followed by industry (9%) and services (55%). The manufacturing sector performed very poorly in the state during 2002-2006, with an average growth rate of 0.38 per cent compared to India's 7.8 per cent. However, now there is rapid growth in manufacturing sector with 36.07 per cent and Bihar has become the second best manufacturing state in India. Bihar had the lowest GDP per capita in India between 1999 and 2008, which grew by 5.1 per cent a year and was below the Indian average of 7.3 per cent. The state achieved 18 per cent growth rate in GDP in 2006-07.

Bihar was the victim of apathetic national policies which created constraints, both structural and institutional, for industrialisation of the state. The policy of freight equalisation introduced after independence stayed for a long period and played havoc in de-industrialisation of the state. As a result of bifurcation, whatever industries worth the name were in the erstwhile Bihar went to Jharkhand. The de-industrialisation of the state on a large scale led to weak infrastructural development with specific implications for the industrial sector. This had an obvious negative impact on the overall economic growth of the state. The existing low level of infrastructure facilities is the major bottleneck in accelerating the process of development in the state.

As on December 2008, there were 1,74,278 registered units in Bihar, consisted of 1,502 small-scale units, 1,02,676 tiny units and 70,100 artisan-based units. The total investment in these units was to the tune of ₹ 1,017.62 crore and it provided employment to 5.68 lakh workers. The government has given top priority to create investment opportunities for big industrial houses like Reliance. Further developments have taken place in the growth of small industries, improvements in information technology (IT) infrastructure, the construction of software park in Patna and the completion of the expressway from the Purvanchal border through Bihar to Jharkhand.

Overview of SLPEs

The first SLPE in Bihar was set up in 1954 and since then there is a steady growth of public enterprises. There were 20 working SLPEs in Bihar as on March 31, 2008. About 30 per cent of them set up during the Fifth Five Year Plan period. The total investment was ₹ 7,974.91 crore consisting of paid-up capital and long-term loans. The capital employed increased by 24.42 per cent in 2007-08. The total number of employees was 22,326 which declined by 8 per cent in 2007-08. The turnover increased by 15.8 per cent from ₹ 1,337.29 crore in 2006-07 to ₹ 1,588.26 crore in 2007-08. The loss of the SLPEs in Bihar was ₹ 907.92 crore in 2007-08. The details are given in Table 5.1.

Table 5.1

Overview of SLPEs in Bihar

(₹ in lakh)

Particulars	*2007-08*	*2006-07*	*2005-06*
Investment			
Paid-up capital			
State Govt.	29875.57	39451.23	38392.41
Central Govt.	2705.78	2705.78	2651.78
Others	5145.02	4908.39	4700.71
Total	37726.37	47065.4	45744.9
Long-term Loan			
Government	681519	671548.2	646417
Others	78245.6	74149.07	71473.94
Total	759764.6	745697.2	717890.9
Total Investment	797491	792762.6	763635.8
Capital Employed	335598.8	253639.1	29306.66
Turnover	158826.3	133729.2	117967.7
Net Profit/Loss	-90791.8	-12170.4	-21035.5
Accumulated Profit/Loss	-277876	-150951	-140870

contd...

...contd...

Particulars	*2007-08*	*2006-07*	*2005-06*
No. of Employees	22326	24196	24638
Total Return on Capital employed	224.3	47740.8	7743.55
Percentage of Total Return on Capital Employed	138.52	164.58	98.13
Subsidies/Grants			
Central Govt.	0	0	0
State Govt.	2300	0	0
Total	2300	0	0

Source: Comptroller and Auditor General (CAG) (Commercial) India, 2007-08.

Categorisation

The SLPEs are classified into five categories: financial, manufacturing, promotional, utility and welfare enterprises. The number of enterprises functioning under each category is shown in Figure 5.1. The promotional, financial and utility enterprises constitute the largest number. The investment increased from ₹ 7,927.63 crore in 2005-06 to ₹ 7,974.91 crore in 2007-08. Nearly 65 per cent of the SLPEs are incurring losses in Bihar.

Figure 5.1

Category-wise SLPEs in Bihar

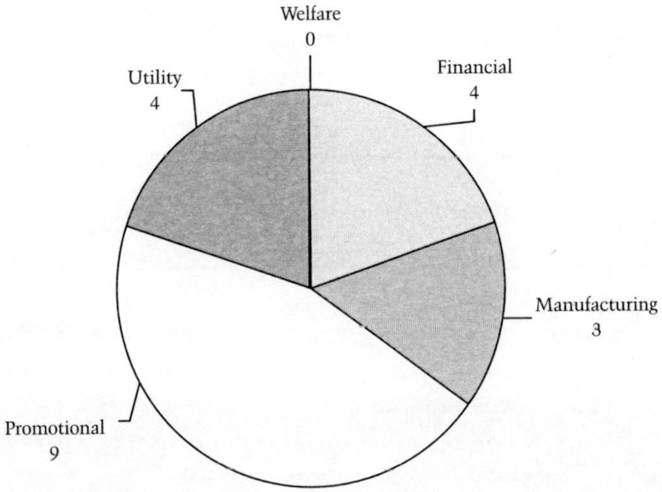

Source: CAG (Commercial) India, 2007-08.

Accumulated Profits and Losses

The accumulated losses of the SLPEs increased from ₹ 1,509.51 crore in 2006-07 to ₹ 2,778.76 crore in 2007-08 by 45.68 per cent. The losses were incurred mostly in the utility sector followed by the promotional and the manufacturing sectors.

Table 5.2

Accumulated Profit and Loss of SLPEs

(₹ in lakh)

S. No.	*Particulars*	*2007-08*	*2006-07*	*2005-06*
1	Financial	-53911	-56539	-55618
2	Manufacturing	-460.28	-324.05	15.67
3	Promotional	-8041.7	-7030.4	-5891.8
4	Utility	-215462	-87058	-79375
5	Welfare	0	0	0
6	Total	-277876	-150951	-140870

Source: CAG (Commercial) India, 2007-08.

Top Five Profit-making and Loss-making Units

Tables 5.3 and 5.4 provide the information on top five profit and loss making units in Bihar. Bihar State Financial Corporation, Bihar State Mineral Development Corporation and Bihar State Warehousing Corporation are ranked first, second and third respectively among the profit making SLPEs.

Table 5.3

Top Five Profit-making Units (2007-08)

(₹ in lakh)

S. No.	*Name of the Enterprise*	*Amount*
1	Bihar State Financial Corp.	2625.9
2	Bihar State Mineral Development Corp.	929.04
3	Bihar State Warehousing Corp.	157.45
4	Bihar State Tourism Development Corp.	82.81
5	Bihar State Forest Development Corp.	27.63

Source: CAG (Commercial) India, 2007-08.

Bihar State Electricity Board (BSEB), Bihar State Road Transport Corporation (BSRTC) and Bihar Sate Hydro Electric Power Corporation (BSHEPC) are the major loss-making units. BSEB incurred losses owing to the mis-allocation of resources in sub-stations. BSRTC incurred loss due to the delay in payment of accidental compensation. The investment in mini hydro-electric project led to recurring loss of ₹ 1.83 crore per annum in BSHEPC.

Table 5.4

Top Five Loss-making Units (2007-08)

(₹ in lakh)

S. No.	*Name of the Enterprise*	*Amount*
1	Bihar State Electricity Board	85461.42
2	Bihar State Road Transport Corp.	5085.59
3	Bihar Sate Hydro Electric Power Corp.	1430.44
4	Bihar State Credit & Investment Corp.	903.36
5	Bihar State Text Book Pub. Corp.	455.62

Source: CAG (Commercial) India, 2007-08.

Budgetary Support

The loans given by the state and central government constitute the major share in the budgetary support followed by the grants and subsidies. The details regarding budgetary outgo towards equity, loans and grants/ subsidies for the period 2005-06 to 2007-08 are given in Table 5.5.

Table 5.5

Budgetary Support to SLPEs (2006-2008)

(₹ in crore)

S. No	*Particulars*	*2005-06*	*2006-07*	*2007-08*
1	Equity	0	11.2	4.05
2	Loans	1176.24	253.64	293.11
3	Grants/subsidies	0	0	23
4	Total	1176.24	264.84	320.16

Source: CAG (Commercial) India, 2007-08.

The budgetary support to the SLPEs has been fluctuating over the years. The budgetary support declined by 78.44 per cent from ₹ 1,176.24

crore in 2005-06 to ₹ 264.84 crore in 2006-07. It increased by 20 per cent in 2007-08. The government has meager equity and has not given any grants and subsidies to the SLPEs. The loans taken constitute a major constituent of the budgetary support of the SLPEs in Bihar.

Performance

Of the 20 SLPEs functioning in the state, 13 units are making losses and 6 enterprises are making profits. The SLPEs turnover to state GDP shows the extent of public enterprises activities in the state. Table 5.6 provides the details of SLPEs contribution to state GDP (SGDP) from 2005-06 to 2007-08.

Table 5.6

SLPEs Contribution to State GDP

(₹ in crore)

S. No.	*Particulars*	*2007-08*	*2006-07*	*2005-06*
1	Turnover	1588.26	1337.29	1179.68
2	State GDP	80993.9	81053.6	67394.2
3	Percentage of Turnover to State GDP	1.96	1.65	1.75

Source: CAG (Commercial) India, 2007-08.

The percentage of turnover to the SGDP has been declining steadily over the years. The decline in the turnover of the financial, manufacturing and promotional sectors showed a drop in their contribution to the state's GDP. The losses of SLPEs are mainly attributable to deficiencies in financial management, planning, implementation of project, running their operations and monitoring. The government initiated revival measures for the development of the state by mobilising the funds for the development of infrastructure, better health facilities, education, etc. The government decided for the closure of 5 working and 12 non-working enterprises. The government needs to consider conversion of loans into equity so as to reduce the interest burden, curb the unproductive staff, for which Voluntary Retirement Scheme (VRS) might be initiated. To revive and restore the SLPEs, the public-private partnership (PPP) is being commenced. The policies implemented in Bihar captivated the interest of Indian and global business leaders to invest in the state.

6 Chhattisgarh

Introduction

Chhattisgarh takes its name from 36 (*chhattis* is 36 and *garh* is fort) princely states that constitute the region. The economy of the state has rapidly grown in recent years with GDP growth of 7.35 per cent from 2004-05 to 2008-09. The gross state domestic product (GSDP) was ₹ 95,204 crore for 2008-09, registering a growth of 19.88 per cent. The per capita income, which is an important indicator of economic development, was ₹ 34,483 during 2008-09. The primary sector which includes agriculture, forest, fisheries and mining recorded a growth of 7.02 per cent; the secondary sector which includes construction, manufacturing, electricity, gas and water supply increased at 14.7 per cent; and the service sector grew at 7.78 per cent in 2008-09.

Nearly 80 per cent of the population depends on agriculture. Chhattisgarh is rich in mineral resources. Twenty per cent of the country's steel and cement is produced in the state. Iron ore, limestone, dolomite, coal, bauxite garnet corundum, quartz, marble and diamonds are found in the state. It is the only tin-ore producing state in the country. The State has private and state owned industries, which are significant part of state's economy. Bhilai steel plant and National Thermal Power Corporation (NTPC) are some of the public enterprises. Balco (sterlite industry), Lafarge and Jindal steel are some of big private companies in the state. There is a sharp increase in the growth rate of manufacturing sector with 8.05 per cent. The state is also launching an ambitious plan to become bio-fuel self-sufficient by 2015 by planting crops of jatropha.

Overview of SLPEs

The SLPEs were initiated from the Ninth Five Year Plan onwards in the state. There were 10 working SLPEs in Chhattisgarh as on March 31,

2008. Nearly 60 per cent of the enterprises were earning profits. The total investment was ₹ 3,151.78 crore consisting of paid-up capital and long-term loans. The capital employed declined from ₹ 2,309.26 crore in 2006-07 to ₹ 2,296.39 crore in 2007-08. The total number of employees was 19,677 in 2007-08 which declined from 19,932 in 2006-07. The turnover increased by 40 per cent from ₹ 2,676.2 crore in 2006-07 to ₹ 4,493.72 crore in 2007-08. The profit of the SLPEs in Chhattisgarh was ₹ 306.53 crore in 2007-08. The details are given in Table 6.1.

Table 6.1

Overview of SLPEs in Chhattisgarh

(₹ *in lakh)*

Particulars	*2007-08*	*2006-07*	*2005-06*
Investment			
Paid-up capital			
State Govt.	4258.21	4158.83	3758.83
Central Govt.	92.4	92.4	92.4
Others	0.07	0.08	15
Total	4350.68	4251.31	3866.23
Long-term Loan			
Government	88615.61	92265.27	82919.32
Others	222211.4	135450.8	12952
Total	310827.1	227716.1	95871.32
Total Investment	315177.7	231967.4	99737.55
Capital employed	229639	230926.6	217885.7
Turnover	449372.5	267620.4	301523.7
Net Profit/Loss	30652.9	13747.48	32890.14
Accumulated Profit/Loss	72851.53	45176.2	31928.37
No. of Employees	19677	19932	20043
Total Return on Capital employed	52273.43	33139.7	44799.34
Percentage of Total Return on Capital Employed	618.38	88.94	116.38
Subsidies/Grants			
Central Govt.	108323.4	65493	1798.95
State Govt.	86367.29	68708.38	18910.15
Total	194690.7	134201.4	20709.1

Source: Comptroller and Auditor General (CAG) (Commercial) India, 2007-08.

Categorisation

The SLPEs are classified into five categories: financial, manufacturing, promotional, utility and welfare sectors. The number of enterprises functioning under each category is shown in Figure 6.1. The manufacturing, promotional and utility enterprises constitute the largest number. There are no SLPEs in the financial and the welfare sectors. A multifold increase in the number of SLPEs during the Tenth Plan period led to a rapid growth of investment in public enterprises. The investment increased by 26 per cent i.e., from ₹ 2,319.67 core in 2005-06 to ₹ 3,151.78 crore in 2007-08. The investments are financed through the budgetary support from the state and central governments and other financial institutions.

Figure 6.1

Category-wise SLPEs in Chhattisgarh

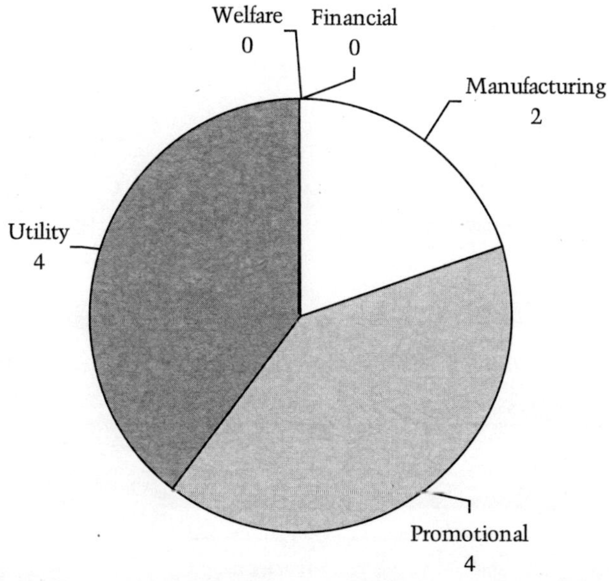

Source: CAG (Commercial) India, 2007-08.

Accumulated Profits and Losses

The accumulated losses of the SLPEs increased from ₹ 1,824.60 crore in 2006-07 to ₹ 2,14,831 in 2007-08 by 15.1 per cent. The losses were incurred mostly in the financial and the welfare sectors. The enterprises in the utility sector were earning profits (Table 6.2).

Table 6.2

Accumulated Profit and Loss of SLPEs

(₹ in lakh)

S. No.	*Particulars*	*2007-08*	*2006-07*	*2005-06*
1	Financial	0	0	0
2	Manufacturing	-15.63	20.16	-0.63
3	Promotional	-1151.84	-3590.96	-3198
4	Utility	74019	48747	35127
5	Welfare	0	0	0
6	Total	72851.53	45176.2	31928.37

Source: CAG (Commercial) India, 2007-08.

Top Five Profit-making and Loss-making Units

Tables 6.3 and 6.4 provide the information on top profit- and loss-making units in Chhattisgarh. Chhattisgarh State Electricity Board, Chhattisgarh State Civil Supplies Corporation and Chhattisgarh State Warehousing Corporation are ranked first, second and third respectively amongst the profit-making SLPEs.

Table 6.3

Top Five Profit-making Units (2007-08)

(₹ in lakh)

S. No.	*Name of the Enterprise*	*Amount*
1	Chhattisgarh State Electricity Board	26884
2	Chhattisgarh State Civil Supplies Corporation Ltd.	2945.79
3	Chhattisgarh State Warehousing Corporation	705.67
4	Chhattisgarh Van Vikas Nigam Ltd.	283.69
5	Chhattisgarh State Beverages Corporation Ltd.	59.39

Source: CAG (Commercial) India, 2007-08.

Chhattisgarh has only three loss-incurring enterprises. Chhattisgarh Mineral Development Corporation Limited (CMDC), Chhattisgarh State Industrial Development Corporation (CSIDC) and Chhattisgarh Infrastructure Development Corporation (CIDC) are the major loss-making units. Lack of planning and delay in the completion of projects resulted in loss for CSIDC. CMDC incurred loss due to the non-utiltisation of resources.

Table 6.4

Top Three Loss-making Units (2007-08)

(₹ in lakh)

S. No.	*Name of the Enterprise*	*Amount*
1	Chhattisgarh Mineral Development Corp.	-81.23
2	Chhattisgarh State Industrial Development Corp.	-78.33
3	Chhattisgarh Infrastructure Development Corp.	-28.01

Source: CAG (Commercial) India, 2007-08.

Budgetary Support

The grants and subsidies given by the state and central government constitute the major share in the budget support followed by the loans. The details regarding budgetary outgo towards equity, loans and grants/subsidies for the period 2005-06 to 2007-08 are given in Table 6.5.

Table 6.5

Budget Support to SLPEs (2006-2008)

(₹ in crore)

S. No.	*Particulars*	*2007-08*	*2006-07*	*2005-06*
1	Equity	1	1	0.50
2	Loans	8.13	5	11
3	Grants/subsidies	863 2/3	687.08	189.51
4	Total	872.8	693.08	201.01

Source: CAG (Commercial) India, 2007-08.

The budgetary support to SLPEs has been increasing over the years. The grants/subsidies from the state government constitute the major part of budgetary support to the SLPEs. Since the government wants to establish the enterprises, there is an increase in the budgetary support by 20.6

per cent in 2007-08. The government is promoting the establishment of industries by way of subsidies and grants.

Performance

Of the 10 SLPEs functioning in the state, 60 per cent of the units are making profits and the enterprises that are making losses are about 30 per cent. SLPEs turnover to state GDP shows the extent of public enterprises activities in the state. Table 6.6 provides the details of SLPEs contribution to state GDP from 2005-06 to 2007-08.

Table 6.6

SLPEs Contribution to State GDP

(₹ in crore)

S. No.	*Particulars*	*2007-08*	*2006-07*	*2005-06*
1	Turnover	4493.72	2676.2	3015.23
2	State GDP	67455	57782	51921
3	Percentage of Turnover to State GDP	6.66	4.63	5.81

Source: CAG (Commercial) India, 2007-08.

The percentage of turnover to the state GDP increased from 4.63 per cent in 2006-07 to 6.66 per cent in 2007-08. There is steady increase in the turnover of SLPEs due to an increase in business activities of the power sector. The losses of SLPEs are mainly attributable to deficiencies in financial management, planning, implementation of project, running their operations and monitoring. The state government need to introduce a performance-based system of accountability for enterprises. The government has taken up various developmental works for the speedy growth of the socioeconomic sector. The national and global investors are being encouraged to establish the industries in the state by providing the subsidies and grants. This transforms the mineral-rich state into a well-developed state benefitting the mass by modernisation, infrastructure development, etc.

7 Delhi

Introduction

Delhi is known as the national capital territory (NCT). Delhi is a major cultural, political and commercial centre which is ranked 12th in all India ranking. Delhi has India's largest and one of the fastest growing retail industries. The manufacturing industry has grown considerably, as many consumer goods industries have established manufacturing units and headquarters in and around Delhi. Construction, power, telecommunications, health and community services, and real estate form integral parts of Delhi's economy. The large consumer market, coupled with the easy availability of skilled labour, attracted foreign investment in Delhi. The key service industries include information technology (IT), telecommunications, hotels, banking, media and tourism. A major part of the gross state domestic product (GSDP) is contributed by finance, insurance, real estate and business services sector followed with trade, hotels and restaurants. The total value of GSDP in 2007-08 is ₹ 1,43,911 crore, to which, the contribution of primary sector is 0.70 per cent (₹ 1,006 crore), 20.25 per cent by the secondary sector (₹ 29,143 crore) and 79.05 per cent by the tertiary sector (₹ 1,13,761 crore). The per capita income of Delhi was ₹ 66,728.

The retail trade is the major economic activity undertaken in the NCT Delhi which has 48.9 per cent share in the total establishments followed by manufacturing (18.19%) and community, social, personal services and other activities (9.99%). Delhi contributes about 3.61 per cent of the total employment in India. The total number of persons employed in establishments was 35.56 lakh. The industrial units which contributed predominantly to employment is manufacturing of food products and beverages, wearing apparel, dressing and dying of fur, leather goods, publishing, printing and reproduction of recorded media, manufacturing of chemical and chemical products, fabricated metal products, machinery and equipment, electrical machinery and apparatus.

Overview of SLPEs

Over the years, the state has seen all-round progress in industrial development and infrastructure development. There were 19 working SLPEs in Delhi as on March 31, 2008. Nearly 64 per cent of the enterprises are making profits and 36 per cent are loss incurring. About 36 per cent

Table 7.1

Overview of SLPEs in Delhi

(₹ in lakh)

Particulars	*2007-08*	*2006-07*	*2005-06*
Investment			
Paid-up Capital			
State Govt.	548280.7	50657.18	51246.73
Central Govt.	1187.7	1187.7	1187.7
Others	32788.75	32702.75	32777.17
Total	582257.2	84547.63	85211.6
Long-term Loan			
Government	704400	946073.2	855677.8
Others	81361.06	99166.02	108243.4
Total	785761.1	1045239	963921.2
Total Investment	1368018	1129787	1049133
Capital Employed	228835	171290.5	215483.1
Turnover	301971.5	828341.4	773421.1
Net Profit/Loss	-114692	-142620	-87093.2
Accumulated Profit/Loss	-1085179	-870277	-810409
No. of Employees	33777	33750	35843
Total Return on Capital Employed	15508.4	-46138.7	-7928.52
Percentage of Total Return on Capital Employed	134.37	107.27	99.87
Subsidies/Grants			
Central Govt.	319	543.44	0
State Govt.	9865.17	20940.93	13133.45
Total	10184.17	21484.37	13133.45

Source: Comptroller and Auditor General (CAG) (Commercial) India, 2007-08.

of the enterprises were set up during the Ninth Plan period. The total investment was ₹ 13,680.18 crore consisting of paid-up capital and long-term loans. The capital employed increased by 25.15 per cent in 2007-08. The total number of employees was 33,777 in 2007-08. The turnover declined from ₹ 8,283.41 crore in 2006-07 to ₹ 3,019.71 crore in 2007-08. The SLPEs in Delhi incurred loss of ₹ 1,146.92 crore in 2007-08. The details are given in Table 7.1.

Categorisation

The SLPEs are classified into five categories: financial, manufacturing, promotional, utility and welfare sectors. The number of enterprises functioning under each category is shown in Figure 7.1. The utility and promotional enterprises constitute the largest number. The growth in the number of SLPEs and the increasing number of profit-making

Figure 7.1

Category-wise SLPEs in Delhi

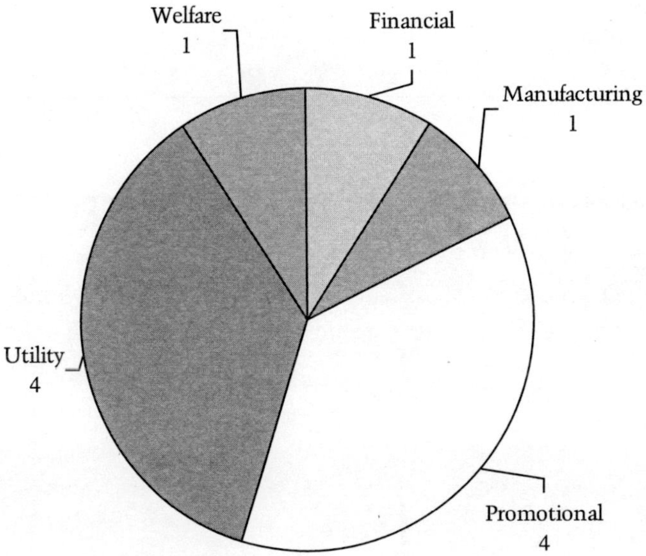

Source: CAG (Commercial) India, 2007-08.

units have increased the total investment levels. The investment was ₹ 11,297.87 crore in 2005-06 which increased to ₹ 13,680.08 crore in 2007-08. The investments are financed through the budgetary support from the state and central governments and other financial institutions.

Accumulated Profits and Losses

The accumulated losses of the SLPEs increased from ₹ 8,702.77 crore in 2006-07 to ₹ 10,851.79 crore in 2007-08 by 19.8 per cent. The losses were incurred mostly in the utility sector mainly by the Delhi Transport Corporation (DTC). The enterprises in the financial, promotional and welfare sectors were the profit earners (see Table 7.2).

Table 7.2

Accumulated Profit and Loss of SLPEs

(₹ in lakh)

S. No.	*Particulars*	*2007-08*	*2006-07*	*2005-06*
1	Financial	4835	4813.8	4344.14
2	Manufacturing	-79.92	-88	-99.39
3	Promotional	11066.55	9648.44	7612.29
4	Utility	-1102649	-885576	-822898
5	Welfare	1648.45	924.45	632.23
	Total	-1085179	-870277	-810409

Source: CAG (Commercial) India, 2007-08.

Top Five Profit-making and Loss-making Units

Tables 7.3 and 7.4 present the top profit- and loss-making units in Delhi. Pragati Corporation, Delhi Transco and Delhi State Industrial Infrastructure are ranked first, second and third amongst the profit-making SLPEs.

Table 7.3

Top Five Profit-making Units (2007-08)

(₹ in lakh)

S. No.	*Name of the Enterprise*	*Amount*
1	Pragati Corporation	9616.26
2	Delhi Transco	5878.63
3	Delhi State Industrial Infrastructure	1802.61
4	Delhi Tourism & Transport Development	1299.91
5	Delhi State Civil Supplies	951.65

Source: CAG (Commercial) India, 2007-08.

Table 7.4

Top Four Loss-making Units (2007-08)

(₹ in lakh)

S. No.	*Name of the Enterprise*	*Amount*
1	Delhi Transport Corporation	95482.32
2	Delhi Power Company	11204.13
3	Indraprastha Power Generation	1562.77
4	Delhi SC/ST/OBC/Mino Finance	0.08

Source: CAG (Commercial) India, 2007-08.

Delhi Transport Corporation (DTC), Delhi Power Company (DPC), Indraprastha Power Generation (IPG) are the major loss-making units. DTC incurred loss due to lack of supervision and mis-management by the authorities in their operations. DPC suffered loss owing to the irregularities in the distribution of finance.

Budgetary Support

Table 7.5 shows the budgetary support to the SLPEs during the year 2006-2008. The loans and grants/subsidies given by the state and central Government constitute the major share in the budget support followed by the equity.

Table 7.5

Budget Support to SLPEs (2006-2008)

(₹ in crore)

S. No.	Particulars	2005-06	2006-07	2007-08
1	Equity	1.81	8.3	1367.34
2	Loans	1397.85	978.66	1222.78
3	Grants/subsidies	131.33	209.41	96.98
4	Total	1530.99	1196.37	2687.10

Source: CAG (Commercial) India, 2007-08.

The budgetary support to the SLPEs has been fluctuating over the years. The budgetary support declined by 27.97 per cent in 2006-07. It increased from ₹ 1,196.37 crore in 2006-07 to ₹ 2,687.10 crore (i.e., by 55.48 per cent in 2007-08). The losses of SLPEs are mainly attributable to deficiencies in financial management, planning, implementation of project, running their operations and monitoring.

Performance

Of the 11 SLPEs functioning in the state, 7 units are making profits and 4 enterprises are making losses. SLPEs turnover to state GDP shows the extent of public enterprises activities in the state. Table 7.6 provides the details of SLPEs contribution to state GDP from 2006-07 to 2007-08.

Table 7.6

SLPEs Contribution to State GDP

(₹ in crore)

S. No.	Particulars	2006-07	2007-08
1	Turnover	8283.41	3019.71
2	State GDP	89487	109201
3	Percentage of Turnover to State GDP	9.26	2.77

Source: CAG (Commercial) India, 2007-08.

The percentage of turnover to the state GDP has been declining steadily over the years. The utility sector has a steep decline in the turnover, though there is a marginal increase in the turnover of the promotional and welfare sectors. So, the SLPEs contribution to the state GDP declined.

The SLPEs can execute their role efficiently only if they are financially self-reliant. There is scope for improvement in overall performance, when the government introduces a performance-based system of accountability and imbibes greater degree of professionalism to ensure efficiency and profitability. The government has taken restructuring measures in the power and the transportation sector. The vision 2021 strives to make Delhi into a world class city with better infrastructure facilities, technological development, public private partnerships and other innovative, well-devised policies and strategies for the development of the state.

8 Goa

Introduction

Goa is the smallest and richest state in India with a GDP per capita of two and a half times that of the country as a whole. It was ranked the best placed state by the Eleventh Finance Commission for its infrastructure and ranked on top for the best quality of life in India by the National Commission on Population. Tourism is the primary industry in Goa with 12 per cent of foreign tourist arrivals in India. Mining forms the second largest industry with focus on ores of iron, bauxite, manganese, clays, limestone and silica. The medium-scale industries include the manufacturing of pesticides, fertilisers, tyres, tubes, footwear, chemicals, pharmaceuticals, wheat products, steel rolling, fruits and fish canning, cashew nuts, textiles and brewery products.

During the last four decades, the industrial sector has grown leaps and bounds. The state has around 7,322 small-scale industrial units and 209 large-scale industries in the organised sector. The value addition sector increased from ₹ 3,294.85 crore in 2005-06 to ₹ 4,400.23 crore in 2008-09 at constant prices. The number of large- and medium-scale industries is 209 with a total investment and employment of ₹ 1,784.40 crore and 4,375 persons respectively. The industrial sector attracts sizeable investment and provides large-scale employment opportunities. The fishing industry provides employment for about 40,000 people. The gross state domestic product (GSDP) at constant prices was ₹ 12,161 crore in 2008-09. The major contribution to the GDP is from the tertiary sector with 53.21 per cent followed by the secondary and the primary sector with the contribution of 36.18 per cent and 10.61 per cent respectively. The industrial policy aims at accelerated industrial development, economic growth, balanced regional growth, environment protection and sustainable employment.

Overview of SLPEs

Over the years, the state has seen all-round progress in industrial development and infrastructure development. There were 17 working SLPEs in Goa as on March 31, 2008. Nearly 35.29 per cent of the enterprises are earning profits in the state. Amongst these, about 24 per cent of the enterprises were set up during the Sixth Plan period. The total investment was ₹ 461.24 crore consisting of paid-up capital and long-term loans. The capital employed increased by 12.5 per cent in 2007-08. The total number of employees was 3,242 which declined by 2.99 per cent in 2007-08. The turnover increased by 37.24 per cent from ₹ 219.41 crore in 2006-07 to ₹ 349.59 crore in 2007-08. The SLPEs in Goa made a profit of ₹ 32.43 crore in 2007-08. The details are given in Table 8.1.

Table 8.1

Overview of SLPEs in Goa

(₹ in lakh)

Particulars	*2007-08*	*2006-07*	*2005-06*
Investment			
Paid-up capital			
State Govt.	18852.75	16048.9	13525.53
Central Govt.	1175.21	1195.21	1175.21
Others	4442.12	4442.12	4683.58
Total	24470.08	21696.23	19384.32
Long-term Loan			
Government	249	185	185
Others	21405.35	25414.1	37242.83
Total	21654.35	25601.1	37429.83
Total Investment	46124.43	47297.33	56814.15
Capital employed	56319.5	49289.45	66249.05
Turnover	34958.78	21941.17	30189.98
Net Profit/Loss	3242.91	105.33	-2587
Accumulated Profit/Loss	-17385.4	-22418.6	-22500.4
No. of Employees	3242	3339	3327
Total Return on Capital Employed	8749.86	4202.37	2470.44
Percentage of Total Return on Capital Employed	19.5	42.59	-69.64
Subsidies/Grants	-		
Central Govt.	0	0	0
State Govt.	8516.32	7775.12	11336.76
Total	8516.32	7775.12	11336.76

Source: Comptroller and Auditor General (CAG) (Commercial) India, 2007-08.

Categorisation

The SLPEs are classified into five categories: financial, manufacturing, promotional, utility and welfare enterprises. The number of enterprises functioning under each category is shown in Figure 8.1. The manufacturing and promotional enterprises constitute the largest number. The growth in the number of SLPEs and the increasing number of profit-making units has reduced the total investment level. The investment was ₹ 472.97 crore in 2005-06 which declined to ₹ 461.24 crore in 2007-08, due to the repayment of loans. The investments are financed through the budgetary support from the state and central governments and other financial institutions.

Figure 8.1

Categorisation of SLPEs in Goa

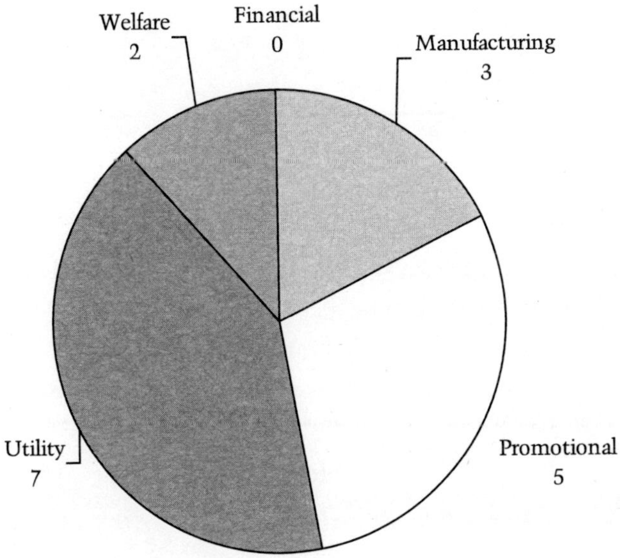

Source: CAG (Commercial) India, 2007-08.

Accumulated Profits and Losses

The accumulated losses of the SLPEs declined from ₹ 224.19 crore in 2006-07 to ₹ 173.85 in 2007-08. The losses were incurred mostly in the manufacturing, financial and utility sectors. There is a decline in the loss of the promotional sectors as the enterprises in this sector were earning profits (Table 8.2).

Table 8.2

Accumulated Profit and Loss of SLPEs

(₹ *in lakh)*

S. No.	*Particulars*	*2007-08*	*2006-07*	*2005-06*
1	Financial	-70.11	-32.78	-213.59
2	Manufacturing	-5286.8	-5181.1	-4959.4
3	Promotional	-4881.7	-10720	-12034
4	Utility	-7146.8	-6484.9	-5293.3
5	Welfare	0	0	0
6	Total	-17385	-22419	-22500

Source: CAG (Commercial) India, 2007-08.

Top Five Profit-making and Loss-making Units

Tables 8.3 and 8.4 provide the information on top five profit- and loss-making units in Goa. The Economic Development Corporation (EDC) Limited, Goa Industries Development Corporation and Goa State Infrastructure Development Corporation Limited are ranked first, second and third respectively amongst the profit-making SLPEs.

Table 8.3

Top Five Profit-making Units (2007-08)

(₹ *in lakh)*

S. No.	*Name of the Enterprise*	*Amount*
1	EDC Limited	4818.49
2	Goa Industries Development Corporation	1080.27
3	Goa State Infrastructure Development Corporation Ltd.	213.42
4	Goa Electronics Ltd.	74.81
5	Goa Handicrafts, Rural and Small Scale Industries Development Corporation Ltd.	48.54

Source: CAG (Commercial) India, 2007-08.

Kadamba Transport Corporation Limited, Goa Antibiotics and Pharmaceuticals Limited and Goa Meat Complex Limited are the major loss-making units.

Table 8.4

Top Five Profit-making Units (2007-08)

(₹ in lakh)

S. No.	*Name of the Enterprise*	*Amount*
1	Kadamba Transport Corporation Ltd.	-556.35
2	Goa Antibiotics and Pharmaceuticals Ltd.	-213.13
3	Goa Meat complex Ltd.	-81.11
4	Info Tech Corporation of Goa Limited	-39.03
5	Goa Auto Accessories Ltd.	-24.5

Source: CAG (Commercial) India, 2007-08.

Budgetary Support

The grants and subsidies given by the state and central government constitute the major share in the budget support followed by the equity. The details regarding budgetary outgo towards equity, loans and grants/subsidies during the year 2005-06 to 2007-08 are given in Table 8.5.

Table 8.5

Budget Support to SLPEs (2006-2008)

(₹ in crore)

S. No.	*Particulars*	*2007-08*	*2006-07*	*2005-06*
1	Equity	26.4	28.3	9.08
2	Loans	1	0	1
3	Grants/subsidies	86.32	74.16	114.68
4	Total	113.72	102.46	124.76

Source: CAG (Commercial) India, 2007-08.

The budgetary support to SLPEs has been varying over the years. The grants/subsidies from the state government constitute the major part of budgetary support to the SLPEs. Since the government wants to revive the enterprises, there is an increase in the budgetary support by 9 per cent.

Performance

Of the 17 SLPEs functioning in the state, more than 35 per cent of the units are making profits and nearly 53 per cent of the enterprises are incurring losses. The SLPEs turnover to state GDP shows the extent of public enterprises activities in the state. Table 8.6 provides the details of SLPEs contribution to state GDP from 2005-06 to 2007-08.

Table 8.6

SLPEs Contribution to State GDP

(₹ in crore)

S. No.	*Particulars*	*2007-08*	*2006-07*	*2005-06*
1	Turnover	349.59	219.41	301.89
2	State GDP	16901	15023	13354
3	Percentage of Turnover to State GDP	2.07	1.46	2.26

Source: CAG (Commercial) India, 2007-08.

The percentage of turnover to the state GDP increased from 1.46 per cent in 2006-07 to 2.07 per cent in 2007-08. In 2007-08, there is a slight increase in contribution to GDP from the SLPEs, owing to an increase in the turnover in all the sectors. The enterprises need to be self-reliant and competitive to ensure efficiency in delivery of the products and run profitably. The state government implemented various policy measures. The performance of the SLPEs is assessed and suitable measures are undertaken to improve revenue mobilisation through revision of the electricity tariff. Further, there is a need for assessment of recovery from economic and social services. To ensure steady growth, effective public expenditure management, accountability and transparency are taken care off. The government focused on the tourism sector, especially development of infrastructure through public-private partnership (PPP).

9 Gujarat

Introduction

Gujarat is one of the leading industrial states in India with world-class production capabilities and facilities in textiles, petrochemicals, pharmaceuticals and agro-based industries. The state has achieved remarkable economic growth which has brought prosperity to the people and enhanced their standard of living. The gross state domestic product (GSDP) at factor cost at constant (1999-2000) prices in 2007-08 has been estimated at ₹ 2,09,584.7 crore as against ₹ 1,85,802 crore in 2006-07, registering a growth of 12.8 per cent during 2007-08. The state is all set to move along the path of development. The state has witnessed impressive development in industrial sector over the years. The number of small industries was just 2,169 in the year 1961, whereas it has gone up to 3.12 lakh in 2006. Its manufacturing sector is constantly growing with the small and medium enterprise (SME) sector playing a significant role in shaping the manufacturing sector. The manufacturing units in the state account for the largest employment of manpower across industries. A good governance practice across the sectors is believed to be the key to success. The delivery of service is efficient and the understanding of technology is excellent and this has enabled Gujarat to position itself as a fast-growing industrial state.

According to the *Annual Survey of Industries* (ASI), Gujarat ranks second in India in terms of state-wise percentage share in net value added by manufacture generated by the factory sector. The ASI also stated that the share of Gujarat in the country's industrial aggregate is: 9.97 per cent of factories, 9.56 per cent of employees, 15.59 per cent of value of output and 13.86 per cent of net value added. The state is targeting an annual GDP growth of 11.02 per cent, agricultural growth of 5.5 per cent and industrial sector growth of 14 per cent during the Eleventh Five Year Plan (2007-2012) period.

Overview of SLPEs

Over the years, the state has seen all-round progress in industrial development and infrastructure development. There are 48 working SLPEs in Gujarat as on March 31, 2008. Majority of enterprises were set up during the Fifth Five Year Plan period. The total investment was ₹ 17,759.49 crore consisting of paid-up capital and long-term loans in 2007-08 and the capital employed is increased by 30.8 per cent. The total number of employees was 58,633 which decreased by 13 per cent in 2007-08. The turnover also decreased by 33.6 per cent from ₹ 52,285.58 crore in 2006-07 to ₹ 34,696.48 crore in 2007-08. In spite of decrease in the manpower employed and turnover, the SLPEs in Gujarat made a profit of ₹ 1,571.89 crore in 2007-08. The details are given in Table 9.1.

Table 9.1

Overview of SLPEs in Gujarat

(₹ in lakh)

Particulars	*2007-08*	*2006-07*	*2005-06*
Investment			
Paid-up Capital			
State Government	2311977	1989585	1660310
Central Government	996.3	996.3	996.31
Others	561759.1	542354.8	542136.1
Total	2874733	2532936	2203442
Long-term Loan			
Government	179037.6	103299.2	140682.4
Others	1596911	1837306	1865316
Total	1775949	1940605	2005999
Total Investment	4650681	4473540	4209441
Capital Employed	5864148	4481721	2877685
Turnover	3469648	5228558	397219.7
Net Profit/Loss	157189	136684	65695.95
Accumulated Profit/Loss	191626	114264.5	40315.15
No. of Employees	58633	67374	68013
Total Return on Capital Employed	313011.1	278705.7	101010.3
Percentage of Total Return on Capital Employed	295.56	375.15	257.94
Subsidies/Grants			
Central Government	36352.41	41414.65	23185.85
State Government	304011.7	260203.6	207585
Total	340364.1	301618.3	230770.9

Source: Comptroller and Auditor General (CAG) (Commercial) India, 2007-08.

Categorisation

The SLPEs are classified into five categories: financial, manufacturing, promotional, utility and welfare enterprises. The number of enterprises functioning under each category is shown in Figure 9.1. The promotional and utility enterprises constitute the largest number followed by enterprises in manufacturing and welfare sectors. The categorisation of SLPEs reveals that out of 48 enterprises, 14 were in the utility sector, 12 in promotional, 6 in financial and 8 in manufacturing and welfare sectors. The total investment in all the 48 enterprises grew by 4 per cent in 2007-08 from ₹ 44,735.40 crore in 2006-07 to ₹ 46,506.81 crore in 2007-08. The increase in this investment during 2007-08 was mainly due to infusion of capital by the state government in utility sector enterprises. The investments are financed through the budgetary support from the state and central governments and other financial institutions.

Figure 9.1

Categorisation of SLPEs in Gujarat (in numbers)

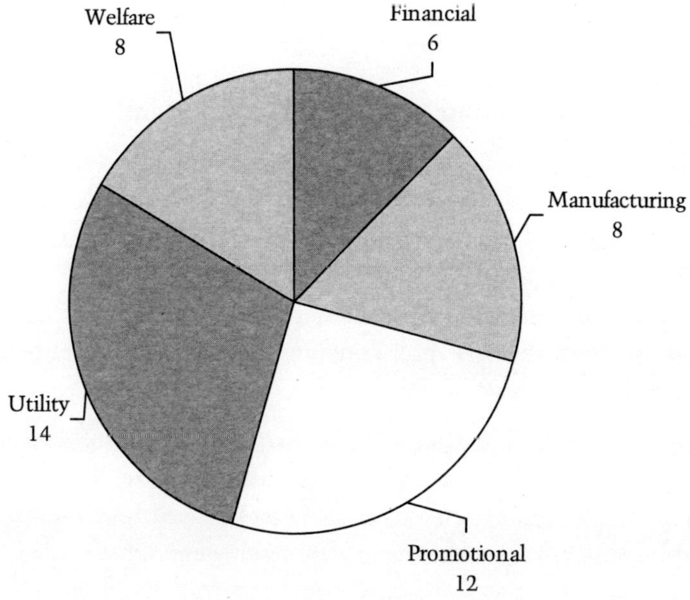

Source: CAG (Commercial) India, 2007-08.

Accumulated Profits and Losses

The accumulated profits of the SLPEs increased from ₹ 1,14,265 lakh in 2006-07 to ₹ 1,91,626 lakh in 2007-08. The enterprises in manufacturing, utility and welfare sectors are the major profit earners. Amongst the profit earners, the SLPEs in the manufacturing sector top the list with an accumulated profit of ₹ 2,40,696 lakh in 2007-08. The losses were incurred mostly in the financial and promotional sectors (Table 9.2).

Table 9.2

Category-wise SLPEs Accumulated Profit and Loss

(₹ in lakh)

Category	*2007-08*	*2006-07*	*2005-06*
Financial	-62937	-67528	-73728
Manufacturing	240696	170254	90981.7
Promotional	-3158.1	-2160	-15092
Utility	16753.6	13490	38070.7
Welfare	271.87	208.29	82.82
Total	191626	114265	40315.2

Source: CAG (Commercial) India, 2007-08.

Top Five Profit-making and Loss-making Units

Tables 9.3 and 9.4 provide the information on top five profit-earning and loss-making enterprises in Gujarat. The Gujarat State Electricity Corporation Limited, Gujarat Mineral Development Corporation Limited, Gujarat State Petroleum Corporation Limited (GSPC Limited) are ranked first, second and third respectively amongst the profit-making SLPEs. Table 9.3 also indicates that the profit making enterprises are centred in the manufacturing and utility sectors.

The SLPEs in the financial sector are the major loss-making enterprises. Table 9.4 indicates that Gujarat State Road Transport Corporation, Gujarat Urja Vikas Nigam Limited and Gujarat State Financial Corporation are the major loss-making enterprises.

Table 9.3

Top Five Profit-making Units (2007-08)

(₹ in lakh)

S. No.	Name of the Enterprise	Amount
1	Gujarat State Electricity Corporation Limited	50748.79
2	Gujarat Mineral Development Corporation Limited	40839.48
3	Gujarat State Petroleum Corporation Limited (GSPC Limited)	30383.00
4	Gujarat Industrial Development Corporation	7938.06
5	GSPC Gas Company Limited	5614.62

Source: CAG (Commercial) India, 2007-08.

Table 9.4

Top Five Loss-making Units (2007-08)

(₹ in lakh)

S. No.	Name of the Enterprise	Amount
1	Gujarat State Road Transport Corporation	6613.86
2	Gujarat Urja Vikas Nigam Limited	3176.47
3	Gujarat State Financial Corporation	1200.67
4	Gujarat State Handloom and Handicraft Development Corporation Limited	219.01
5	Gujarat State Land Development Corporation Limited	117.13

Source: CAG (Commercial) India, 2007-08.

Budgetary Support

Table 9.5 shows the budgetary support to the SLPEs from the year 2005-06 to 2007-08. The grants and subsidies given by the state and central governments constitute the major share in the budget support followed by the equity.

Table 9.5

Budget Support to SLPEs (2006-2008)

(₹ in crore)

S. No.	Particulars	2005-06	2006-07	2007-08
1	Equity	1478.15	2697.93	3249.73
2	Loans	371.62	263.13	369.51
3	Grants/subsidies	2432.35	2966.29	3402.6
4	Total	4282.12	5927.35	7021.84

Source: CAG (Commercial) India, 2007-08.

The budgetary support to SLPEs has been increasing over the years. The grants and subsidies from the state and central governments constitute the major part of budgetary support to the SLPEs followed by the equity. In 2007-08, the state government increased the share of grants/subsidies in the total budgetary support to a tune of 14.7 per cent. The state government is making industrial policies in keeping view the balanced regional development and employment generation.

Performance

Of the 48 SLPEs functioning in the state, the major number of enterprises is profit-making enterprises. SLPEs turnover to state GDP shows the extent of public enterprises activities in the state. Table 9.6 provide the details of SLPEs contribution to state GDP from 2005-06 to 2007-08.

Table 9.6

SLPEs Contribution to State GDP

(₹ in crore)

S. No.	*Particulars*	*2007-08*	*2006-07*
1	Turnover	34696.48	52285.58
2	State GDP	280086	254533
3	Percentage of Turnover to State GDP	12.4	20.5

Source: CAG (Commercial) India, 2007-08.

It can be seen from the above table that the percentage of turnover to the state GDP has been declined from 20.5 per cent in 2006-07 to 12.4 per cent in 2007-08. This is due to overall declining turnover in general and turnover of promotional enterprises in particular, which also constitute 25 per cent of the total SLPEs in the state. The state government of Gujarat is actively working on phase-wise restructuring of SLPEs. In the first phase, the government has short listed 12 enterprises for restructuring. As a first step towards restructuring, it has also completed reorganisation of Gujarat Electricity Board (GEB), which earlier was a major loss-incurring enterprise.

The government has also laid a policy framework through a series of policy and vision documents. Various industrial policies designed by the Government of Gujarat have been facilitating flow of private investment by offering investment and other subsidies, entrepreneurial training, export promotion and technological upgradation to improve production efficiency and turnover in the SLPEs. The Gujarat Infrastructure Development Agenda, 2010, has laid down the roadmap for infrastructure development in the state. The 'Gujarat Infrastructure Development Act, 1999,' has been also enacted to provide a framework for private sector participation in the financing, construction, maintenance and operation of various infrastructure projects in the state.

10 Haryana

Introduction

Haryana means the Abode of God. It is derived from Sanskrit words *Hari* (the Hindu God Vishnu) and *ayana* (home) and also referred to the lush green landscape of the state. The state has always given high priority to the expansion of electricity infrastructure, as it is one of the most important inputs for the development of the state. It was the first state in the country to achieve 100 per cent rural electrification in 1970, link all villages with all-weather roads and provide safe drinking water facilities throughout the state. Haryana now ranks 3rd amongst states in software exports from India. More than a thousand medium and large industries with a capital investment of ₹ 2,000 billion are established in the state mainly at Gurgaon, Panchkula, Panipat, Faridabad and Bahadurgarh. As a result, Haryana's share in national production is 50 per cent in passenger cars, motorcycles, 30 per cent in refrigerators, 25 per cent in tractors, bicycles and sanitary ware and 20 per cent of the country's export of scientific instruments.

The gross state domestic product (GSDP) of Haryana at constant (1999-2000) prices was ₹ 1,11,420.13 crore in 2008-09 as against ₹ 1,03,244.09 crore in 2007-08 recording a growth of 7.9 per cent during 2008-09. The contribution of primary sector to the state GDP was 19.8 per cent, while the secondary sector contributed 28.8 per cent and tertiary sector had a major share of 51.4 per cent in 2008-09. Haryana has the 2nd highest per capita income in the country.

Overview of SLPEs

Over the years, the state has seen all-round progress in industrial development and infrastructure development. There were 21 working

SLPEs in Haryana as on March 31, 2008. Nearly 67 per cent of the enterprises are making profits and 29 per cent are incurring losses. The total investment was ₹ 17,449.66 crore consisting of paid-up capital and long-term loans. The capital employed increased by 27.8 per cent in 2007-08. The total number of employees declined from 1.32 lakh in 2006-07 to 0.39 lakh in 2007-08. The turnover increased by 43.8 per cent from ₹ 8,248.11 crore in 2006-07 to ₹ 14,668 crore in 2007-08. The SLPEs in Haryana were incurring a loss of ₹ 486.24 crore in 2007-08. The details are given in Table 10.1.

Table 10.1

Overview of SLPEs in Haryana

(₹ in lakh)

Particulars	*2007-08*	*2006-07*	*2005-06*
Investment			
Paid-up Capital			
State Government	594941.8	594941.8	287185.5
Central Government	2503.51	2489.09	2085.57
Others	112196.3	99198.13	99195.41
Total	709641.6	528719.7	388466.5
Long-term Loan			
Government	16814.05	53692.86	56887.67
Others	1036934	779755	708663.5
Total	1035324	833447.8	765551.2
Total Investment	1744966	1362167	1154018
Capital Employed	1368677	988466.1	854053.3
Turnover	1466800	824811.3	759619.6
Net Profit/Loss	-48624.5	-26094.7	-38526.2
Accumulated Profit/Loss	-240503	-176069	-139559
No. of Employees	38757	132201	40256
Total Return on Capital Employed	33510.88	27657.1	13666.13
Percentage of Total Return on Capital Employed	124.16	117.92	126.12
Subsidies/Grants			
Central Government	5318.27	2529.96	18311.91
State Government	264363.7	378183.8	135309.5
Total	269681.9	380713.7	154191.4

Source: Comptroller and Auditor General (CAG) (Commercial) India, 2007-08.

Categorisation

The SLPEs are classified into five categories: financial, manufacturing, promotional, utility and welfare enterprises. The number of enterprises functioning under each category is shown in Figure 10.1. The manufacturing and promotional enterprises constitute the largest number. The growth in the number of SLPEs and the increasing number of profit-making units has increased the total investment level. The investment was ₹ 13,621.67 crore in 2005-06 which increased to ₹ 17,449.66 crore in 2007-08. The investments are financed through the budgetary support from the state and central governments and other financial institutions.

Figure 10.1

Category-wise SLPEs in Haryana

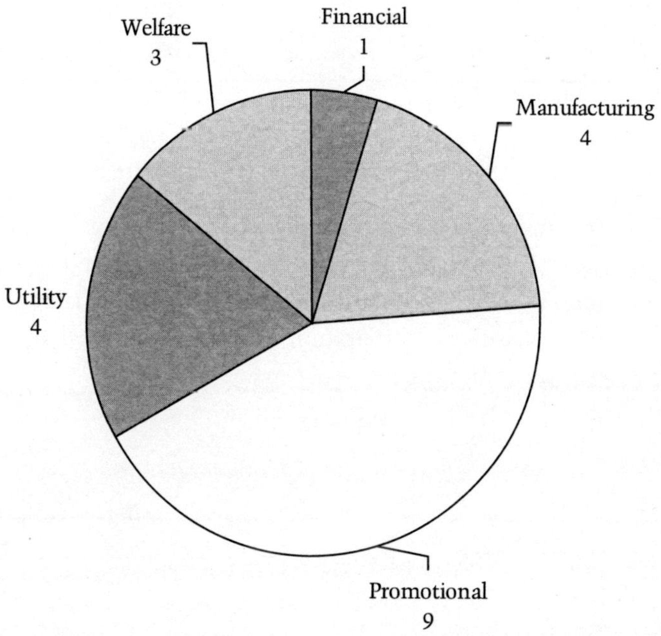

Source: CAG (Commercial) India, 2007-08.

Accumulated Profits and Losses

The accumulated losses of the SLPEs increased from ₹ 1,760.69 crore in 2006-07 to ₹ 2,405.03 crore in 2007-08 by 15.1 per cent. The losses were incurred mostly in the utility and the financial sectors. The enterprises in the promotional sector were earning profits during the same period (Table 10.2).

Table 10.2

Accumulated Profit and Loss of SLPEs

(₹ in lakh)

S. No.	*Particulars*	*2007-08*	*2006-07*	*2005-06*
1	Financial	-13521.9	-15032	-15991
2	Manufacturing	539.73	419.04	529.34
3	Promotional	10484.58	9869.73	6375.66
4	Utility	-237511	-170823	-129798
5	Welfare	-494.56	-502.34	-675.14
	Total	-240503	-176069	-139559

Source: CAG (Commercial) India, 2007-08.

Top Five Profit-making and Loss-making Units

Tables 10.3 and 10.4 provide the information on top five profit- and loss-making units in Haryana. Haryana Vidyut Prasaran Nigam Limited, Haryana Warehousing Corporation and Haryana State Industrial and Infrastructure Development Corporation Limited are ranked first, second and third respectively amongst the profit-making SLPEs.

Table 10.3

Top Five Profit-making Units (2007-08)

(₹ in lakh)

S. No.	*Name of the Enterprise*	*Amount*
1	Haryana Vidyut Prasaran Nigam Limited	16145.98
2	Haryana Warehousing Corporation	3145.08
3	Haryana State Industrial and Infrastructure Development Corporation Limited	2625.90
4	Haryana Agro Industries Corporation Limited	196.86
5	Haryana Tourism Corporation Limited	141.22

Source: CAG (Commercial) India, 2007-08.

Uttar Haryana Bijli Vitran Nigam Limited (UHBVN), Dakshin Haryana Bijli Vitran Nigam Limited (DHBVN) and Haryana Financial Corporation (HFC) are the major loss-making units. HFC was incurring losses due to non-recovery of loans and failure in mobilising the funds. UHBVN and DHBVN incurred losses owing to an increase in the expenditure on purchase of transformers, poles, etc.

Table 10.4

Top Five Loss-making Units (2007-08)

(₹ in lakh)

S. No.	*Name of the Enterprise*	*Amount*
1	Uttar Haryana Bijli Vitran Nigam Limited	30149.6
2	Dakshin Haryana Bijli Vitran Nigam Limited	28482.49
3	Haryana Financial Corporation	10285
4	Haryana State Road and Bridges Development Corp.	2503.34
5	Haryana State Minor Irrigation and Tube wells Corp.	944.33

Source: CAG (Commercial) India, 2007-08.

Budgetary Support

Table 10.5 shows the budgetary support to the SLPEs during the years 2006-2008. The grants and subsidies given by the state and central government constitute the major share in the budget support followed by the equity.

Table 10.5

Budget Support to SLPEs (2006-2008)

(₹ in crore)

S. No.	*Particulars*	*2005-06*	*2006-07*	*2007-08*
1	Equity	351.47	789.96	920.97
2	Loans	5.09	202.68	2.51
3	Grants/subsidics	1316	3781.31	2643.2
4	Total	1672.66	4773.95	3566.68

Source: CAG (Commercial) India, 2007-08.

The budgetary support to the SLPEs has been fluctuating over the years. The budgetary support increased from ₹ 1,672.66 crore in 2005-06 to ₹ 4,773.95 crore in 2006-07 by 64.9 per cent. It declined by 33 per cent in

2007-08. The increase in the number of profit-making enterprises resulted in the decline in the budgetary support due to restructuring measures taken in the state.

Performance

Of the 21 SLPEs functioning in the state, more than 14 units are making profits and 6 enterprises are making losses. The SLPEs turnover to state GDP shows the extent of public enterprises activities in the state. Table 10.6 provides the details of SLPEs contribution to state GDP from 2005-06 to 2007-08.

Table 10.6

SLPEs Contribution to State GDP

(₹ in crore)

S. No.	*Particulars*	*2005-06*	*2006-07*	*2007-08*
1	Turnover	7596.19	8248.11	14668
2	State GDP	106732	130033	153087
3	Percentage of Turnover to State GDP	7.12	6.34	9.58

Source: CAG (Commercial) India, 2007-08.

The percentage of turnover to the state GDP has been declining steadily over the years. Though there is an increase in the turnover of the promotional, utility and the welfare sectors, their contribution to the state GDP declined owing to a decline in the turnover of the manufacturing sector. The losses of SLPEs are mainly attributable to deficiencies in financial management, planning, implementation of projects, running their operations and monitoring. The restructuring measures were taken up in various sectors to ensure the effective growth in the enterprises. The government granted autonomy to SLPEs to bring greater efficiency in their functioning as well as accountability.

11 Himachal Pradesh

Introduction

Himachal Pradesh was also known as *Deva Bhumi* (the land of the Gods). The economy of the state is highly dependent on hydroelectric power, tourism and agriculture. Himachal Pradesh is extremely rich in hydroelectric resources with about 25 per cent of the total potential of the nation. It has been estimated that about 20,300 MW of hydroelectric power can be generated in the state by constructing various major, medium, small and mini/micro hydel projects on the five river basins. The gross state domestic product (GSDP) was ₹ 24,817 crore in 2007-08 as against ₹ 22,854 crore in 2006-07 registering a growth of 8.6 per cent. The per capita income at current prices grew at 9.1 per cent as it increased from ₹ 36,781 in 2006-07 to ₹ 40,134 in 2007-08. The increase in GSDP is mainly attributed to 11.8 per cent in secondary sectors, 7.2 per cent in primary sector, 3.8 per cent in transport and trade and 6.1 per cent in services sector.

Agriculture is the main source of income and employment. Over 93 per cent of the population depends upon agriculture which provides employment to 71 per cent of its people. Himachal has a rich heritage of handicrafts. The state made significant achievements in the field of industrialisation in the past few years with the ushering of the liberalised economy and consequent delicensing and notification of special package of incentives. The flow of investment increased manifold resulting in very good response for setting up new industrial ventures in the state. As on December 31, 2008, there were 401 medium- and large-scale industries and 35,427 small-scale industries with a total investment of about ₹ 7,737.73 crore working in the state. These industries provide employment to about 2.24 lakh workers.

Overview of SLPEs

Over the years, the state has seen all-round progress in industrial development and infrastructure development. There were 19 working SLPEs in Himachal Pradesh as on March 31, 2008. About 36 per cent of the enterprises were set up during the Fourth Plan period. Nearly 42 per cent of the enterprises are making profits and 53 per cent are incurring loss. The total investment was ₹ 3,837.46 crore consisting of paid-up capital and long-term loans. The capital employed declined by 12.64 per cent in 2007-08. The total number of employees increased by 29.2 per cent i.e., from 29,978 in 2006-07 to 42,371 in 2007-08. There is an increase in the turnover by 14.73 per cent from ₹ 2,995.34 crore in 2006-07 to ₹ 3,512.83 crore in 2007-08. The SLPEs in Himachal Pradesh incurred a loss of ₹ 71.46 crore in 2007-08. The details are given in Table 11.1.

Table 11.1

Overview of SLPEs in Himachal Pradesh

(₹ in lakh)

Particulars	*2007-08*	*2006-07*	*2005-06*
Investment			
Paid-up Capital			
State Govt.	88581.78	71609.38	67672.93
Central Govt.	1903.05	1903.05	1903.05
Others	1394.05	1434.05	1375.63
Total	91878.88	74946.48	70951.61
Long-term Loan			
Government	5843.37	6326	6330.48
Others	286022.8	307359.7	297062.2
Total	291867.2	313685.7	303392.7
Total Investment	383746	388632	374344.3
Capital Employed	352015.6	396507.8	423258.6
Turnover	351283.2	299533.7	252832.4
Net Profit/Loss	-7146.24	-7443.92	-403.66
Accumulated Profit/Loss	-100262	-88519.5	-81702.7
No. of Employees	42371	29978	40257
Total Return on Capital Employed	13810.2	9522	15202.08
Percentage of Total Return on Capital Employed	85.71	87.55	137.6
Subsidies/Grants			
Central Govt.	7777.87	7631.9	9617.72
State Govt.	323.86	5697.13	13081
Total	8101.73	13329.03	22698.72

Source: Comptroller and Auditor General (CAG) (Commercial) India, 2007-08.

Categorisation

The SLPEs are classified into five categories: financial, manufacturing, promotional, utility and welfare enterprises. The number of enterprises functioning under each category is shown in Figure 11.1. The promotional, utility and manufacturing enterprises constitute the largest number. The increase in the number of loss-making SLPEs led to a decline in the total investment level. The investment was ₹ 3,886.32 crore in 2006-07 which declined to ₹ 3,837.46 crore in 2007-08. The investments are financed through the budgetary support from the state and central governments and other financial institutions.

Figure 11.1

Category-wise SLPEs in Himachal Pradesh

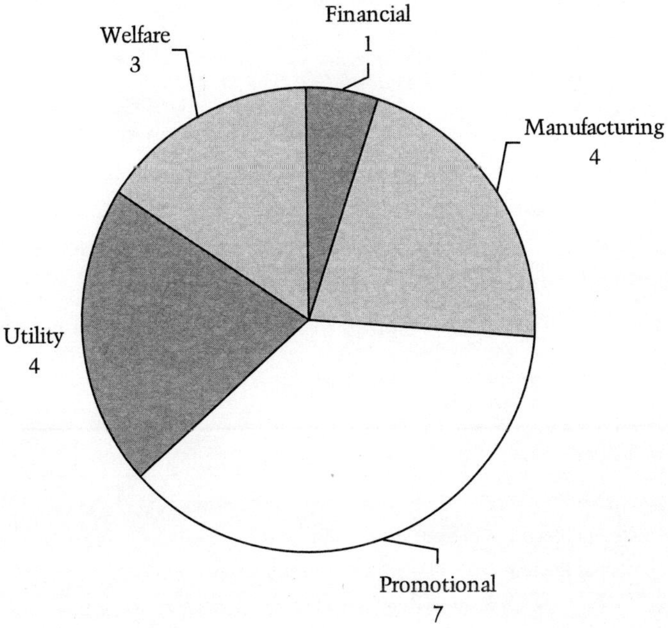

Source: CAG (Commercial) India, 2007-08.

Accumulated Profits and Losses

The accumulated losses of the SLPEs increased from ₹ 885.19 crore in 2006-07 to ₹ 1,002.62 crore in 2007-08 by 11.71 per cent. The losses were incurred mostly in the utility and the promotional sector. The enterprises in the manufacturing, financial and the welfare sector were earning profits, so there is a decline in the accumulated losses (Table 11.2).

Table 11.2

Accumulated Profit and Loss of SLPEs

(₹ in lakh)

S. No.	*Particulars*	*2007-08*	*2006-07*	*2005-06*
1	Financial	-9572.57	-10225.9	-8959.22
2	Manufacturing	-1370.9	-1560.45	-1545.79
3	Promotional	-15257.8	-12505.1	-10588.6
4	Utility	-74076.6	-64265.1	-60629.2
5	Welfare	16.27	36.96	20.18
	Total	-100262	-88519.5	-81702.7

Source: CAG (Commercial) India, 2007-08.

Top Five Profit-making and Loss-making Units

Tables 11.3 and 11.4 provide the information on top five profit- and loss-making units in Himachal Pradesh. Himachal Pradesh State Industrial Development Corporation, Himachal Pradesh Financial Corporation and Himachal Pradesh State Electronics Development Corporation are ranked first, second and third amongst the profit-making SLPEs.

Table 11.3

Top Five Profit-making Units (2007-08)

(₹ in lakh)

S. No.	*Name of the Enterprise*	*Amount*
1	Himachal Pradesh State Industrial Development Corp.	680.9
2	Himachal Pradesh Financial Corp.	673.71
3	Himachal Pradesh State Electronics Development Corp.	151.96
4	Himachal Pradesh State Civil Supplies Corp.	113.09
5	Himachal Pradesh General Industries Corp.	73.64

Source: CAG (Commercial) India, 2007-08.

Himachal Pradesh Road Transport Corporation (HPRTC), Himachal Pradesh State Electricity Board (HPSEB) and Agro Industrial Packaging India Limited are the major loss-making units. HPRTC incurred loss owing to the uneconomic operation of the services. HPSEB suffered loss due to delay in formulation and execution of various policies, resulting excess in unproductive expenditure.

Table 11.4

Top Five Loss-making Units (2007-08)

(₹ in lakh)

S. No.	*Name of the Enterprise*	*Amount*
1	Himachal Pradesh Road Transport Corporation	-4009.45
2	Himachal Pradesh State Electricity Board	-2538.23
3	Agro industrial Packaging India Ltd.	-819.06
4	Himachal Pradesh Horticulture Produce Marketing & Processing corp.	-626.07
5	Himachal Pradesh Tourism Development Corporation	-621.36

Source: CAG (Commercial) India, 2007-08.

Budgetary Support

Table 11.5 shows the budgetary support to the SLPEs during the years 2006-2008. The grants and subsidies given by the state and central government constitute the major share in the budget support followed by the equity.

Table 11.5

Budgetary Support to SLPEs (2006-2008)

(₹ in crore)

S. No.	*Particulars*	*2005-06*	*2006-07*	*2007-08*
1	Equity	13.99	14.36	164.83
2	Loans	1.97	7.93	0.5
3	Grants/subsidies	130.81	56.97	213.49
4	Total	146.77	79.26	378.82

Source: CAG (Commercial) India, 2007-08.

The budgetary support to the SLPEs has been fluctuating over the years. The budgetary support declined from ₹ 146.77 crore in 2005-06 to ₹ 79.26 crore in 2006-07. It increased by 79.08 per cent in 2007-08. There is an increase in the budgetary support as the government invested in 10 SLPEs in the state.

Performance

Of the 19 SLPEs functioning in the state, 8 units are making profits and 10 enterprises are making losses. The SLPEs turnover to state GDP shows the extent of public enterprises activities in the state. Table 11.6 provides the detail of SLPEs contribution to state GDP from 2005-06 to 2007-08.

Table 11.6

SLPEs Contribution to State GDP

(₹ *in crore)*

S. No.	*Particulars*	*2005-06*	*2006-07*	*2007-08*
1	Turnover	2528.32	2995.34	3512.83
2	State GDP	25471	28358	31974
3	Percentage of Turnover to State GDP	9.93	10.56	10.99

Source: CAG (Commercial) India, 2007-08.

The percentage of turnover to the state GDP is slightly increasing over the years. The increase in the turnover of the manufacturing, financial and utility sectors, led to an increase in their contribution to the state GDP, though there is a decline in the turnover of the promotional sector. The losses of SLPEs are mainly attributable to deficiencies in financial management, planning, implementation of projects, running their operations and monitoring. The Government of Himachal Pradesh has taken initiatives like modernisation and technological upgradation through innovative research, design and development, human resource development through skill upgradation and training, infrastructure development, simplified procedures and good governance for the socioeconomic development of the state. The Industrial Renewal and Revival Scheme, 2004, was set off for the industrial development of small, medium- and large-scale units in the state. The other incentives given by the government were to encourage investment and optimum utiltisation of the resources of the state, namely, power, land, capital, manpower and raw material in terms of employment and revenue generation.

12 Jammu & Kashmir

Introduction

Jammu & Kashmir (J&K) is the only state in India which enjoys special autonomy under Article 370 of the Constitution of India. The economy is mainly dependent on agriculture and allied activities. Horticulture plays a vital role in the economic development of the state. This sector is the next biggest source of income with an annual turnover of over ₹ 300 crore, apart from foreign exchange of over ₹ 80 crore. Industrial development in the state faces several major constraints including extreme mountainous landscape and power shortage. Though small, the manufacturing and services sector is growing rapidly, especially in the Jammu division. In recent years, several consumer companies have opened manufacturing units in the region. The Associated Chambers of Commerce and Industry of India (ASSOCHAM) identified several industrial sectors which can attract investment in the state, and accordingly, it is working with the union and the state government to set up industrial parks and special economic zones.

The gross state domestic product (GSDP) at current prices was about US$ 7.9 billion in 2007-08. The average annual GSDP growth rate from 1999-2000 to 2007-08 was about 11.3 per cent. The tertiary sector contributed 56.9 per cent to the state GSDP in 2007-08. It was followed by the primary sector at 34.6 per cent. The secondary sector's share in GSDP was 8.4 per cent in 2007-08. The mining and quarrying registered an average growth rate of 10 per cent between 1999-2000 and 2007-08. Indian government commenced work on the Kashmir Railway project which is being constructed by Konkan Railway Corporation and IRCON at a cost of more than US$ 2.5 billion to economically integrate J&K with the rest of India and improve the infrastructure in the state.

Overview of SLPEs

Over the years, the state has been attempting for the progress in industrial and infrastructure development There were 20 working SLPEs in J&K as on March 31, 2008. About 25 per cent of them were set up during the Fourth Plan period. Nearly 35 per cent of the enterprises are making profits and 55 per cent are incurring losses. The total investment was ₹ 4,761.03 crore consisting of paid-up capital and long-term loans. The capital employed increased by 10.92 per cent in 2007-08. The total number of employees increased from 29,698 in 2006-07 to 30,011 in 2007-08. There is an increase in the turnover by 25.22 per cent from ₹ 2,689.17 crore in 2006-07 to ₹ 3,595.92 crore in 2007-08. The profits of the SLPEs in J&K increased by 25 per cent i.e., from ₹ 151.67 crore in 2006-07 to ₹ 202.64 crore in 2007-08. The details are given in Table 12.1.

Table 12.1

Overview of SLPEs in Jammu & Kashmir

(₹ in lakh)

Particulars	*2007-08*	*2006-07*	*2005-06*
Investment			
Paid-up Capital			
State Government	32500.31	32380.31	32130.31
Central Government	5237.47	5187.03	5119.78
Others	2290.15	2290.15	2290.15
Total	40027.93	39857.49	39540.24
Long-term Loan	0	0	0
Government	113887.2	106052.3	118620.9
Others	322188.2	296785.9	161892.2
Total	436075.3	402838.1	280513.2
Total Investment	476103	442695.6	320053.4
Capital Employed	2141565	1907651	844744.3
Turnover	359592	268916.6	255367.5
Net Profit/Loss	20263.62	15167.68	7116.86
Accumulated Profit/Loss	-127419	-121917	-61808.8
No. of Employees	30011	29698	29669
Total Return on Capital Employed	189658.3	136953.9	117937.3
Percentage of Total Return on Capital Employed	74.43	75.48	-478.07
Subsidies/Grants	0	0	0
Central Government	6839	17381.58	10143.48
State Government	1217.96	18755.46	21812.68
Total	8056.96	36137.04	31956.36

Source: Comptroller and Auditor General (CAG) (Commercial) India, 2007-08.

Categorisation

The SLPEs are classified into five categories: financial, manufacturing, promotional, utility and welfare enterprises. The number of enterprises functioning under each category is shown in Figure 12.1. The promotional and manufacturing enterprises constitute the largest number. The increase in the number of profit-making SLPEs led to an increase in the total investment level. The investment was ₹ 4,426.95 crore in 2006-07 which increased to ₹ 4,761.03 crore in 2007-08. The investments are financed through the budgetary support from the State and Central governments and other financial institutions.

Figure 12.1

Category-wise SLPEs in Jammu & Kashmir

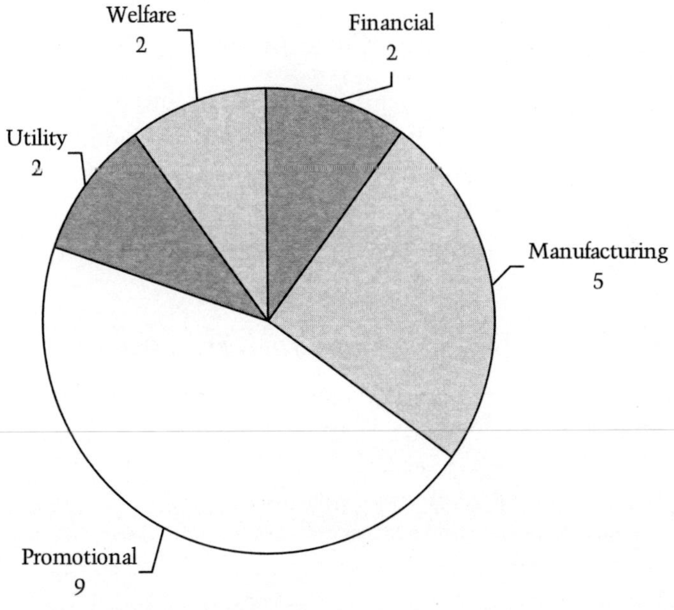

Source: CAG (Commercial) India, 2007-08.

Accumulated Profits and Losses

The accumulated losses of the SLPEs increased from ₹ 1,219.17 crore in 2006-07 to ₹ 1,274.19 crore in 2007-08 by 4.32 per cent. The losses were incurred mostly in the utility sector. The enterprises in the manufacturing and the promotional sector were earning profits, so there was a decline in the accumulated losses (Table 12.2).

Table 12.2

Accumulated Profit and Loss of SLPEs

(₹ in lakh)

S. No.	*Particulars*	*2007-08*	*2006-07*	*2005-06*
1	Financial	-19249.9	-19249.9	-19713.5
2	Manufacturing	-26689.1	-26659.5	-24072
3	Promotional	-10825.5	-11817.9	-10558.1
4	Utility	-70650.7	-64185.7	-7465.2
5	Welfare	-3.8	-3.8	0
	Total	-127419	-121917	-61808.8

Source: CAG (Commercial) India, 2007-08.

Top Five Profit-making and Loss-making Units

Tables 12.3 and 12.4 provide the information on top five profit- and loss-making units in J&K. Jammu & Kashmir Bank Limited, Jammu & Kashmir State Financial Corporation and Jammu & Kashmir Small Scale Industries Development Corporation are ranked first, second and third respectively amongst the profit-making SLPEs.

Table 12.3

Top Five Profit-making Units (2007-08)

(₹ in lakh)

S. No.	*Name of the Enterprise*	*Amount*
1	Jammu & Kashmir Bank Limited	36000.4
2	Jammu & Kashmir State Financial Corporation	463.64
3	Jammu & Kashmir Small Scale Industries Development Corp.	73.06
4	Jammu & Kashmir Cements Limited	54.75
5	Jammu & Kashmir State Agro Industries Development Corp.	47.96

Source: CAG (Commercial) India, 2007-08.

Jammu & Kashmir State Power Development Corporation (JKSPDC), Jammu & Kashmir State Road Transport Corporation (JKSRTC) and Jammu & Kashmir Industries Limited (JKIL) are the major loss-making units. JKSRTC incurred losses owing to lack of coordination between the departments and failure to recover the renewal fees. JKSPDC was running in loss due to the delay in the completion of projects and excess in expenditure.

Table 12.4

Top Five Loss-making Units (2007-08)

(₹ in lakh)

S. No.	*Name of the Enterprise*	*Amount*
1	Jammu and Kashmir State Power Development Corp.	64650.2
2	Jammu and Kashmir State Road Transport Corp.	5467.14
3	Jammu and Kashmir Industries Limited	2179.48
4	Jammu and Kashmir State Industrial Development Corp.	626.56
5	Jammu and Kashmir State Horticultural Produce, Marketing and Processing Corp.	607.01

Source: CAG (Commercial) India, 2007-08.

Budgetary Support

Table 12.5 shows the budgetary support to the SLPEs during the years 2006-2008. The grants and subsidies given by the state and central governments constitute the major share in the budget support followed by the equity.

Table 12.5

Budgetary Support to SLPEs (2006-2008)

(₹ in crore)

S. No.	*Particulars*	*2005-06*	*2006-07*	*2007-08*
1	Equity	7.55	2.5	1.2
2	Loans	34.92	36.07	42.75
3	Grants/subsidies	218.13	187.55	12.18
4	Total	260.6	226.12	56.13

Source: CAG (Commercial) India, 2007-08.

The budgetary support to the SLPEs has been declined over the years. The budgetary support declined from ₹ 260.6 crore in 2005-06 to ₹ 56.13 crore in 2007-08. There is a steep fall in the budgetary support as the government has reduced its grants and subsidies to the loss-making units to carry out day-to-day activities as well as to meet their wage bills. A few sick and loss-making units are closed down.

Performance

Of the 20 SLPEs functioning in the state, 7 enterprises are making profits and 11 enterprises are making losses. The SLPEs turnover to state GDP shows the extent of public enterprises activities in the state. Table 12.6 provides the details of SLPEs contribution to state GDP from 2005-06 to 2007-08.

Table 12.6

SLPEs Contribution to State GDP

(₹ in crore)

S. No.	*Particulars*	*2005-06*	*2006-07*	*2007-08*
1	Turnover	2553.68	2689.17	3595.92
2	State GDP	26537	29030	31793
3	Percentage of Turnover to State GDP	9.62	9.26	11.31

Source: CAG (Commercial) India, 2007-08.

The percentage of turnover to the state GDP has increased by 2 per cent in 2007-08. There is an increase in the turnover of the manufacturing, financial and promotional sectors, which led to an increase in the contribution to the state GDP, inspite of the decline in the turnover of the utility sector. The losses of SLPEs are mainly attributable to deficiencies in financial management, planning, implementation of project, running their operations and monitoring. The state government has taken numerous initiatives to encourage modernisation of the enterprises, provide financial support and better infrastructure facilities to achieve higher productivity, energy efficiency and thus improve its sustainability in the competitive environment. The government had explored the privatisation and disinvestment strategies but could not get the desired results, as the manufacturing industries are quite few and most of the units are engaged in the service sector. The industrial policy of 2004 has implemented various strategies for the rapid development of the industrial sector.

13 Jharkhand

Introduction

Jharkhand is known as the *land of jungles* (forests) and *jharis* (bushes). The highly industrialised cities such as Jamshedpur, Ranchi, Bokaro Steel City and Dhanbad are concentrated in the state. Jharkhand has immense mineral resources ranging from iron ore, coal, copper ore, gold, silver, mica, bauxite, manganese, limestone, china clay, fire clay graphite, kainite, chromite, asbestos, thorium, sillimanite, uranium and several other minerals. The large deposits of coal and iron ore led to the concentration of industry in Jamshedpur, Bokaro and Ranchi. The gross state domestic product (GSDP) was ₹ 69,752 crore in 2006-07. The sectoral contribution to GDP was from agriculture (23.6%), industry (42.2%) and tertiary sector (34.2%) in 2006-07. The per capita income was ₹ 21,465 in 2008-09. The state is all set to move along the path of development. The state has witnessed impressive development in industrial sector over the years.

Overview of SLPEs

Over the years, the state has seen all-round progress in industrial development and infrastructure development. There were nine working SLPEs in Jharkhand as on March 31, 2008. Amongst these, about 56 per cent of the enterprises were set up during the Ninth Plan period. Nearly 33 per cent of the enterprises are making profits and 44 per cent are incurring losses. The total investment was ₹ 3,673.29 crore consisting of paid-up capital and long-term loans. The capital employed increased by 11.78 per cent in 2007-08. The total number of employees increased by 6.8 per cent i.e., from 8,427 in 2006-07 to 9,042 in 2007-08. There is an increase in the turnover by 91.57 per cent from ₹ 30 crore in 2006-07 to ₹ 364.90 crore in 2007-08. The SLPEs in Jharkhand were incurring a loss of ₹ 121.39 crore in 2007-08. The detailed information is given in Table 13.1.

Table 13.1

Overview of SLPEs in Jharkhand

(₹ in lakh)

Particulars	*2007-08*	*2006-07*	*2005-06.*
Investment			
Paid-up Capital			
State Govt.	12240	1330	780
Central Govt.	0	0	0
Others	0	0	0
Total	12240	1330	780
Long-term Loan			
Government	348534.9	247211	240053
Others	6554	6554	6554
Total	355088.9	253765	246607
Total Investment	367328.9	255095	247387
Capital Employed	498902.8	440143	439856.4
Turnover	36490.13	3076.7	15122.53
Net Profit/Loss	-12139.5	-4885.77	-4764.22
Accumulated Profit/Loss	-26545.4	-4289.73	-4386
No. of Employees	9042	8427	7899
Total Return on Capital Employed	23672.81	24184.14	24071.06
Percentage of Total Return on Capital Employed	673.53	173.5	171.86
Subsidies/Grants			
Central Govt.	0	0	0
State Govt.	127258	31250	32351
Total	127258	31250	32351

Source: Comptroller and Auditor General (CAG) (Commercial) India, 2007-08.

Categorisation

The SLPEs are classified into five categories: financial, manufacturing, promotional, utility and welfare enterprises. The number of enterprises functioning under each category is shown in Figure 13.1. The promotional enterprises constitute the largest number. There are no enterprises in the financial and welfare sectors in Jharkhand. The inclusion of enterprises increased the total investment level. The investment was ₹ 2,550.95 crore in 2006-07 which increased to ₹ 3,673.29 crore in 2007-08 by 30.55 per cent. The investments are financed through the budgetary support from the state and central governments and other financial institutions.

Figure 13.1

Category-wise SLPEs in Jharkhand

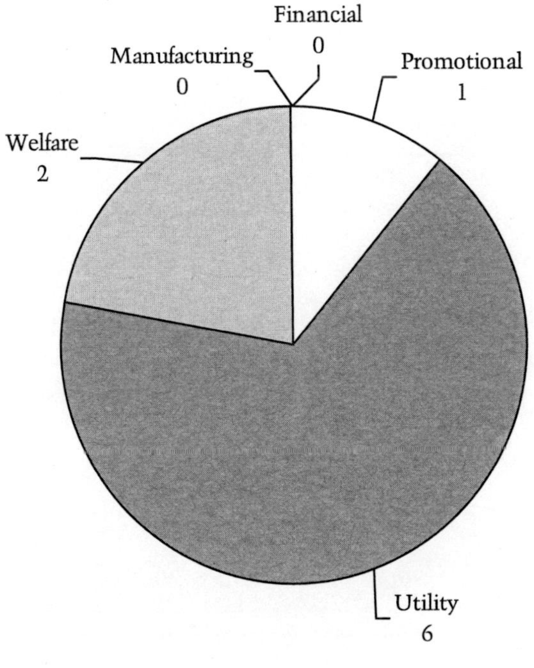

Source: CAG (Commercial) India, 2007-08.

Accumulated Profits and Losses

The accumulated losses of the SLPEs increased from ₹ 42.87 crore in 2006-07 to ₹ 265.45 crore in 2007-08 by 83.84 per cent. The losses were incurred mostly in the utility sector. The incorporation of Tenughat Vidyut Nigam Limited (TVNL) in the SLPEs increased the accumulated losses.

Table 13.2

Accumulated Profit and Loss of SLPEs

(₹ *in lakh)*

S. No.	*Particulars*	*2007-08*	*2006-07*	*2005-06*
1	Financial	0	0	0
2	Manufacturing	0	0	0
3	Promotional	582.22	655.05	558.78
4	Utility	-27128	-4944.8	-4944.8
5	Welfare	0	0	0
	Total	-26545	-4289.7	-4386

Source: CAG (Commercial) India, 2007-08.

Top Profit-making and Loss-making Units

Tables 13.3 and 13.4 provide the information on top profit- and loss-making units in Jharkhand. Jharkhand Industrial Infrastructure Development Corporation Limited, Jharkhand Tourism Development Corporation Limited and Jharkhand Police Housing Corporation Limited are ranked first, second and third amongst the profit-making SLPEs.

Table 13.3

Top Profit-making Units (2007-08)

(₹ *in lakh)*

S. No.	*Name of the Enterprise*	*Amount*
1	Jharkhand Industrial Infrastructure Development Corp. Ltd.	24.77
2	Jharkhand Tourism Development Corp. Ltd.	19.92
3	Jharkhand Police Housing Corporation Ltd.	11.50

Source: CAG (Commercial) India, 2007-08.

Tenughat Vidyut Nigam Limited (TVNL), Jharkhand State Electricity Board (JSEB) and Jharkhand Forest Development Corporation Limited (JFDC) are the major loss-making units. TVNL incurred loss due to mis-management by the authorities which increased the amount of accumulated losses than it's paid-up capital. JSEB incurred loss owing to the lack of monitoring by the management on the operational and financial activities of the enterprise.

Table 13.4

Top Four Loss-making Units (2007-08)

(₹ in lakh)

S. No.	*Name of the Enterprise*	*Amount*
1	Tenughat Vidyut Nigam Limited	7093.85
2	Jharkhand State Electricity Board	4944.78
3	Jharkhand Forest Development Corp. Ltd.	109.1
4	Jharkhand Hill Area Lift Irrigation Corp. Ltd.	48

Source: CAG (Commercial) India, 2007-08.

Budgetary Support

Table 13.5 shows the budgetary support to the SLPEs during the years 2006-2008. The grants and subsidies given by the state and central government constitute the major share in the budget support followed by the loans.

Table 13.5

Budgetary Support to SLPEs (2006-2008)

(₹ in crore)

S. No.	*Particulars*	*2005-06*	*2006-07*	*2007-08*
1	Equity	3.25	2.5	4.10
2	Loans	321.26	60	347.34
3	Grants/Subsidies	0	250	921.14
4	Total	324.51	312.5	1272.58

Source: CAG (Commercial) India, 2007-08.

The budgetary support to the SLPEs has been varying over the years. The budgetary support declined by 3.8 per cent from ₹ 324.51 crore in 2005-06 to ₹ 312.5 crore in 2006-07. The budgetary support increased by 75.44 per cent in 2007-08. There is an increase in the amount of grants and subsidies given to SLPEs which led to a rise in the budgetary support by the government. Nearly 72 per cent of the subsidy was received by the JSEB i.e., ₹ 921.14 crore by the government for the restructuring and revival of the enterprise.

Performance

Of the nine SLPEs functioning in the state, three enterprises are making profits and four enterprises are making losses. There is an increase in the turnover of the utility sector. The losses of SLPEs are mainly attributable to deficiencies in financial management, planning, implementation of project, running their operations and monitoring. The government initiated the Jharkhand Rehabilitation and Resettlement Policy, 2008, and the Memorandum of Understanding (MoU) were signed with the large enterprises for the development of industries in the state. The government is encouraging the entrepreneurs for setting up new industries by providing various subsidies and schemes. The infrastructure facilities are developed for providing easy access for the rapid industrial and economic development of the state. The loss-making and sick industrial units are being revived under the rehabilitation scheme by providing the requisite incentives.

14 Karnataka

Introduction

Karnataka is one of the high economic growth states in India with gross state domestic product (GSDP) of US$ 58.23 billion in 2008-09 at current prices. On the sectroal contribution front, the tertiary sector contributed US$ 31.6 billion (55%), followed by the secondary sector contributed US$ 17 billion (29%) and the primary sector's contribution amounted to US$ 9.5 billion (16%) to the GSDP in 2008-09. With the establishment of largest public sector industries like Hindustan Aeronautics Limited, National Aerospace Laboratories, Bharat Heavy Electricals Limited, Indian Telephone Industries, Bharat Earth Movers Limited, Bharat Electronics Limited, Hindustan Machine Tools, etc., the state has evolved as the manufacturing hub of India.

The state has had a strong tradition of state sector-led industrialisation. Moving on to the SLPEs in Karnataka, the princely state of Mysore, which was quite rich in natural resources, has started its industrial activities before India's independence (Mendon, 1964). The noteworthy initiatives of Sir M. Visveshvarayya, started several ventures like Mysore Iron Works (later the Mysore Iron and Steel Works), the Mysore Sugar Factory, the Mysore Soap Factory, the Mysore Paper Mills, the Mysore Silk Weaving Factory, etc., created employment and generated other economic spin-offs. Bangalore owes much of its development to the establishment of several state public sector enterprises in the 1950s. After Independence, the state government of Karnataka successively expanded the horizons of SLPEs in the state.

The present paper analyses the current status of SLPEs in Karnataka, their performance and highlights various recent government policy measures for the development of these enterprises in the state.

The Growth Story

On an analysis of the growth of the SLPEs in Karnataka, it can be observed that 10 (23% of total enterprises) public sector enterprises were set up during the Fifth Five Year Plan (see Figure 14.1). The period during 1985-2007 can be termed as a remarkable period for the public sector in Karnataka because about 33 enterprises were established during this period. The total number of enterprises went up to 65 by the end of 2008. The current status of enterprises in the state does not include the enterprises which have been wound up or merged with others. It has also been observed that mostly the enterprises were set up in the manufacturing and welfare sectors.

Figure 14.1

Plan-wise Growth of SLPEs in Karnataka

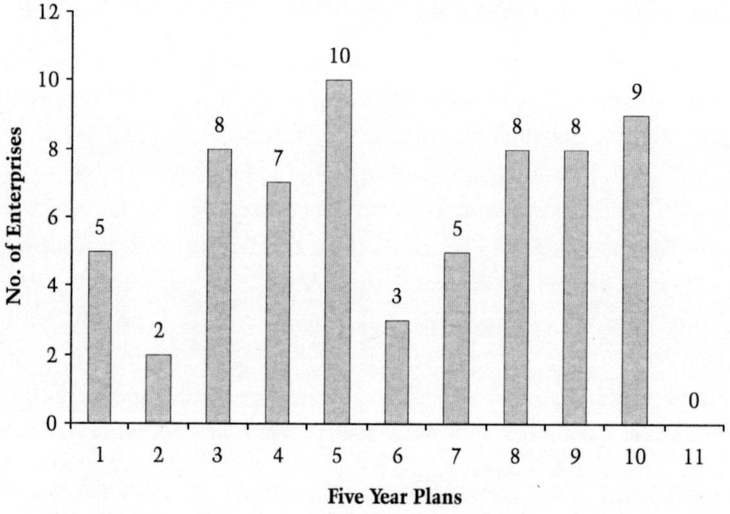

Source: Comptroller and Auditor General (CAG) (Commercial) Government of India and the author's calculations.

Overview of SLPEs

Karnataka occupies third place amongst the working SLPEs in India. Over the years, the enterprises have developed gradually. There were 65 working SLPEs in Karnataka as on March 31, 2008. Nearly 67 per cent of the enterprises were making profits and 20 per cent were incurring losses. The total investment was ₹ 47,813.29 crore consisting of paid-up capital and long-term loans. The capital employed increased by 7.6 per cent in 2007-08. The total number of employees was 1.69 lakh which increased by 5.8 per cent in 2007-08. The turnover increased by 10 per cent from ₹ 25,284.68 crore in 2006-07 to ₹ 28,218.05 crore in 2007-08. The SLPEs in Karnataka made a profit of ₹ 996.02 crore in 2007-08. The details are given in Table 14.1.

Table 14.1

Overview of SLPEs in Karnataka

(₹ in lakh)

Particulars	*2007-08*	*2006-07*	*2005-06*
Investment			
Paid-up Capital			
State Government	2330987	2069938	1847734
Central Government	29780.36	15980.36	12980.36
Others	30686.47	32185.21	26634.45
Total	2391466	2118104	1887349
Long-term Loan			
Government	746453.8	702706.4	694972.9
Others	1643409	1606328	1569142
Total	2389863	2309035	2264114
Total Investment	4781329	4427138	4151463
Capital Employed	5159088	4766086	4873473
Turnover	2821805	2528468	2104271
Net Profit/Loss	99602.06	93472.51	60570.79
Accumulated Profit/Loss	214831.4	182459.5	210566.3
No. of Employees	168811	159104	156480
Total Return on Capital Employed	250963	235283.5	179999.2
Percentage of Total Return on Capital Employed	787.96	627.6	662.19
Subsidies/Grants			
Central Government	26651.61	7921.23	1300.64
State Government	230379.5	623621.6	307951.9
Total	257031.1	631542.8	309252.5

Source: CAG (Commercial) India, 2007-08.

Categorisation

On the basis of the commodities and services these enterprises are dealing with, the SLPEs are classified into five categories: financial, manufacturing, promotional, utility and welfare enterprises. The number of enterprises functioning under each category is shown in Figure 14.2. The manufacturing and promotional enterprises constitute the largest number. The growth in the number of SLPEs and the increasing number of profit making units has increased the total investment levels. The investment was ₹ 44,271.38 crore in 2006-07 which increased to ₹ 47,813.29 crore in 2007-08. The investments are financed through the budgetary support from the state and central governments and other financial institutions.

Figure 14.2

Category-wise SLPEs in Karnataka

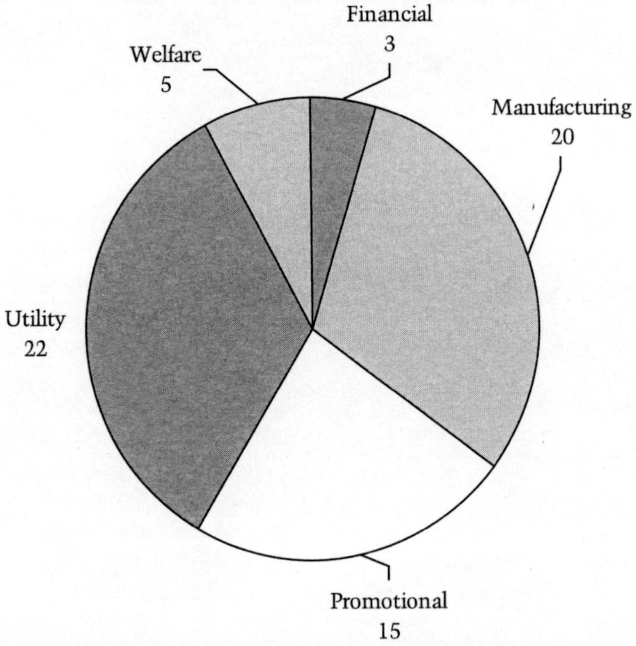

Source: CAG (Commercial) India, 2007-08.

Performance

The Government of Karnataka is constantly reviewing the role of SLPEs in the state and facilitating all the enterprises to enhance performance and turn around of all enterprises on one hand and to restore discipline and realize full potential of social justice special purpose vehicles on the other hand. Given the massive investment in the SLPEs, it is essential to examine the overall view of their performance. The sector-wise performance of SLPEs reveals that the enterprises in the financial and welfare sectors are running under losses or with high levels of government subsidy. The accumulated losses of the SLPEs increased from ₹ 1,824.60 crore in 2006-07 to ₹ 2,148.31 crore in 2007-08, registering a growth of 15.1 per cent. Table 14.2 shows the sector-wise accumulated profits and losses of the SLPEs from 2005-06 to 2007-08.

Table 14.2

Accumulated Profit and Loss of SLPEs

(₹ in lakh)

S. No.	*Particulars*	*2007-08*	*2006-07*	*2005-06*
1	Financial	-97257.3	-107804	5622.94
2	Manufacturing	20875.29	3847.14	-10030.3
3	Promotional	20731.45	21346.9	18204.95
4	Utility	274014.5	268637.3	199787.2
5	Welfare	-3532.57	-3567.98	-3018.46
	Total	214831	182460	210566

Source: CAG (Commercial) India, 2007-08.

Tables 14.3 and 14.4 present information on the top five profit- and loss-making units in Karnataka. Karnataka Power Corporation Limited, Hutti Gold Mines Company Limited and Bangalore Metropolitan Transport Corporation are ranked first, second and third respectively amongst the profit-making SLPEs.

Table 14.3

Top Five Profit-making Units (2007-08)

(₹ in lakh)

S. No.	Name of the Enterprise	Amount
1	Karnataka Power Corporation Limited	25022.67
2	Hutti Gold Mines Company Limited	14489.81
3	Bangalore Metropolitan Transport Corporation	14022.65
4	Karnataka Power Transmission Corporation Limited	12488.15
5	Mysore Minerals Limited	9820.03

Source: CAG (Commercial) India, 2007-08.

North Western Karnataka Road Transport Corporation (NWKRTC), Mysore Sugar Company Limited (MSCL) and Karnataka Road Development Corporation Limited (KRDCL) are the major loss-making units. KRDCL incurred loss owing to the inefficiency in the execution of the projects. MSCL was running in loss due to the non-availability of resources.

Table 14.4

Top Five Loss-making Units (2007-08)

(₹ in lakh)

S. No.	Name of the Enterprise	Amount
1	North Western Karnataka Road Transport Corporation	6706.7
2	Mysore Sugar Company Limited	2221.33
3	Karnataka Road Development Corporation Limited	776.59
4	Karnataka Land Army Corporation Limited	597.81
5	Karnataka State Agro Corn Products Limited	441.92

Source: CAG (Commercial) India, 2007-08.

Thus, it can be summarised that both financial and welfare enterprises are loss-making sectors in the aggregated sense. On the other hand, the services sectors such as the promotional and the utilities sectors are performing well. According to the Public Enterprises Surveys and CAG reports of the Government of India (GoI), because of the political interventions, bad managerial decisions, excessive employed manpower, etc., these organisations are not able to make profits. These surveys have shown that many enterprises in the financial and welfare sectors degenerated into chronic loss-making enterprises and which forced the state government of Karnataka to re-think its policies and measures towards the development of SLPEs in the state.

Figure 14.3

Human Resources in SLPEs in Karnataka

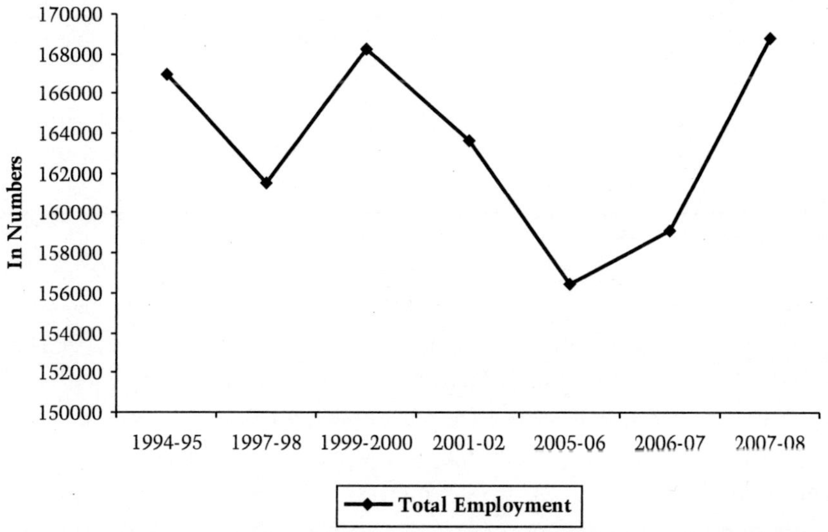

Source: CAG (Commercial), GoI.

As far as the human resources are concerned, even after the initiation of the overall economic reforms in 1990-91, the growth rate of employment in the state SLPEs has been positive till 1994-95, but has started falling in 1997-98. It can be observed from Figure 14.3 that the total employment in SLPEs fell over the years till 2005-06, but it has gone up from 1,56,480 in 2005-06 to 1,68,811 in 2007-08. Most interestingly, the overemployment seems to be the major obstacle for the government's commitment to make the SLPEs competitive in the liberalised, privatised and globalised world.

Budgetary Support

The data on budgetary support shows a decline in the government support in terms of grants and subsidies to the SLPEs in 2007-08. Interestingly, the grants and subsidies given by the state and central government constitute the major share in the budget support followed by the equity. Table 14.5 shows the budgetary support to the SLPEs from 2005-06 to 2007-08.

Table 14.5

Budget Support to SLPEs (2006-2008)

(₹ in crore)

S. No.	*Particulars*	*2005-06*	*2006-07*	*2007-08*
1	Equity	3248.34	2173.68	2610.65
2	Loans	222.07	124.07	481.01
3	Grants/subsidies	3008.99	6063.82	2252.79
4	Total	6479.4	8361.57	5344.45

Source: CAG (Commercial) India, 2007-08.

The budgetary support to the SLPEs has been fluctuating over the years. The budgetary support increased from ₹ 6,479.4 crore in 2005-06 to ₹ 8,361.57 crore in 2006-07, registering a growth rate of 22.5 per cent. On the other hand, it has declined by 56 per cent in 2007-08. The point to be noted here is that usually the borrowings of the SLPEs are from the state government and when these enterprises fail to repay the loans, the government has to convert these loans into an investment. It has also been observed that the major reasons for the inability to repay the loans by these enterprises are deficiencies in financial management, lack of proper planning, lack of project implementation mechanism, lack of operations and monitoring capabilities.

Contribution to the State GDP

Karnataka occupies the first place in the country with most of the enterprises making profits. Of the 65 SLPEs functioning in the state, more than 40 units are making profits and the enterprises that are making losses are 13 in number. SLPEs turnover to state GDP shows the extent of public enterprises activities in the state. Table 14.6 provides the details of SLPEs contribution to state GDP from 2005-06 to 2007-08.

Table 14.6

SLPEs Contribution to State GDP

(₹ in crore)

S. No.	Particulars	2005-06	2006-07	2007-08
1	Turnover	28218.05	25284.7	21042.7
2	State GDP	186209	200922	233802
3	Percentage of Turnover to State GDP	15.15	12.58	9.00

Source: CAG (Commercial) India, 2007-08.

The percentage of turnover to the state GDP has been declining steadily over the years. Though there is an increase in the turnover of the manufacturing, promotional and utility sectors, their contribution to the state GDP declined. The SLPEs can discharge their role efficiently only if they are financially self-reliant. There is scope for improvement in overall performance, when the government introduces a performance-based system of accountability and imbibes greater degree of professionalism to ensure efficiency and profitability.

Government Reforms and Policy Initiatives

In 1980s, the state government of Karnataka initiated steps to improve the performance of SLPEs. As a first step towards the evaluation of the state government policies relating to these enterprises, the government formed a committee in August 1988 and another Cabinet sub-committee was formed in 1990, which recommended for privatisation of the loss-making SLPEs in the state. But, due to the lack of proper implementation mechanism and political will, the recommendations of the sub-committee were not materialised. Again in March 2000, the government formed a committee on 'Public Sector Restructuring' with the following objectives:

1. To evaluate the performance of SLPEs and suggest appropriate measures to promote greater productivity and profitability.
2. To suggest measures to promote autonomy of SLPEs.
3. To enable the government in identifying the enterprises that need state support or complete privatisation, those that need strategic

partners to reduce dependence on state budgetary support, those for which restructuring measures could be suggested, etc.

4. to safeguard the interests of the human resources.

Memorandum of Understanding (MoU) was introduced with a vision to know the performance of SLPEs. The document of MoU mentions self-imposed physical and financial targets for coming three years and promises made to the government about enhancement of performance. This created competition amongst the SLPEs and the private sector. The SLPEs were encouraged, restructured and amalgamated to become prosperous, healthy and efficient vehicles surging forward delivery of developed assets to the people, the nation so that the state becomes prosperous and self-reliant. The executives of the SLPEs have imparted training in various reputed institutes.

Conclusion

The Government of Karnataka is continuously reviewing the role and performance of the public sector enterprises from various aspects. The most important are states presence in any sector of public service like utilities, welfare, etc., advances in technology, new realities of pricing and marketing strategies, issues in human resource management, etc. It has also been realised that whatever the sectors, manufacturing or welfare or financial or utilities, the ultimate performance can be judged by their ability to sustain in the globally competitive world and to generate their own resources for growth. In the past, SLPEs used to come before government only with grievances and problems. Now there is a change in trend, i.e., SLPEs are coming before the government with good performance, so that they will be awarded and rewarded.

15 Kerala

Introduction

Since Independence, Kerala was managed as a democratic socialist welfare economy and the 1990s liberalisation helped the state in achieving economic expansion, job creation, higher foreign direct investments (FDI), etc. The state leads many other Indian states in terms of GDP per capita and economic productivity. According to the *Economic Survey*, Government of India (GoI), Kerala's nominal gross state domestic product (GSDP) was ₹ 162,414.79 crore in 2007-08. The most vibrant service sector dominates the economy. The state has around 180,000 small-scale industries, 511 medium- and large-scale manufacturing firms with traditional industries manufacturing such items as coir, handlooms and handicrafts employing around one million people.

Public sector enterprises are an important segment of various economies, whether they are mixed or socialist economies. SLPEs form an important part of state economies and have played a very critical role in the overall development of the state. The Government of Kerala conceived the SLPEs as instruments of social equitable opportunity for the common man and creating and distributing wealth. The major objectives behind setting up of these enterprises in Kerala are for employment generation, providing public utility services such as water supply, gas and electricity supply, providing public transport and development of business opportunities in the state. The government is also preparing policy frameworks to tap the potential of SLPEs and spurring them to high levels of productivity and professionalism in the globalised scenario.

The present paper outlines the growth and classification of SLPEs, the current status and the performance of these enterprises, and the state government initiatives and strategies for the development of SLPEs in Kerala.

Overview of SLPEs

Over the years, the number of SLPEs has gone up phenomenally in Kerala. Perhaps the state stands in the forefront in India in terms of having a large number of SLPEs in a single state. On the analysis front, the growth of the SLPEs in Kerala can be observed from the Figure 15.1. The Fifth Five Year Plan records the setting up of highest number of SLPEs compared to the other plan periods. About 23 per cent of total enterprises in the state were set up during the Fifth Five Year Plan. The growth in the number of these enterprises was highest during 1970s. The total number of enterprises went up to 88 by the end of 2008. The current status of enterprises in the state does not include the enterprises which have been wound up or merged with others.

Figure 15.1

Plan-wise Growth of SLPEs in Kerala

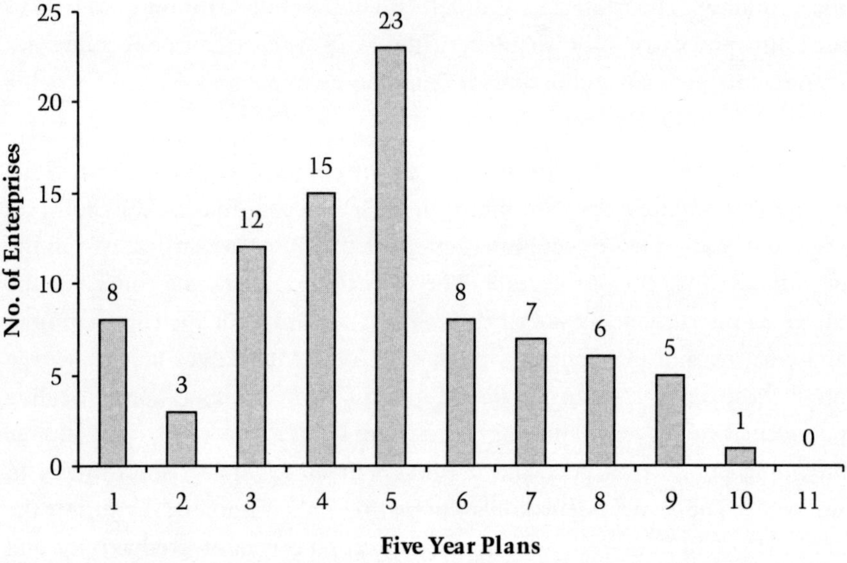

Source: Comptroller and Auditor General (CAG) (Commercial) Government of India and the author's calculations.

Currently, Kerala has the largest number of SLPEs in India. There were 88 working SLPEs in Kerala as on March 31, 2008, accounting for about 10 per cent of the total SLPEs of the country. About 23 per cent of the enterprises were set up during the Fifth Plan period. Identifying the potential of SLPEs in powering the growth in wealth creation through enhanced industrial production, job creation and social equity, the state government of Kerala has infused huge amount of resources into these enterprises. The total investment in these enterprises was ₹ 7,24,985.9 lakh consisting of paid-up capital and long-term loans. The capital employed was ₹ 13,23,273 lakh, which increased by 16 per cent in 2007-08 compared to 2006-07. The total number of employees was 86,305 which increased by 2.5 per cent in 2007-08. The turnover increased by 14.3 percent from ₹ 9,01,203.81 lakh in 2006-07 to ₹ 10,30,267.29 lakh in 2007-08. The SLPEs in Kerala made a profit of ₹ 20,135.84 lakh in 2007-08. An overview of the SLPEs in Kerala is shown in Table 15.1.

Table 15.1

Overview of SLPEs in Kerala

(₹ in lakh)

Parameters	*2007-08*	*2006-07*	*2005-06*
Investment			
Paid-up Capital			
State Govt.	310038.8	304826.2	301472.1
Central Govt.	6365.92	6189.61	5552.86
Others	9865.43	9865.33	9554.37
Total	327270.1	320881.1	316579.4
Long-term Loan	0	0	0
Government	90192.98	83305.17	110682.6
Others	307522.8	370082.8	538900.9
Total	397715.8	453388	649582.9
Total Investment	724985.9	774269.1	966162.2
Capital Employed	1323273	1106614	1393674
Turnover	1030267	901203.8	842501.2
Net Profit/Loss	20135.84	11420.35	830.08
Accumulated Profit/Loss	-113345	-34060.7	-165609
No. of Employees	86305	84222	89788
Total Return on Capital Employed	109082.8	111189.8	112944.1
Percentage of Total Return on Capital Employed	-12.98	-1088.29	-166.41
Subsidies/Grants	0	0	0
Central Govt.	16185.39	5347.88	9319.49
State Govt.	14503.83	5123.725	453802.7
Total	30886.22	10471.61	463122.2

Source: CAG (Commercial) India.

Categorisation

The SLPEs are classified into five categories: financial, manufacturing, promotional, utility and welfare enterprises. The number of enterprises functioning under each category is shown in Figure 15.2. The manufacturing and promotional enterprises constitute the largest number. The growth in the number of SLPEs and the increasing number of profit making units has reduced the total investment levels. The investment was ₹ 9,66,162.202 lakh in 2005-06 which declined to ₹ 7,24,985.892 lakh in 2007-08. The investments are financed through the budgetary support from the state and central governments and other financial institutions.

Figure 15.2

Categorisation of SLPEs in Kerala

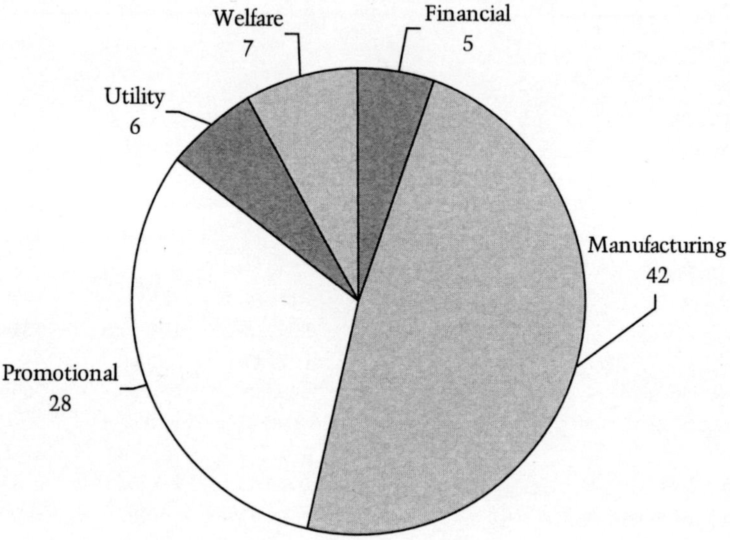

Source: CAG (Commercial) India.

Performance

The state government of Kerala is continuously putting efforts to convert Kerala into an investment friendly destination and to achieve consistently high economic growth with specific thrust on social objectives, without adversely affecting ecology and environment and to create employment opportunities for the people of Kerala. The government is also focusing on restructuring and retaining potentiality of SLPEs in the state.

The category-wise performance of the SLPEs in Table 15.2 describes that the financial and welfare sectors are the profit-making sectors in all the years during the study period mentioned in the table. But, the enterprises in manufacturing, promotional and utilities sectors continuously incurred losses from 2005-06 to 2007-08. There are numerous reasons identified for these heavy losses in these sectors, such as lack of corporate culture, low profitability, lack of professionalism in management, poor marketing approaches and financial difficulties. The accumulated losses of the SLPEs increased from ₹ 34,060.73 lakh in 2006-07 to ₹ 1,13,345.05 lakh in 2007-08. The details of the category-wise accumulated profits and losses of SLPEs are shown in the Table 15.2.

Table 15.2

Category-wise Accumulated Profit and Loss of SLPEs

(₹ in lakh)

S. No.	*Category*	*2007-08*	*2006-07*	*2005-06*
1	Financial	11446.91	12334.54	8300.4
2	Manufacturing	-36448.99	-73281.14	-65244.2
3	Promotional	-51214.96	-54276.43	-54401.01
4	Utility	-39270.72	79952.19	-54508.36
5	Welfare	2142.71	1210.11	243.86
	Total	-113345.05	-34060.73	-165609.31

Source: CAG (Commercial) India.

Tables 15.3 and 15.4 present the top five profit- and loss-making enterprises in Kerala. Among the profit-making enterprises, Kerala State Electricity Board (KSEB) topped the list with ₹ 217.42 crore, followed by the Kerala State Beverages (Manufacturing & Marketing) Corporation Limited and Kerala State Financial Enterprises Limited.

Table 15.3

Top Five Profit-making Units (2007-08)

(₹ in lakh)

S. No.	Name of the Enterprise	Amount
1	Kerala State Electricity Board	21742.0
2	Kerala State Beverages (Manufacturing & Marketing) Corporation Limited	5158.43
3	The Kerala State Financial Enterprises Limited	3918.67
4	The Kerala Minerals and Metals Limited	2243.24
5	Kerala Industrial Development Corporation Limited (KSIDC)	2097.92

Source: CAG (Commercial) India.

Kerala State Road Transport Corporation led the list of the loss-making SLPEs, which was followed by Kerala State Civil Supplies Corporation Limited and the Kerala State Cashew Development Corporation Limited.

Table 15.4

Top Five Loss-making Units (2007-08)

(₹ in lakh)

S. No.	Name of the Enterprise	Amount
1	Kerala State Road Transport Corporation	15103.88
2	The Kerala State Civil Supplies Corporation Limited	7404.32
3	The Kerala State Cashew Development Corporation Limited	4098.09
4	Kerala Financial Corporation	2815.28
5	Travancore Titanium Products Limited	1552.91

Source: CAG (Commercial) India.

The government is monitoring the performance of SLPEs and suggesting appropriate course-corrections to help the weaker ones turn around fast and making them to perform well in today's competitive environment. But some of the areas of differentiation of the SLPEs from their private sector counterparts have been the commercial orientation, professionalism, economic productivity and profit consciousness. Due to the lack of the above-said aspects, some of the SLPEs have become cost-centres rather than revenue-generators.

The total employment in the SLPEs in the state during 2007-08 was 86,305 (Figure 15.3). The average investment per employee during 2007-08 was ₹ 11.90 lakh as against ₹ 9.30 lakh in 2005-06. The state government signaled a fresh wave of change by the policy perspectives ensuring co-operation of the state and safeguarding interests of these establishments. In this context, the government has provided an opportunity to the SLPEs in the state to improve the efficiency of operations, enhance the quality, diversify the delivery mechanisms and channels, tone up the distribution systems, speed up the collection mechanism and to modernise the management of these enterprises.

Figure 15.3

Total Human Resources in SLPEs in Kerala

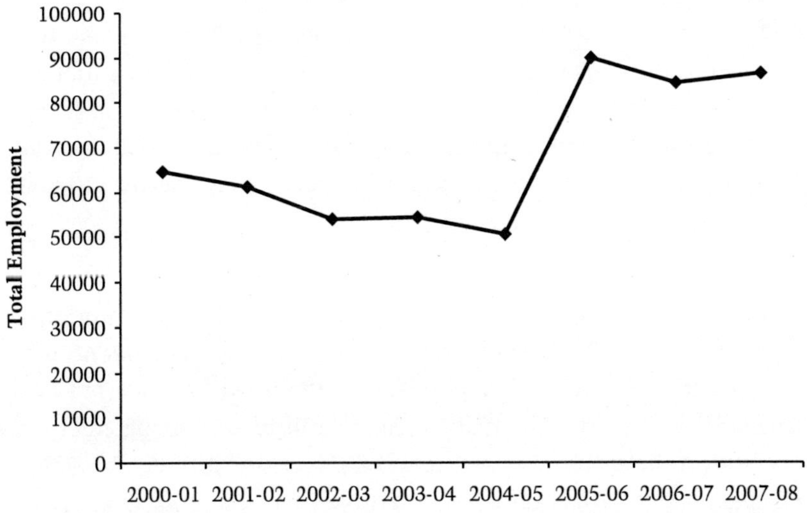

Source: CAG (Commercial), GoI.

Budgetary Support

The budgetary assistance to SLPEs during 2007-08 and the two preceding years is shown in Table 15.5. During the year under review, the assistance to SLPEs amounted to ₹ 336.71 crore, which increased by 62 per cent over the year 2006-07. The loans from various financial agencies and grant and subsidies given by the state and central governments constitute the major share in the budgetary support followed by the equity.

Table 15.5

Budgetary Support to SLPEs

(₹ in crore)

S. No.	*Particulars*	*2005-06*	*2006-07*	*2007-08*
1	Equity	12.02	31.69	56.81
2	Loans	136.5	145.98	147.11
3	Grants/subsidies	28.85	30.17	132.79
4	Total	177.37	207.84	336.71

Source: CAG (Commercial) India.

The budgetary support to SLPEs has been increasing over the years. The loans from the various state financial agencies constitute the major part of budgetary support to the SLPEs. Under the effort and initiative of reviving the enterprises and pull them out from the clutches of the crisis, in 2007-08, the state government has increased the share of grants/subsidies in the total budgetary support to a tune of 340 per cent compared to 2006-07.

SLPEs Contribution to State GDP

The year 2007-08 has witnessed a positive note in the working of SLPEs in the state. Of the 88 enterprises functioning in the state, more than 45 enterprises made profits and the enterprises that incurred losses are about 40 in number. The growing number of profit-making enterprises in the state is indicative of new energies that are driving the various enterprises. In 2005-06, only 12 enterprises earned profits, whereas it increased to more than 45 in 2007-08. The SLPEs turnover to state GDP shows the extent of public enterprises activities in the state. Table 15.6 provides the details of SLPEs contribution to state GDP from 2005-06 to 2007-08.

Table 15.6

SLPEs Contribution to State GDP

(₹ in crore)

S. No.	Particulars	2007-08	2006-07	2005-06
1	Turnover	10302.67	9012.04	8425.01
2	State GDP	148485	132739	118998
3	Percentage of Turnover to State GDP	6.9	6.8	7.1

Source: CAG (Commercial) India.

It can be observed from Table 15.6 that the percentage of turnover to the state GDP is declining steadily over the years. This is due to the decline in turnover of manufacturing enterprises. In 2007-08, owing to an increase in the turnover in welfare enterprise, there is a slight increase in contribution to GDP from the SLPEs.

Government Reforms and Measures

The state government is not only helping the SLPEs to overcome their crises, but is trying to pulling them out of the red. The state government is also making efforts to increase the number of profit-making SLPEs by following a 10-step success plan, such as:

1. Strategic alliances/equity participation with CPSUs.
2. Mandatory product purchase by government departments.
3. Cleaning up of balance sheets with the government writing off long-pending dues.
4. Induction of professionals as directors on boards.
5. Investment in modernisation.
6. Selection board for CEOs and trebling of their salaries and perks and wage revision for all employees.
7. One-time settlements of bank dues, budgetary support and annual auditing.
8. Increasing productivity through daily monitoring and fresh recruitment.

9. Trade unions refraining from strikes.

10. Cost-cutting exercises.

Conclusion

The SLPEs in Kerala herald a new era by following the principle of cooperation and joint ventures with the Central Public Sector Enterprises. At the same time, the government also felt the need for professionalism in management of the units by building a well-trained team of highly professional managerial talent pool. Apart from professionalisation of the boards and the management of public sector units (PSUs), training in corporate governance with support from the Commonwealth Secretariat, Academy of Corporate Governance (ACG), Global Corporate Governance Forum (GCGF), and high-end training in re-engineering and restructuring for both government nominee directors and other directors are on the anvil.

16 Madhya Pradesh

Introduction

Madhya Pradesh was founded on November 1, 1956. The state was bifurcated into Madhya Pradesh and Chhattisgarh on November 1, 2000. It is known as the "Heart of India". The state occupies seventh rank in terms of population and second in terms of area. The growth rate of population has come down from 27.24 per cent in the previous decade to 24.34 per cent during 1991-2001. The net state domestic product (NSDP) of the state, at current prices, increased from ₹ 1,02,795.68 crore in 2005-06 to ₹ 1,50,296.12 crore in 2008-09 thus registering an increase of 46.21 per cent, while at constant prices it is 23.62 per cent. The major contribution to NSDP is made by the tertiary sector followed by the primary and the secondary sectors. The per capita income at constant prices increased from ₹ 12,384 in 1999-2000 to ₹ 14,918 in 2008-09. The economy largely depends on agriculture, industries and minerals. Nearly 70 per cent of the total work force of the state depends directly or indirectly on agriculture. Mines and industries play important roles in economic development of the state. There are many flourishing textile mills in the state and artificial silk manufacturing plants located at Ujjain, Nagda, Indore and Gwalior.

Madhya Pradesh is one of the leading states in the country in mineral production. Industries in the areas of electronics, telecommunications, automobiles, etc., are set up. The state produces optical fibre for telecommunication needs. The public sector enterprises in the state are Bharat Heavy Electrical Limited (BHEL) at Bhopal, Security Paper Mill at Hoshangabad, Bank Note Press at Dewas, Newsprint Factory at Nepanagar and Alkaloid Factory at Neemuch. The state is known for its traditional handicrafts and handloom cloths manufactured in Chanderi and Maheshwar. The literacy rate of the State is 70.53 per cent. The state is home to some of the premier educational and research institutions of India such as the Indian Institute of Technology (IIT) Indore, Indian Institute of

Information Technology and Management (IIITM), Gwalior, National Law Institute University (NLIU) Bhopal, Indian Institute of Forest Management, Maulana Azad National Institute of Technology Bhopal, etc.

Overview of SLPEs

The first SLPE in Madhya Pradesh was set up in 1955 and since then there is a steady growth in number of public enterprises. There were 35 working SLPEs in Madhya Pradesh as on March 31, 2008. About 20 per cent of them were set up during the Sixth Plan period. The total investment was ₹ 8,993.49 crore consisting of paid-up capital and long-term loans. The capital employed declined by 5.5 per cent in 2006-07. The total number of employees was 35,674 which declined by 5.5 per cent in 2007-08. The turnover declined by 11.38 per cent from ₹ 14257.18 crore in 2006-07 to ₹ 12,800.73 crore in 2007-08. The loss of the SLPEs in Madhya Pradesh was ₹ 1,668.65 crore in 2007-08. The details are given in Table 16.1.

Table 16.1

Overview of SLPEs in Madhya Pradesh

(₹ in lakh)

Particulars	*2007-08*	*2006-07*	*2005-06*
Investment			
Paid-up Capital			
State Govt.	713848.4	520282.5	453011.1
Central Govt.	3579.95	3579.95	3579.95
Others	6840.62	24940.62	5878.27
Total	724269	548803.1	462469.3
Long-term Loan			
Government	196405.9	543202.5	480377.8
Others	702943.4	938831	936787.2
Total	899349.3	1482034	1417165
Total Investment	1623618	2030837	1879634
Capital Employed	2197001	2317718	1260780
Turnover	1280073	1425718	737532.2
Net Profit/Loss	-166865	55577.89	124213.3
Accumulated Profit/Loss	-603246	-316089	-236412
No. of Employees	35674	83232	83229
Total Return on Capital Employed	9305.63	128621.8	163644.5
Percentage of Total Return on Capital Employed	833.41	355.18	223.46
Subsidies/Grants			
Central Govt.	11648.39	9800.35	23638.93
State Govt.	146467.4	29282.02	52811.81
Total	158115.7	39082.37	76450.74

Source: Comptroller and Auditor General (CAG) (Commercial) India, 2007-08.

Categorisation

The SLPEs are classified into five categories: financial, manufacturing, promotional, utility and welfare enterprises. The number of enterprises functioning under each category is shown in Figure 16.1. The promotional and utility enterprises constitute the largest in number. The investment declined from ₹ 14,820.34 crore in 2006-07 to ₹ 8,993.49 crore in 2007-08. Nearly 57 per cent of the SLPEs are making profits in Madhya Pradesh.

Figure 16.1

Category-wise SLPEs in Madhya Pradesh

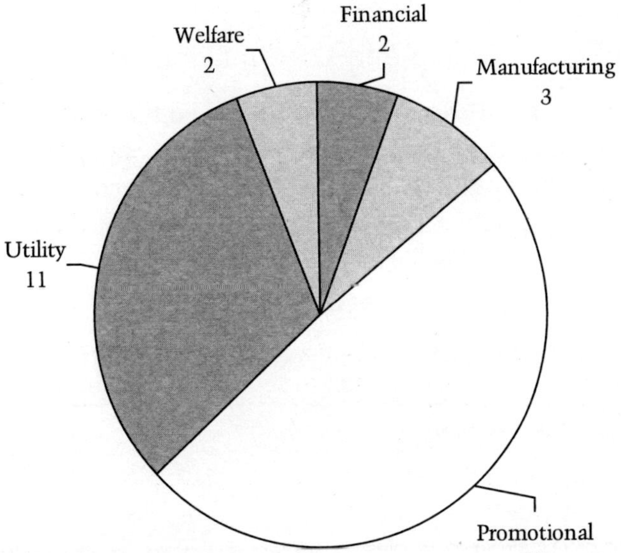

Source: CAG (Commercial) India, 2007-08.

Accumulated Profits and Losses

The accumulated losses of the SLPE's increased by 47.6 per cent from ₹ 3,160.89 crore in 2006-07 to ₹ 6,032.46 crore in 2007-08. The losses were incurred mostly in the utility sector. There is an increase in profits in the manufacturing and welfare sectors. The loss declined in the financial and promotional sectors over the years.

Table 16.2

Accumulated Profit and Loss of SLPEs

(₹ in lakh)

S.No.	*Particulars*	*2007-08*	*2006-07*	*2005-06*
1	Financial	-23341	-23696	-22103
2	Manufacturing	4825.05	3770.73	3758.46
3	Promotional	-41368	-43954.8	-47022.7
4	Utility	-543562	-252277	-173048
5	Welfare	199.36	68.05	2003.6
	Total	-603246	-316089	-236412

Source: CAG (Commercial) India, 2007-08.

Top Five Profit-making and Loss-making Units

Tables 16.3 and 16.4 provide information on top five profit- and loss-making units in Madhya Pradesh. Madhya Pradesh State Electricity Board, Madhya Pradesh State Civil Supplies Corporation and Madhya Pradesh State Mining Corporation are ranked first, second and third respectively amongst the profit-making SLPEs.

Table 16.3

Top Five Profit-making Units (2007-08)

(₹ in lakh)

S.No.	*Name of the Enterprise*	*Amount*
1	MP State Electricity Board	9399.33
2	MP State Civil Supplies Corporation	2932.1
3	MP State Mining Corporation	1909.96
4	MP Laghu Udyog Nigam	1177.39
5	MP Police Housing Corporation	1013.78

Source: CAG (Commercial) India, 2007-08.

Madhya Pradesh Paschim Kshetra Vidyut Vitran, Madhya Pradesh Purva Kshetra Vidyut Vitran and Madhya Pradesh Madhya Kshetra Vidyut Vitran are the major loss-making units. The enterprises incurred losses owing to the lack of efficiency in assessment of requirement and utiltisation of material.

Table 16.4

Top Five Loss-making Units (2007-08)

(₹ in lakh)

S.No.	Name of the Enterprise	Amount
1	MP Paschim Kshetra Vidyut Vitran	67980.32
2	MP Purva Kshetra Vidyut Vitran	61377.7
3	MP Madhya Kshetra Vidyut Vitran	49422.36
4	MP Power Transmission Company Limited	3993.83
5	MPS Industrial Development Corporation	1762.89

Source: CAG (Commercial) India, 2007-08.

Budgetary Support

Table 16.5 shows the budgetary support to the SLPEs during 2005-06 to 2007-08. The equity given by the state and central governments constitute the major share in the budgetary support followed by the grants and subsidies.

Table 16.5

Budgetary Support to SLPEs (2006-2008)

(₹ in crore)

S. No.	Particulars	2005-06	2006-07	2007-08
1	Equity	3261.29	983.61	1541.19
2	Loans	742.47	196.79	638.71
3	Grants/subsidies	528.12	293.8	1464.68
4	Total	4531.88	1474.2	3644.58

Source: CAG (Commercial) India, 2007-08.

The budgetary support to the SLPEs has been fluctuating over the years. The budgetary support declined by 67.47 per cent from ₹ 4,531.88 crore in 2005-06 to ₹ 1,474.2 crore in 2006-07. It increased by 59.55 per cent in 2007-08. The government invested mostly in the power sector in the form of equity and loan inspite of the enterprises incurring losses. The equity taken constitutes a major constituent of the budgetary support of the SLPEs in Madhya Pradesh. The government invested in 15 SLPEs in 2007-08 and repaid the loan of ₹ 2.92 crore on behalf of the M.P. State Industrial Development Corporation Limited.

Performance

Of the 35 SLPEs functioning in the state, 13 units are making losses and 20 enterprises are making profits. The SLPEs turnover to state GDP shows the extent of public enterprises activities in the state. Table 16.6 provides the detail of SLPEs contribution to state GDP from 2005-06 to 2007-08.

Table 16.6

SLPEs Contribution to State GDP

(₹ in crore)

S. No.	Particulars	2005-06	2006-07	2007-08
1	Turnover	7375	14257	12801
2	State GDP	116932	130571	142499
3	Percentage of Turnover to State GDP	6.31	10.92	8.98

Source: CAG (Commercial) India, 2007-08.

The percentage of turnover to the state GDP has been varying over the years. The decline in the turnover of the utility sector showed a drop in their contribution to the state GDP. The losses of SLPEs are mainly attributable to deficiencies in financial management, planning, implementation of project, running their operations and monitoring. The State has tremendous potential for fast industrial growth due to its rich natural resources, fast developing infrastructure, central location, peaceful industrial climate, progressive industrial policy and improved human resources. The major thrust by the government is on developing industrial infrastructure, which includes industrial areas, industrial growth centres, various industrial parks, special economic zones (SEZs), information technology (IT) parks, etc., and efficient management of the same. A dedicated freight corridor between Delhi and Mumbai (Delhi-Mumbai Industrial Corridor; DMIC) is under perception. To build a strong economic base, Ratlam-Nagda and Pithampur-Dhar-Mhow investment regions and industrial areas of Neemuch and Shajapur are included in the DMIC.

The state is likely to attract an investment of more than ₹ 50,000 crore in large and medium industries during the Eleventh Plan. Around 70,000 new micro, small and medium enterprises (MSMEs) are targeted to be set up during the same period. These units will provide employment opportunities to nearly 2,00,000 people. In addition, around 1,00,000 people are supposed to be benefitted through micro sector and service enterprises. The Department of Industries is also playing a key role in promoting the growth of MSMEs. The objectives of the new industrial promotion policy is to create industry friendly administration, maximise employment opportunities, tackle industrial sickness, rationalise rates of commercial taxes, enlist participation of private sector in the efforts of industrialisation and promote balanced regional development. The beverages industries, food processing, sericulture, agro-based, electrical and electronics industries, drug and pharmaceuticals, chemical and petro-chemical industries, handloom and handicrafts industries, etc., are given prominence in the industrial policy. The government formulated special packages for removing the industrial sickness and attracting foreign investment in the state.

17 Maharashtra

Introduction

Maharashtra is India's leading industrial state with implementation of constructive economic policies. The gross state domestic product (GSDP) at constant prices was ₹ 4,16,248 crore during 2007-08, as against ₹ 3,81,247 crore in 2006-07, showing an increase of 9.2 per cent. The per capita national income at current prices was ₹ 33,283 in 2007-08. The sectoral composition of GSDP comprises the agriculture & allied activities ₹ 81,591 crore (13.8%), industry sector ₹ 1,62,223 crore (27.5%) and services sector ₹ 3,47,181 crore (58.7%). Maharashtra's industrial sector contributes 15 per cent of national industrial output and over 40 per cent of India's national revenue. Major industries are chemical and allied products, electrical and non-electrical machinery, textiles, petroleum and allied products. Other important industries include metal products, wine, jewellery, pharmaceuticals, engineering goods, machine tools, steel and iron castings and plastic wares. Prominent Indian and foreign automobile makers such as Tata Motors, Mahindra & Mahindra, Mercedes Benz, Audi, Skoda Auto, Fiat, General Motors and Volkswagen are also either based in or have a manufacturing unit in the state.

The state has information technology (IT) software parks in Pune, Mumbai, Navi Mumbai, Aurangabad, Nagpur and Nashik. Over the years, the state has emerged as the second largest exporter of software with annual exports of ₹ 18,000 crore (US$ 3.91 billion) and accounts for more than 30 per cent of the country's software exports, with over 1,200 software units. It ranks first in coal-based thermal electricity as well as nuclear electricity generation with national market shares of over 13 per cent and 17 per cent respectively. Mumbai, financial capital of India, is the headquarters of almost all major banks, financial institutions, insurance companies and mutual funds in India. India's largest stock exchange Bombay Stock Exchange (BSE), the oldest in Asia, is also located in the city. An international cargo hub (Multi-modal International Cargo Hub and Airport at Nagpur, MIHAN) is being developed at Nagpur. MIHAN will be used for handling heavy cargo coming from Southeast Asia and Middle-East Asia. This is the biggest development project in India.

Overview of SLPEs

There were 53 working SLPEs in Maharashtra as on March 31, 2008. About 26 per cent of them were set up under the Tenth Plan period. Nearly 49 per cent of the enterprises are making profits and 41 per cent are incurring losses. The total investment was ₹ 28,241.35 crore consisting of paid-up capital and long-term loans. The capital employed increased by 16.4 per cent in 2007-08. The total number of employees declined from 2.32 lakh in 2006-07 to 2.16 lakh in 2007-08. The turnover increased by 23.9 per cent from ₹ 25,993.22 crore in 2006-07 to ₹ 34,169 crore in 2007-08. The SLPEs in Maharashtra incurred a loss of ₹ 661.88 crore in 2007-08. The details are given in Table 17.1.

Table 17.1

Overview of SLPEs in Maharashtra

(₹ in lakh)

Particulars	*2007-08*	*2007-06*	*2006-05*
Investment			
Paid-up capital			
State Govt.	194018.6	175625.7	159695
Central Govt.	13243.13	13233.13	12145.03
Others	892746.8	845343	510064
Total	1100009	1034202	681904
Long-term Loan			
Government	82218.67	192293	195385.3
Others	1641908	1201080	962685.6
Total	1724127	1393373	1158071
Total Investment	2824135	2427575	1839975
Capital Employed	2964605	2477801	656054.4
Turnover	3416909	2599322	457352
Net Profit/Loss	-66188	-18024.4	-38409.1
Accumulated Profit/Loss	-464558	-274562	-291055
No. of Employees	216157	232187	222986
Total Return on Capital Employed	159596.1	91709.08	10415.51
Percentage of Total Return on Capital Employed	338.28	908.06	221.68
Subsidies/Grants			
Central Govt.	9478.55	230685.3	17554.97
State Govt.	344655	38992.47	77170.61
Total	354133.5	269677.8	94725.58

Source: Comptroller and Auditor General (CAG) (Commercial) India, 2007-08.

Categorisation

The SLPEs are classified into five categories: financial, manufacturing, promotional, utility and welfare enterprises. The number of enterprises functioning under each category is shown in Figure 17.1. The promotional and utility enterprises constitute the largest in number. The growth in the number of SLPEs and the increasing number of profit-making units increased the total investment level. The investment was ₹ 24,275.75 crore in 2005-06 which increased to ₹ 28,241.35 crore in 2007-08. The investments are financed through the budgetary support from the state and central governments and other financial institutions.

Figure 17.1

Category-wise SLPEs in Maharashtra

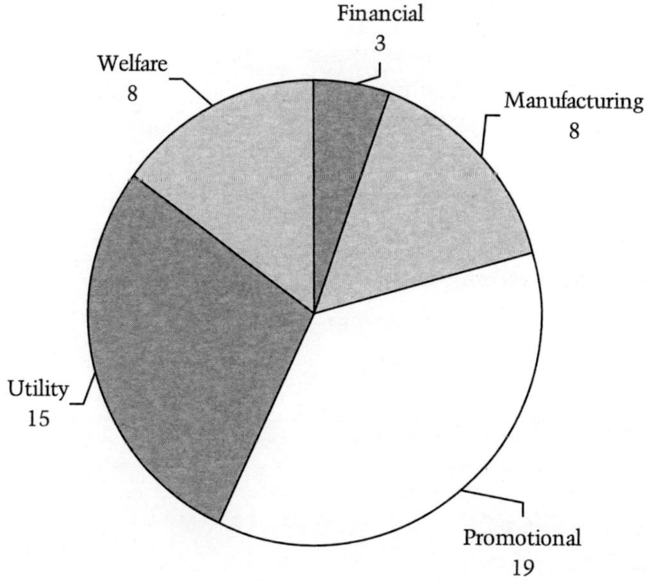

Source: CAG (Commercial) India, 2007-08.

Accumulated Profits and Losses

The accumulated losses of the SLPEs increased by 41 per cent from ₹ 2,745.62 crore in 2006-07 to ₹ 4,645.58 crore in 2007-08. The losses were incurred mostly in the utility, manufacturing and financial sectors.

The enterprises in the promotional sector were earning profits, but the loss incurred in the utility sector increased the accumulated losses of these enterprises (Table 17.2).

Table 17.2

Accumulated Profit and Loss of SLPEs

(₹ *in lakh*)

S.No.	*Particulars*	*2007-08*	*2006-07*	*2005-06*
1	Financial	-62228	-62229	-61512
2	Manufacturing	-7281.6	-7167.9	-7272.8
3	Promotional	20532.2	9967.66	7179
4	Utility	-416672	-215645	-229595
5	Welfare	1090.83	511.61	146.24
	Total	-464558	-274562	-291055

Source: CAG (Commercial) India, 2007-08.

Top Five Profit-making and Loss-making Units

Tables 17.3 and 17.4 provide information on top five profit- and loss-making units in Maharashtra. Maharashtra State Power Generation Company, Maharashtra State Electricity Transmission Company and Maharashtra State Road Transport Corporation are ranked first, second and third respectively amongst the profit-making SLPEs.

Table 17.3

Top Five Profit-making Units (2007-08)

(₹ *in lakh)*

S.No.	*Name of the Enterprise*	*Amount*
1	Maharashtra State Power Generation Company	26406.34
2	Maharashtra State Electricity Transmission Company	17933
3	Maharashtra State Road Transport Corporation	15803
4	Forest Development Corporation of Maharashtra	4460.77
5	Maharashtra Industrial Development	3228

Source: CAG (Commercial) India, 2007-08.

Maharashtra State Electricity Distribution, Maharashtra State Electricity Board and Maharashtra State Road Development Corporation are the major loss-making units. The electricity distribution increased its expenses due to huge shortfall of power which led to an increase of load shedding ranging from 2.5 to 15 hours. It resorts to purchase of costly power from outside agencies. The state road transportation suffered a loss of ₹ 21.31 crore due to adoption of lower traffic growth rate contrary to government notification, incorrect rates of toll and incurred wasteful expenditure of ₹ 70.26 lakh on construction of temporary site office.

Table 17.4

Top Five Loss-making Units (2007-08)

(₹ in lakh)

S.No.	*Name of the Enterprise*	*Amount*
1	Maharashtra State Electricity Distribution	60661
2	Maharashtra State Electricity Board	42129.26
3	Maharashtra State Road Development Corporation	33179.03
4	Maharashtra State financial Corporation	975
5	Maharashtra State Farming Corporation	973.86

Source: CAG (Commercial) India, 2007-08.

Budgetary Support

Table 17.5 shows the budgetary support to the SLPEs during the year 2007-08. The loans, grants and subsidies given by the state and central governments constitute the major share in the budget support followed by the equity.

Table 17.5

Budget Support to SLPEs (2007-08)

(₹ in crore)

S. No.	*Particulars*	*2005-06*	*2006-07*	*2007-08*
1	Equity	210.47	578.65	327.75
2	Loans	1260.98	94.87	86.59
3	Grants/subsidies	771.71	2631.04	3382.78
4	Total	2243.16	3304.56	3797.12

Source: CAG (Commercial) India, 2007-08.

The budgetary support to the SLPEs has been increasing over the year. The budgetary support increased from ₹ 2,243.16 crore in 2005-06 to ₹ 3,304.56 crore in 2006-07 by 32.12 per cent. It increased by 12.97 per cent in 2007-08. The investment made in enterprises increased the budgetary support in the state.

Performance

Of the 53 SLPEs functioning in the state, more than 26 units are making profits and 21 enterprises are making losses. The SLPEs turnover to state GDP shows the extent of public enterprises activities in the state. Table 17.6 provides the detail of SLPEs contribution to state GDP from 2005-06 to 2007-08.

Table 17.6

SLPEs Contribution to State GDP

(₹ in crore)

S. No.	*Particulars*	*2005-06*	*2006-07*	*2007-08*
1	Turnover	4573.52	25993.22	34169.09
2	State GDP	432413	509356	590995
3	Percentage of Turnover to State GDP	1.06	5.10	5.78

Source: CAG (Commercial) India, 2007-08.

The percentage of turnover to the state GDP increased from 1.06 per cent in 2005-06 to 5.1 per cent in 2006-07. In 2008, the percentage of turnover to GDP was 5.78 per cent. There is an increase in the turnover of all the sectors mainly the utility and the welfare. There contribution to the state GDP meagerly increased owing to a minute increase in the turnover of the manufacturing and promotional sectors. The losses of SLPEs are mainly attributable to deficiencies in financial management, planning, implementation of project, running their operations and monitoring. The state is recognised as the country's industrial powerhouse and holds the position of being the most industrialised state in the economy. The state is pioneer in small-scale industries. It has been attracting industrial investments from both domestic as well as foreign institutions on one hand and boasting largest number of special export promotion zones on the other. During the year 2007-08, about 27 per cent of the exports from the country are from the state.

The state occupies a front place in sustaining industrial growth and creating environment conducive to industrial development. The investment friendly industrial policies, excellent infrastructure, strong and productive human resource base have made it a favoured destination for the manufacturing, export, distribution and financial service sectors. The state is well diversified in terms of human resource with positive work culture, excellent educational facilities and quality infrastructure thriving partnership with enterprising entrepreneurs, backed by continuity and consistency in government policies on investments. The objective of the government is to achieve higher and sustainable economic growth with emphasis on balanced regional development and employment generation through greater private and public investments in industrial and infrastructure development. The new industrial policy focus on much better ease of doing business, especially for the micro, small and medium enterprises (MSMEs) sector, which is the backbone of the state's industry. Further, the policy laid emphasis on transparent and stakeholder friendly policy and procedure for land acquisition.

18 Manipur

Introduction

Manipur is known as a land of jewels. Agriculture & allied activities provide the backbone to the economy, while weaving and pisciculture are other important and traditional means of livelihood in the valley. Manipur is rich in natural resources but due to difficult terrain, inadequate infrastructural facilities and varying climatic conditions, the state could not develop much in the industrial sector of its economy. The revival and revitalisation of the traditional handlooms and handicrafts was given priority by the government. The GDP of Manipur was ₹ 4,31,770 lakh in 2007 with a growth rate of 5.23 per cent. The per capita income was ₹ 15,047 lakh in 2006-07 with the growth rate of 3.35 per cent. The contribution of agricultural sector to GDP is 26.82 per cent, industrial sector contributes 29.64 per cent and the service sectors contribution is 43.54 per cent in 2006-07. The state government has made persistent efforts for rapid industrialisation of the state thereby generating more employment opportunities, alleviation of poverty and removal of economic disparities. The government is focusing on the small scale- and agro-based industries without discouraging the medium- and large-scale industries.

Overview of SLPEs

There were 8 working SLPEs in Manipur as on March 31, 2008, and about 50 per cent of them were set up during the Sixth Plan period. Nearly 38 per cent of the enterprises are making profits and 37 per cent are incurring losses. The total investment was ₹ 43.49 crore consisting of paid-up capital and long-term loans. The capital employed declined by 34.57 per cent in 2007-08. The total number of employees declined by 20 per cent i.e., from 269 in 2006-07 to 224 in 2007-08. There was an increase in the turnover by 5.27 per cent with ₹ 6.39 crore in 2006-07 to ₹ 6.75 crore in

2007-08. The SLPEs in Manipur earned a profit of ₹ 0.80 crore in 2007-08. The details are given in Table 18.1.

Table 18.1

Overview of SLPEs in Manipur

(₹ in lakh)

Particulars	*2007-08*	*2006-07*	*2005-06*
Investment			
Paid-up Capital			
State Govt.	2396.26	2396.56	2296.6
Central Govt.	538	538	538
Others	0	0	0
Total	2934.26	2934.26	2836.6
Long-term Loan			
Government	185.38	185.38	200.38
Others	1230	818	1702
Total	1415.38	1003.38	1902.38
Total Investment	4349.64	3937.64	4738.98
Capital Employed	2628.11	1719.65	1669.73
Turnover	674.99	639.39	642.11
Net Profit/Loss	80.2	44.65	76.86
Accumulated Profit/Loss	46.79	-53.14	-1.35
No. of Employees	224	269	181
Total Return on Capital Employed	172.12	120.85	150.59
Percentage of Total Return on Capital Employed	62.7	65.77	65.77
Subsidies/Grants			
Central Govt.	0	0	0
State Govt.	0	0	0
Total	0	0	0

Source: Comptroller and Auditor General (CAG) (Commercial) India, 2007-08.

Categorisation

The SLPEs are classified into five categories: financial, manufacturing, promotional, utility and welfare enterprises. The number of enterprises functioning under each category is shown in Figure 18.1. The promotional and manufacturing enterprises constitute the largest in number. The investment in the SLPEs increased by 9.47 per cent i.e., from ₹ 39.38 crore in 2006-07 to ₹ 43.49 crore in 2007-08. The investments are financed through the budgetary support from the state and central governments and other financial institutions.

Figure 18.1

Category-wise SLPEs in Manipur

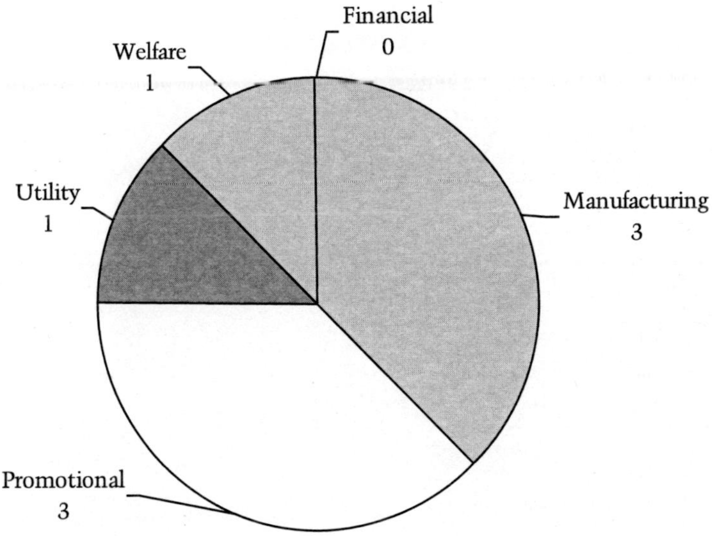

Source: CAG (Commercial) India, 2007-08.

Accumulated Profits and Losses

The accumulated losses of the SLPEs were ₹ 0.53 crore in 2006-07. The enterprises in the promotional and welfare sectors were earning profits, so there was a move from the accumulated loss to profit in 2007-08. The losses were incurred mostly in the manufacturing sector.

Table 18.2

Accumulated Profit and Loss of SLPEs

(₹ in lakh)

S. No.	*Particulars*	*2007-08*	*2006-07*	*2005-06*
1	Financial	0	0	0
2	Manufacturing	-159.54	-159.54	-107.75
3	Promotional	202.8	102.87	102.87
4	Utility	0	0	0
5	Welfare	3.53	3.53	3.53
	Total	46.79	-53.14	-1.35

Source: CAG (Commercial) India, 2007-08.

Top Profit-making and Loss-making Units

Tables 18.3 and 18.4 provide the information on top three profit- and loss-making units in Manipur. Manipur Industrial Development Corporation, Manipur Police Housing Corporation and Manipur Electronics Development Corporation are ranked first, second and third respectively amongst the profit-making SLPEs.

Table 18.3

Top Three Profit-making Units (2007-08)

(₹ in lakh)

S. No.	*Name of the Enterprise*	*Amount*
1	Manipur Industrial Development Corp.	99.94
2	Manipur Police Housing Corp.	24.3
3	Manipur Electronics Development Corp.	11.19

Source: CAG (Commercial) India, 2007-08.

Manipur Handlooms and Handicrafts Development Corporation (MHHDC), Manipur Tribal Development Corporation (MTDC) and Manipur Film Development Corporation (MFDC) are the major loss-making units. MHHDC incurred loss owing to the inconsistency in the decisions of the management. The misappropriation of finance led MTDC to acquire loss. MFDC suffered loss as it would not generate its revenue.

Table 18.4

Top Three Loss-making Units (2007-08)

(₹ in lakh)

S. No.	*Name of the Enterprise*	*Amount*
1	Manipur Handlooms and Handicrafts Dev. Corp.	-2.33
2	Manipur Tribal Development Corp.	-2.33
3	Manipur Film Development Corp.	-1.11

Source: CAG (Commercial) India, 2007-08.

Budgetary Support

Table 18.5 shows the budgetary support to the SLPEs during the years 2006-2008. A clear view of the budgetary support could not be made as the SLPEs had to finalise their accounts.

Table 18.5

Budgetary Support to SLPEs (2006-2008)

(₹ in crore)

S. No.	Particulars	2005-06	2006-07	2007-08
1	Equity	0.05	0	0
2	Loans	0	0	0
3	Grants/subsidies	0	0	0
4	Total	0.05	0	0

Source: CAG (Commercial) India, 2007-08.

Performance

Manipur has eight SLPEs functioning in the state; out of which three units are making profits and three enterprises are making losses. The remaining two enterprises have to commence their operations. The SLPEs turnover to state GDP shows the extent of public enterprises activities in the state. Table 18.6 provides the detail of SLPEs contribution to state GDP from 2005-06 to 2007-08.

Table 18.6

SLPEs Contribution to State GDP

(₹ in crore)

S. No.	Particulars	2005-06	2006-07	2007-08
1	Turnover	6.42	6.4	6.75
2	State GDP	4693	6501	5704
3	Percentage of Turnover to State GDP	0.14	0.10	0.12

Source: CAG (Commercial) India, 2007-08.

The percentage of turnover to the state GDP has been varying over the years. There is a decline in the turnover of the SLPEs, leading to changes in their contribution to the state GDP. The SLPEs can discharge their role efficiently only if they are financially self-reliant. There is scope for improvement in overall performance, when the government introduces a performance-based system of accountability and imbibes greater degree of professionalism to ensure efficiency and profitability. Manipur remained an economically and industrially backward state due to its isolated position and geographical barriers. To overcome the obstacles for development, the government has acknowledged the information technology (IT) industry for economic growth, employment, infrastructure development and power supply. E-governance is introduced to upgrade the standard and quality of administration and to provide efficient and cost-effective government.

19 Meghalaya

Introduction

Meghalaya is predominantly an agrarian economy. Nearly two-third of the total workforce is engaged in agriculture & allied activities. Agriculture is characterised by low productivity and unsustainable farm practices, giving rise to a high incidence of rural poverty. As a result, despite the large percentage of population engaged in agriculture, the state is still dependent upon imports from other states for most food items such as meat, eggs, food grains, etc. The state has a rich base of natural resources. These include minerals such as coal, limestone, sillimanite, kaolin and granite among others. It also has a large forest cover, rich biodiversity and numerous water bodies. The low level of industrialisation and the relatively poor infrastructure base in the state act as an impediment for the exploitation of these natural resources. The gross state domestic product (GSDP) at current prices increased from ₹ 8,472 crore in 2007-08 to ₹ 9,611 crore in 2008-09 indicating an increase of 13 per cent. The per capita income increased from ₹ 33,644 in 2007-08 to ₹ 37,718 in 2008-09. The contribution of the primary sector to the state GDP is 19.40 per cent. The service sector contributes around 47.52 per cent and the industrial sector contributes 33.08 per cent.

Overview of SLPEs

There were 13 working SLPEs in Meghalaya as on March 31, 2008. About 61 per cent of them were set up during the Fifth Plan period. Nearly 31 per cent of the enterprises are making profits and 69 per cent are incurring losses. The total investment was ₹ 1,372.41 crore consisting of paid-up capital and long-term loans. The capital employed increased by 13.18 per cent in 2007-08. The total number of employees declined from 5,996 in 2006-07 to 5,313 in 2007-08. There was an increase in the turnover by 23.89 per cent from ₹ 278.18 crore in 2006-07 to ₹ 365.47 crore in 2007-08. The SLPEs in Meghalaya incurred a loss of ₹ 10.77 crore in 2007-08. The details are given in Table 19.1.

Table 19.1

Overview of SLPEs in Meghalaya

(₹ *in lakh)*

Particulars	*2007-08*	*2006-07*	*2005-06*
Investment			
Paid-up Capital			
State Govt.	39009.27	38393.17	36983.91
Central Govt.	710.64	710.64	833.2
Others	693.24	693.24	570.68
Total	40413.15	39797.05	38387.79
Long-term Loan			
Government	36731.07	37619.63	15862.76
Others	60096.61	51617.16	35429.04
Total	96827.68	89236.79	51291.8
Total Investment	137240.8	129033.8	89679.59
Capital Employed	93222.76	80934.96	70855.01
Turnover	36547.49	27817.79	30063.84
Net Profit/Loss	-1076.76	-9935.94	-7075.22
Accumulated Profit/Loss	-52412.7	-50871.5	-40334.4
No. of Employees	5313	5996	6067
Total Return on Capital Employed	2731.01	-6724.59	-1936.89
Percentage of Total Return on Capital Employed	14.72	7.32	6.57
Subsidies/Grants			
Central Govt.	0	0	0
State Govt.	3713.78	2774.94	1817.32
Total	3713.78	2774.94	1817.32

Source: Comptroller and Auditor General (CAG) (Commercial) India, 2007-08.

Categorisation

The SLPEs are classified into five categories: financial, manufacturing, promotional, utility and welfare enterprises. The number of enterprises functioning under each category is shown in Figure 19.1. The enterprises in Meghalaya are mostly in three sectors. There are no enterprises in the financial and the welfare sectors. The enterprises in the manufacturing sector constitute large in number. The investment was ₹ 1,290.34 crore in 2006-07 which increased to ₹ 1,372.41 crore in 2007-08 i.e., by 5.98 per cent. It increased due to an increase in the equity of Mawmluh Cherra Cements, Meghalaya Industrial Development Corporation (MIDC) and Meghalaya Handloom and Handicraft Development Corporation.

Figure 19.1

Category-wise SLPEs in Meghalaya

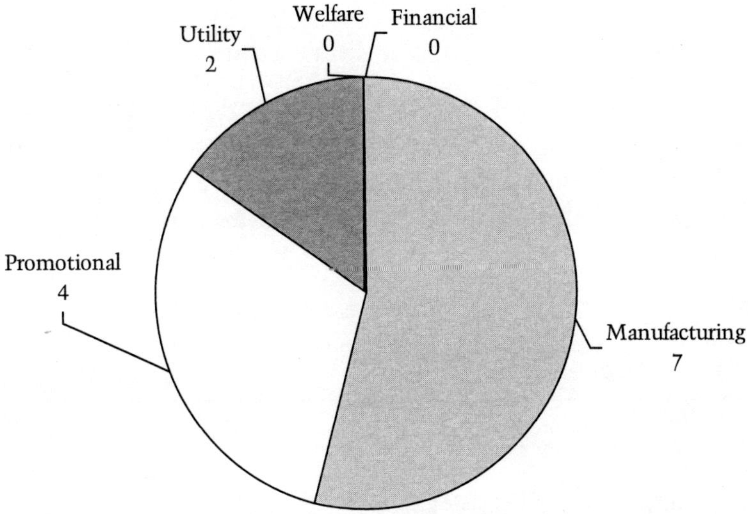

Source: CAG (Commercial) India, 2007-08.

Accumulated Profits and Losses

The accumulated losses of the SLPES have increased by 2.94 per cent, i.e., from ₹ 508.71 crore in 2006-07 to ₹ 524.13 crore in 2007-08. The losses were incurred mostly in the manufacturing and the promotional sectors.

Table 19.2

Accumulated Profit and Loss of SLPEs

(₹ in lakh)

S. No.	*Particulars*	*2007-08*	*2006-07*	*2005-06*
1	Financial	0	0	0
2	Manufacturing	-5980.43	-5136.55	-4359.21
3	Promotional	-328.14	-293.72	-284.51
4	Utility	-46104	-45441	-35691
5	Welfare	0	0	0
	Total	-52413	-50872	-40334

Source: CAG (Commercial) India, 2007-08.

Top Profit-making and Loss-making Units

Tables 19.3 and 19.4 provide the information on top profit- and loss-making units in Meghalaya. Meghalaya State Electricity Board, Maemluhcherra Cements Limited and Meghalaya State Warehousing Corporation are ranked first, second and third respectively amongst the profit-making SLPEs.

Table 19.3

Top Four Profit-making Units (2007-08)

(₹ in lakh)

S. No.	*Name of the Enterprise*	*Amount*
1	Meghalaya State Electricity board	133.76
2	Mawmluh Cherra Cements Limited	145.07
3	Meghalaya State Warehousing Corp.	5.27
4	Meghalaya Industrial Development Corp.	4.25

Source: CAG (Commercial) India, 2007-08.

Meghalaya Transport Corporation (MTC), Meghalaya Electronics Development Corporation (MEDC) and Meghalaya Mineral Development Corporation (MMDC) are the major loss-making units. MTC incurred loss owing to the mismanagement.

Table 19.4

Top Five Loss-making Units (2007-08)

(₹ in lakh)

S. No.	Name of the Enterprise	Amount
1	Meghalaya Transport Corp.	-463.55
2	Meghalaya Electronics Development Corp.	-336.7
3	Meghalaya Mineral Development Corp.	-169.85
4	Meghalaya Bamboo Chips Limited	-151.31
5	Meghalaya Watches Limited	-94.79

Source: CAG (Commercial) India, 2007-08.

Budgetary Support

Table 19.5 shows the budgetary support to the SLPEs during the years 2006-2008. The grants and subsidies given by the state and central governments constitute the major share in the budgetary support followed by the equity.

Table 19.5

Budgetary Support to SLPEs (2006-2008)

(₹ in crore)

S. No.	Particulars	2005-06	2006-07	2007-08
1	Equity	20.78	12.95	10.38
2	Loans	8.52	9.66	8.43
3	Grants/subsidies	18.18	27.75	37.14
4	Total	47.48	50.36	55.95

Source: CAG (Commercial) India, 2007-08.

The budgetary support to the SLPEs has been rising over the years. The budgetary support increased from ₹ 47.48 crore in 2005-06 to ₹ 50.36 crore in 2006-07. The budgetary support increased by 15.14 per cent during 2006-2008. There is an increase in the budgetary support as the government supported the loss-making enterprises in the form of grants and equity in the state.

Performance

Of the 13 SLPEs functioning in the state, 4 units are making profits and 9 enterprises are making losses. The SLPEs turnover to state GDP shows the extent of public enterprises activities in the state. Table 6 provides the details of SLPEs contribution to state GDP from 2005-06 to 2007-08.

Table 19.6

SLPEs Contribution to State GDP

(₹ *in crore)*

S. No.	*Particulars*	*2005-06*	*2006-07*	*2007-08*
1	Turnover	300.64	278.18	365.47
2	State GDP	6445	7330	8472
3	Percentage of Turnover to State GDP	4.66	3.80	4.31

Source: CAG (Commercial) India, 2007-08.

The percentage of turnover to the state GDP has been fluctuating over the years. Though there is an increase in the turnover of the utility sector, their contribution to the state GDP increased marginally owing to a decline in the turnover of the manufacturing and promotional sector. The losses of SLPEs are mainly attributable to deficiencies in financial management, planning, implementation of project, running their operations and monitoring. The government has taken numerous measures for the socioeconomic development of the state. The North East Industrial and Investment Promotion Policy (NEIIPP), 2007, offers fiscal incentives and other concessions to the entrepreneurs for the industrial development of the state. The government is providing incentives to various sectors like the infrastructure development, horticulture, power generation, mineral base industries, etc. Due attention is given to human resources by providing training for the upgradation of skills and enhancing the efficiency. An analytical study is being conducted for the sick/closed industrial units to view their future.

20 Mizoram

Introduction

Mizoram is known as the land of peace with rolling hills, valleys, rivers and lakes. Mizoram lags behind economically within India with little development due to lack of market networks and raw materials. The contribution of industry both registered and unregistered accounts for one per cent of the gross state domestic product (GSDP). Cottage industry and other small-scale industries play an important role in the economy. Nearly 70 per cent of the population is engaged in agriculture. The activities like tailoring, furniture making, automobile repairs, bakery, handloom weaving and black smithing account for more than 80 per cent of the total number of enterprise in the state. There is migration of workforce from agriculture to non-agriculture sector as the government has given priority to agro-based industries.

Mizoram is expected to achieve a growth rate of 6.46 per cent during 2008-09. The per capita income of Mizoram for the year 2008-09 is estimated at ₹ 29,576. Agriculture & allied sector contributes about 14 per cent of the state GDP. The industrial sector contributes about 20 per cent. The tertiary sector (service) remains the driver of the state economy by contributing about 65 per cent. The total employment in the state is 1,06,706 with 13481 (12.6%) employed in agricultural enterprise and 93,225 (87.4%) are in non-agricultural enterprises. A number of oil and gas exploration activities are taking place due to the geographical condition with which Mizoram has been formed, leading to the possibilities and high expectation that reserves would be confirmed. France, Russia and Cyprus as well as several Indian companies have signed a 12 per cent oil and 10 per cent gas royalty arrangement with proceeds going direct to Mizoram state on any production. The hydro power is being developed as the state has rich potential.

Overview of SLPEs

The state has seen an all-round progress in industrial development and infrastructure development, over the years. There were five working SLPEs in Mizoram as on March 31, 2008. About 60 per cent of them were set up during the Seventh Plan period. All the enterprises are incurring losses. The total investment was ₹ 92.96 crore consisting of paid-up capital and long-term loans. The capital employed increased by 10.59 per cent in 2007-08. The total number of employees was 266 in 2007-08. There is an increase in the turnover by 44.7 per cent from ₹ 0.99 crore in 2006-07 to ₹ 1.79 crore in 2007-08. The SLPEs in Mizoram were incurring a loss of ₹ 5.34 crore in 2007-08. The details are given in Table 20.1.

Table 20.1

Overview of SLPEs in Mizoram

(₹ in lakh)

Particulars	*2007-08*	*2006-07*	*2005-06*
Investment			
Paid-up Capital			
State Govt.	5278.11	5402.61	4765.01
Central Govt.	136	173	173
Others	428	0	453
Total	5842.11	5575.61	5391.01
Long-term Loan	0	0	0
Government	185	0	0
Others	3268.47	3347.5	2285.94
Total	3453.47	3347.5	2285.94
Total Investment	9295.58	8923.11	7676.95
Capital Employed	5973.59	5340.88	5071.85
Turnover	179.19	99.1	96.67
Net Profit/Loss	-534.29	-519.41	-502.58
Accumulated Profit/Loss	-3330.21	-3114.04	-2837.86
No. of Employees	266	267	261
Total Return on Capital Employed	-319.93	-385.84	-369.01
Percentage of Total Return on Capital Employed	0	0	0
Subsidies/Grants	0	0	0
Central Govt.	167.51	276.03	40.19
State Govt.	150.2	222	112
Total	317.71	498.03	152.19

Source: Comptroller and Auditor General (CAG) (Commercial) India, 2007-08.

Categorisation

The SLPEs are classified into five categories: financial, manufacturing, promotional, utility and welfare enterprises. The number of enterprises functioning under each category is shown in Figure 20.1. In Mizoram, the enterprises are in the manufacturing and the promotional sector only. There are no enterprises in the remaining sectors. The increase in the number of loss-making SLPEs led to an increase in the investment. The investment was ₹ 89.23 crore in 2006-07 which increased to ₹ 92.91 crore in 2007-08. The investments are financed through the budgetary support from the state and central governments and other financial institutions.

Figure 20.1

Category-wise SLPEs in Mizoram

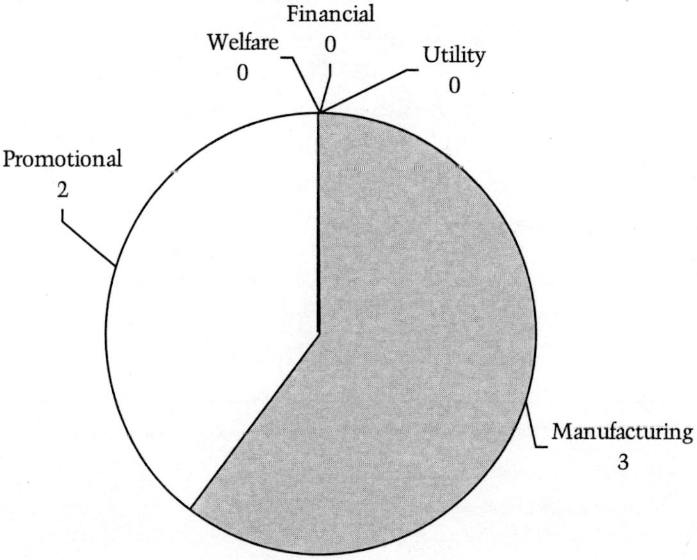

Source: CAG (Commercial) India, 2007-08.

Accumulated Profits and Losses

The accumulated losses of the SLPEs increased from ₹ 31.14 crore in 2006-07 to ₹ 33.30 crore in 2007-08 by 6.49 per cent. The losses were incurred mostly in the promotional sector.

Table 20.2

Accumulated Profit and Loss of SLPEs

(₹ in lakh)

S. No.	*Particulars*	*2007-08*	*2006-07*	*2005-06*
1	Financial	0	0	0
2	Manufacturing	-1644.8	-1644.8	-1449
3	Promotional	-1685.4	-1469.23	-1388.88
4	Utility	0	0	0
5	Welfare	0	0	0
	Total	-3330.2	-3114	-2837.9

Source: CAG (Commercial) India, 2007-08.

Top Loss-making Units

Table 20.3 presents the top loss-making units in Mizoram. Zoram Industrial Development Corporation (ZIDC), Mizoram Food and Allied Industries Corporation (MIFCO) and Mizoram Agri Marketing Development Corporation are the top loss-making SLPEs. ZIDC incurred loss owing to the irregularities in planning, organising and implementation of the financial activities. The outdated machinery, high cost of production and inadequate supply of raw material were the main reasons for the losses incurred by MIFCO.

Table 20.3

Top Five Loss-making Units (2007-08)

(₹ in lakh)

S. No.	*Name of the Enterprise*	*Amount*
1	Zoram Industrial Development Corp.	216.17
2	Mizoram Food and Allied Industries Corp.	148.98
3	Mizoram Agri Marketing Development Corp.	79.11
4	Zoram Electronics Development Corp.	46.85
5	Mizoram Handloom and Handicrafts Development Corp.	43.18

Source: CAG (Commercial) India, 2007-08.

Budgetary Support

Table 20.4 shows the budgetary support to the SLPEs during the years 2006-2008. The grants and subsidies given by the state and central governments constitute the major share in the budgetary support followed by the equity. The details regarding budgetary provision towards equity, loans and grants/subsidies for past three years are given in Table 20.4.

Table 20.4

Budgetary Support to SLPEs (2006-2008)

(₹ in crore)

S. No.	Particulars	2005-06	2006-07	2007-08
1	Equity	6.16	2.1	2.8
2	Loans	0	0	0
3	Grants/subsidies	1.12	2.22	1.5
4	Total	7.28	4.32	4.3

Source: CAG (Commercial) India, 2007-08.

The budgetary support to the SLPEs has been declining over the years. The budgetary support declined from ₹ 7.28 crore in 2005-06 to ₹ 4.32 crore in 2006-07. There was a further decline in the budgetary support in 2007-08. The increase in the equity is due to the investment made by the government in the food processing, electronics and the handloom industries in the state.

Performance

Of the five SLPEs functioning in the state, all the enterprises are incurring losses. The SLPEs turnover to state GDP shows the extent of public enterprises activities in the state. Table 20.5 provides the details of SLPEs contribution to state GDP from 2005-06 to 2007-08.

Table 20.5

SLPEs Contribution to State GDP

(₹ in crore)

S. No.	Particulars	2005-06	2006-07	2007-08
1	Turnover	0.97	0.99	1.79
2	State GDP	2693.96	2984.99	3305.09
3	Percentage of Turnover to State GDP	0.04	0.03	0.04

Source: CAG (Commercial) India, 2007-08.

The percentage of turnover to the state GDP is varying over the years. Though there is an increase in the turnover of the promotional sector, there contribution to the state GDP declined owing to consistency in the manufacturing sector. The losses of SLPEs are mainly attributable to deficiencies in financial management, planning, implementation of project, running their operations and monitoring. The agro-based industries are given priority owing to the geographical barriers in the industrial sector. The government is promoting the setting up of industries in various sectors like energy, mining, horticulture, tourism, food processing, information technology (IT) and others as there is a scope for their development. The infrastructural facilities are given higher priority for the rapid industrial development in the state. North East Industrial and Investment Promotion Policy (NEIIPP), 2007, facilitates establishment and promotion of industries in various sectors.

21 Nagaland

Overview

Nagaland is a flamboyant hill state located in the extreme north-east of India. There were 5 working SLPEs in Nagaland as on March 31, 2008. Nearly 80 per cent of the enterprises are incurring losses. The total investment was ₹ 65.19 lakh consisting of paid-up capital and long-term loans. The capital employed increased by 42.85 per cent in 2007-08. The total number of employees declined from 247 in 2006-07 to 226 in 2007-08. There was an increase in the turnover by 48.92 per cent with ₹ 1.89 lakh in 2006-07 to ₹ 3.7 lakh in 2007-08. The net loss of the SLPEs in Nagaland was ₹ 1.33 lakh in 2007-08. The details are given in Table 21.1.

Categorisation

The SLPEs are classified into five categories: financial, manufacturing, promotional, utility and welfare enterprises. The number of enterprises functioning under each category is shown in Figure 21.1. The manufacturing enterprises constitute the largest number in Nagaland. There are no enterprises in the financial and the welfare sectors. The increase in the number of loss-making SLPEs led to an increase in the total investment level. The investment increased by 8.36 per cent i.e., from ₹ 59.74 lakh in 2006-07 to ₹ 65.19 lakh in 2007-08. The investments are financed through the budgetary support from the state and central governments and other financial institutions.

Table 21.1

Overview of SLPEs in Nagaland

(₹ in lakh)

Particulars	2007-08	2006-07	2005-06
Investment			
Paid-up Capital			
State Govt.	18.63	17.04	16.6
Central Govt.	1.14	1.22	1.22
Others	5.13	5.13	5.13
Total	24.9	23.39	22.95
Long-term Loan			
Government	11.22	11.22	11.76
Others	29.07	25.13	26.78
Total	40.29	36.35	38.54
Total Investment	65.19	59.74	61.49
Capital Employed	34.63	19.79	19.88
Turnover	3.7	1.89	1.89
Net Profit/Loss	-1.33	-1.63	-1.63
Accumulated Profit/Loss	-12.25	-12.26	-12.26
No. of Employees	226	247	235
Total Return on Capital Employed	1.33	0.95	0.95
Percentage of Total Return on Capital Employed	203	6.76	6.79
Subsidies/Grants			
Central Govt.	0	0	0
State Govt.	9.8	5.34	3.34
Total	9.8	5.34	3.34

Source: Comptroller and Auditor General (CAG) (Commercial) India, 2007-08.

Accumulated Profits and Losses

The accumulated losses of the SLPEs declined by 0.08 per cent i.e., from ₹ 12.26 lakh in 2006-07 to ₹ 12.25 lakh in 2007-08. The losses were incurred mostly in the promotional sector. The enterprises in the manufacturing sector were earning profits, which led to marginal decline in the accumulated losses.

Figure 21.1

Category-wise SLPEs in Nagaland

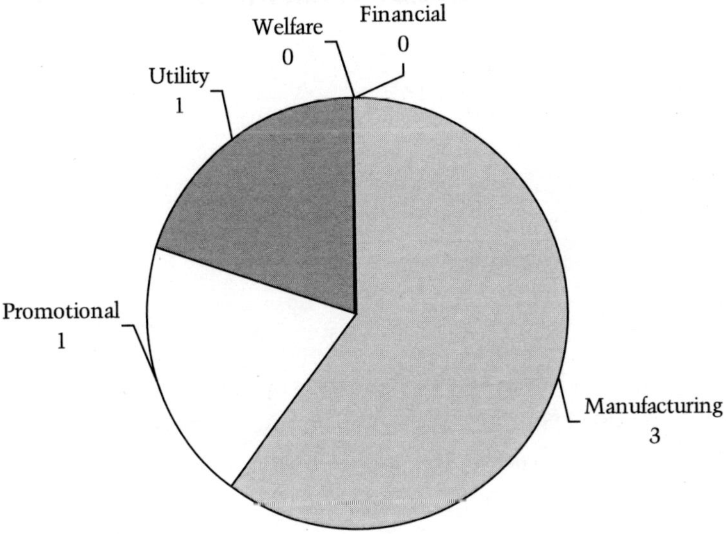

Source: CAG (Commercial) India, 2007-08.

Table 21.2

Accumulated Profit and Loss of SLPEs

(₹ in lakh)

S. No.	*Particulars*	*2007-08*	*2006-07*	*2005-06*
1	Financial	0	0	0
2	Manufacturing	-1.2	-1.66	-1.66
3	Promotional	-11.05	-10.6	-10.6
4	Utility	0	0	0
5	Welfare	0	0	0
	Total	-12.25	-12.26	-12.26

Source: CAG (Commercial) India, 2007-08.

Top Loss-making Units

Table 21.3 presents the top loss-making units in Nagaland. Nagaland State Mineral Development Corporation, Nagaland Industrial Development Corporation and Nagaland Handloom & Handicraft Development

Corporation are the top loss-making units. Lack of proper planning and coordination in execution of their strategies resulted in losses for the enterprises.

Table 21.3

Top Loss-making Units (2007-08)

(₹ in lakh)

S. No.	*Name of the Enterprise*	*Amount*
1	Nagaland State Mineral Deve. Corp	0.57
2	Nagaland Industrial Deve. Corp.	0.45
3	Nagaland Handloom & Handicraft Deve. Corp.	0.3
4	Nagaland Industrial Raw Material & Supply Corp.	0.01

Source: CAG (Commercial) India, 2007-08.

Budgetary Support

Table 21.4 shows the budgetary support to the SLPEs during 2005-06 to 2007-08. The grants and subsidies given by the state and central governments have the major share in the budgetary support followed by the equity.

Table 21.4

Budgetary Support to SLPEs (2005-06 to 2007-08)

(₹ in crore)

S. No.	*Particulars*	*2005-06*	*2006-07*	*2007-08*
1	Equity	0.5	0.45	0.47
2	Loans	4.34	0	7.15
3	Grants/subsidies	5.34	5.34	9.8
4	Total	10.18	5.79	17.42

Source: CAG (Commercial) India, 2007-08.

The budgetary support to the SLPEs has been fluctuating over the years. The budgetary support declined from ₹ 10.18 crore in 2005-06 to ₹ 5.79 crore in 2006-07. There was an increase in the budgetary support in 2007-08 to ₹ 17.42 crore by 66.8 per cent. The increase in the loans and the grants/subsidies given to the SLPEs increased the budgetary support. These investments were made for the revival of the enterprises in the state.

Performance

Of the five SLPEs functioning in the state, four enterprises are incurring losses and one enterprise has not finalised its accounts. The SLPEs turnover to state GDP shows the extent of public enterprises activities in the state. Table 21.5 provides the details of SLPEs contribution to state GDP from 2005-06 to 2007-08.

Table 21.5

SLPEs Contribution to State GDP

(₹ in crore)

S. No.	*Particulars*	*2005-06*	*2006-07*	*2007-08*
1	Turnover	0.02	0.02	0.04
2	State GDP	6374.56	6957.97	7168.52
3	Percentage of Turnover to State GDP	0.000	0.000	0.001

Source: CAG (Commercial) India, 2007-08.

The percentage of turnover to the state GDP is almost nil in the state. Though there is an increase in the turnover of the promotional and the manufacturing sector, their contribution to the state GDP has not progressed. The losses of SLPEs are mainly attributable to deficiencies in financial management, planning, implementation of project, running their operations and monitoring. The Industrial Policy (2000) and the North East Industrial and Investment Promotion Policy (NEIIPP), 2007, facilitated for the rapid industrial development in the state. The state government is providing incentives in the form of subsidies and tax exemption for the promotion of industries and creation of income and employment. The food processing, floriculture, sericulture, handloom and handicrafts, electronics, information technology (IT), petrochemicals and bio-tech are given significance in the state.

22 Orissa

Introduction

Orissa is the ninth largest state in India, and the eleventh largest by population. The state is one of the most vibrant states in the eastern part of India, which is also know for its vast natural resources, investor friendly government and favourable climate. The state has vast mineral deposits and ranks sixth in mineral production in India. Various mineral resources such as bauxite, coal resources, iron ore, nickel, chromite, etc., are found in the state. Orissa contains a fifth of India's coal, a quarter of its iron ore, a third of its bauxite reserves and most of the chromite. The Rourkela Steel Plant was regarded as the first integrated steel plant in the public sector in India.

Over the past few years, the state has grown remarkably in terms of gross state domestic product (GSDP). The GSDP of the state has improved impressively at a growth rate of 9.53 per cent between 1999-2000 and 2005-06. The state has registered an annual average growth rate of 8.73 per cent in first three years of the Eleventh Five Year Plan and the state economy has grown at an annual average rate of 9.51 per cent during the Tenth Five Year Plan period. Since 1990, with the state economy undergoing a structural change, remarkable growth has been observed in all the three sectors, primary sector (comprising agriculture and livestock, fishing and mining and quarrying), secondary sector (comprising manufacturing, construction, electricity, gas and water supply) and tertiary sector (comprising communication, financial services, real estate and related services, public administration and other services). Notably, the secondary and tertiary sectors have contributed a lot towards the development of the state economy.

In 2007, the Government of Orissa has formulated the famous Industrial Policy Resolution 2007 and Vision 2020 documents, which solely focus on the private sector as the main vehicle of growth. It is also highlighted that the state aims at achieving faster growth in sectors such as mining, tourism, handicrafts and other manufacturing sub-sectors.

Development and Objectives

Prior to Independence, the state had a very low level of industrialisation. The state had a few sugar and soap factories to its credit. Inspite of the government's encouraging policies and assistance, industrialisation could not pick up in the initial years. Therefore, the government decided to accelerate the pace of development by setting up SLPEs with the following objectives (Mishra and Lakshmi Kumari, 2006):

- To achieve rapid industrialisation,
- To reduce regional disparities,
- To develop infrastructure facilities,
- To exploit the natural and mineral resources, and
- To generate employment and earn profits.

Overview of SLPEs

There were 32 working SLPEs in Orissa as on March 31, 2008. About 19 per cent of the enterprises were set up during the Fifth Plan period. Nearly 59 per cent of the enterprises are making profits and 34 per cent are incurring losses. The total investment was ₹ 8,021.80 crore consisting of paid-up capital and long-term loans. The capital employed increased by 8.08 per cent in 2007-08. The total number of employees declined by 14.34 per cent i.e., from 31,453 in 2006-07 to 27,508 in 2007-08. There is an increase in the turnover by 16.25 per cent i.e., from ₹ 6,071.68 crore in 2006-07 to ₹ 7,250.07 crore in 2007-08. The SLPEs in the state earned a profit of ₹ 1,279.44 crore in 2007-08. The details are given in Table 22.1.

Table 22.1

Overview of SLPEs in Orissa

(₹ in lakh)

Particulars	*2007-08*	*2006-07*	*2005-06*
Investment			
Paid-up Capital			
State Govt.	179910.9	151811.7	151805.4
Central Govt.	5586.48	1697.54	1697.54
Others	31447.52	35336.46	36194.58
Total	216944.9	188845.7	189697.6
Long-term Loan			
Government	274268	414173.2	320043.9
Others	310967.3	325525.4	452754.1
Total	585235.3	739698.6	772798
Total Investment	802180	928544	962495
Capital Employed	937945	862146.9	923247.3
Turnover	725007.4	607167.7	211981.6
Net Profit/Loss	127943.8	38771.8	76085.54
Accumulated Profit/Loss	25753.45	-114287	-124720
No. of Employees	27508	31453	20999
Total Return on Capital Employed	175114.6	95905.63	140154.8
Percentage of Total Return on Capital Employed	663.43	614.2	377.1
Subsidies/Grants			
Central Govt.	35326	11711.54	7479
State Govt.	5499.95	5132.63	5940.56
Total	40825.95	16844.17	13419.56

Source: Comptroller and Auditor General (CAG) (Commercial) India, 2007-08.

Categorisation

According to the nature of the operations, the SLPEs in the state are classified into five categories: financial, manufacturing, promotional, utility and welfare enterprises. The number of enterprises functioning under each category is shown in Figure 22.1. The promotional, manufacturing and utility enterprises constitute the largest number. There is a decline in the total investment by 15.75 per cent owing to the decline in the loans given to SLPEs in power and finance sectors. The investment was ₹ 9,285.44 crore in 2006-07 which declined to ₹ 8,021.80 crore in 2007-08. The investments are financed through the budgetary support from the state and central governments and other financial institutions.

Figure 22.1

Category-wise SLPEs in Orissa

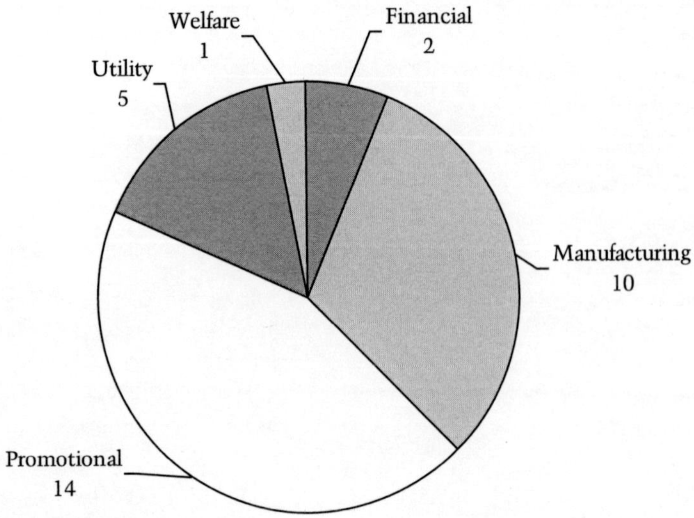

Source: CAG (Commercial) India, 2007-08.

Accumulated Profits and Losses

The accumulated losses of the SLPEs declined from ₹ 1,142.87 crore in 2006-07 and started earning a profit of ₹ 257.53 crore in 2007-08. The enterprises in the manufacturing, financial, utility and welfare sectors were earning profits, leading to declining accumulated losses. Only the SLPEs in the promotional sector were incurring losses.

Table 22.2

Accumulated Profit and Loss of SLPEs

(₹ in lakh)

S. No.	*Particulars*	*2007-08*	*2006-07*	*2005-06*
1	Financial	-37938	-38158	-38158
2	Manufacturing	75752.39	45339.35	37791.35
3	Promotional	-23774	-23184	-20410.1
4	Utility	11495.4	-98483	-103881
5	Welfare	217.56	199.62	-61.63
	Total	25753.5	-114287	-124720

Source: CAG (Commercial) India, 2007-08.

Top Five Profit-making and Loss-making Units

Tables 22.3 and 22.4 present the top five profit- and loss-making units in Orissa. GRIDCO Limited, Orissa Mining Corporation Limited and Orissa Power Generation Corporation Limited are ranked first, second and third respectively amongst the profit-making SLPEs.

Table 22.3

Top Five Profit-making Units (2007-08)

(₹ in lakh)

S. No.	*Name of the Enterprise*	*Amount*
1	GRIDCO Limited	56605.07
2	Orissa Mining Corporation Limited	39966.59
3	Orissa Power Generation Corporation Limited	18152.54
4	Orissa Hydro Power Corporation Limited	12139.41
5	IDCOL Kalinga Iron Works Limited	1613.25

Source: CAG (Commercial) India, 2007-08.

Orissa Forest Development Corporation Limited (OFDC), Orissa Power Transmission Corporation Limited (OPTC) and Orissa Small Industries Corporation Limited are the major loss-making units. OFDC is under the restructuring plan of the state government. OPTC incurred loss due to undue favour to private parties for availing loans and non-recovery of service tax and interest from beneficiaries.

Table 22.4

Top Five Loss-making Units (2007-08)

(₹ in lakh)

S. No.	*Name of the Enterprise*	*Amount*
1	Orissa Forest Development Corporation Limited	1592.5
2	Orissa Power Transmission Corporation Limited	905.88
3	Orissa Small Industries Corporation Limited	477.7
4	Orissa Agro Industries Corporation Limited	230.53
5	Orissa Bridge and Construction Corp. Limited	133.34

Source: CAG (Commercial) India, 2007-08.

Budgetary Support

Table 22.5 shows the budgetary support of the SLPEs during the years 2006-2008. The grants and subsidies given by the state and central governments constitute the major share in the budgetary support followed by the equity. The details regarding budgetary provision towards equity, loans and grants/subsidies for past three years are given in Figure 22.2.

Table 22.5

Budgetary Support to SLPEs (2006-2008)

(₹ *in crore)*

S. No.	*Particulars*	*2005-06*	*2006-07*	*2007-08*
1	Equity	7.21	0	9.95
2	Loans	0	234.12	75.4
3	Grants/subsidies	0.25	49.26	56.79
4	Total	7.46	283.38	142.14

Source: CAG (Commercial) India, 2007-08.

The budgetary support to the SLPEs has been varying over the years. The budgetary support increased by 97.37 per cent from ₹ 7.46 crore in 2005-06 to ₹ 283.38 crore in 2006-07. It declined by almost half in 2007-08. There was a decline in the amount of loans given to SLPEs which led to a decrease in the budgetary support by the government. The SLPEs were earning profits in almost all the sectors; so, there is an increase in equity and subsidies

Performance

Of the 32 SLPEs functioning in the state, 19 units are making profits and 11 enterprises are making losses. The SLPEs turnover to state GDP shows the extent of public enterprises activities in the state. Table 22.6 provides the detail of SLPEs contribution to state GDP from 2005-06 to 2007-08.

Table 22.6

SLPEs Contribution to State GDP

(₹ *in crore)*

S. No.	*Particulars*	*2005-06*	*2006-07*	*2007-08*
1	Turnover	2119.81	6071.68	7250.07
2	State GDP	78953	93374	106466
3	Percentage of Turnover to State GDP	2.68	6.50	6.81

Source: CAG (Commercial) India, 2007-08.

The percentage of turnover to the state GDP increased by almost 4.18 per cent in 2006-07. There was a marginal increase in the GDP percentage in 2007-08. Though there is an increase in the turnover of the manufacturing, financial and utility sectors, their contribution to the state GDP is not up to the mark. The losses of SLPEs are mainly attributable to deficiencies in financial management, planning, implementation of project, running their operations and monitoring. The government constituted a task force on Public Enterprise Reform on October 10, 2000, for framing a policy of public enterprise reforms. The Orissa medium term fiscal reform programme was implemented in two phases: Phase I (2002-2005) and Phase II (2005-2007) which included public sector restructuring. Nearly seven enterprises are under the restructuring plan in Phase II which are about to be completed.

Industrial Policy Resolution 2007 laid thrust on development of infrastructure, increase the flow of credit, support measures for marketing, promotion of exports, technology upgradation, rehabilitation and revival of viable sick units. This policy also gave priority to entrepreneurship development and skill upgradation by providing fiscal incentives through single window mechanism.

23 Puducherry

Introduction

The economy of Puducherry can be characterised as an 'open' economy with flows of virtually all factors of production including natural resources, labour, capital and technology. The economy is largely based on the sectors like engineering, food processing, chemicals, metals, tourism, textiles and information technology. Approximately half of the population in Puducherry is dependent on agriculture and rice, pulses, sugarcane, coconuts, and cotton are some of the crops grown extensively. On industrial scenario front, Puducherry has nearly 5,500 small-scale industries apart from 23 large-scale and 80 medium-scale industries.

Overview of SLPEs

Pondicherry is renamed as Puducherry which means new village in Tamil. There were 13 working SLPEs in Puducherry as on March 31, 2007, and about 38 per cent of them were set up during the Seventh Plan period. Nearly 38 per cent of the enterprises are making profits and 38 per cent are incurring losses. The total investment was ₹ 604.45 crore consisting of paid-up capital and long-term loans. The capital employed increased by 25.98 per cent in 2006-07. The total number of employees increased from 4,114 in 2005-06 to 30,011 in 2006-07. There was an increase in the turnover by 39.01 per cent i.e., from ₹ 209.40 crore in 2005-06 to ₹ 343.31 crore in 2006-07. The loss of the SLPEs in Puducherry increased by 63.38 per cent i.e., from ₹ 5.57 crore in 2005-06 to ₹ 15.2 crore in 2006-07. The details are given in Table 23.1.

Table 23.1

Overview of SLPEs in Puducherry

(₹ in lakh)

Particulars	*2006-07*	*2005-06*
Investment		
Paid-up Capital		
State Govt.	55368.76	46328.26
Central Govt.	167.77	167.77
Others	868.65	868.65
Total	56405.18	47364.68
Long-term Loan		
Government	93.5	0
Others	3946.7	681.29
Total	4040.2	681.29
Total Investment	60445.38	48045.97
Capital Employed	53082.41	39293.47
Turnover	34331.28	20940.02
Net Profit/Loss	-1519.96	-556.58
Accumulated Profit/Loss	-14473.6	-11572
No. of Employees	5599	4114
Total Return on Capital Employed	-1133.54	-185.45
Percentage of Total Return on Capital Employed	83.84	86.26
Subsidies/Grants		
Central Govt.	1288.34	47.61
State Govt.	2297.89	2233.68
Total	55368.76	811.29

Source: Comptroller and Auditor General (CAG) (Commercial) India, 2007-08.

Categorisation

The SLPEs are classified into five categories: financial, manufacturing, promotional, utility and welfare enterprises. The number of enterprises functioning under each category is shown in Figure 23.1. The promotional and manufacturing enterprises constitute the largest number. The increase in the investment in the industrial and electronic sectors led to an increase in the total investment. The investment was ₹ 480.46 crore in 2005-06, which increased to ₹ 604.45 crore in 2006-07. The investments are financed through the budgetary support from the state and central governments and other financial institutions.

Figure 23.1

Category-wise SLPEs in Puducherry

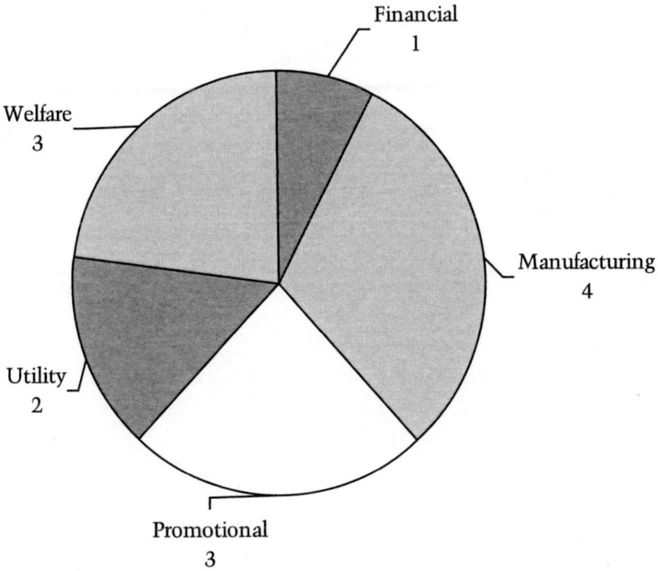

Source: CAG (Commercial) India, 2007-08.

Accumulated Profits and Losses

The accumulated losses of the SLPEs increased by 20.05 per cent during 2005-07 i.e., from ₹ 115.72 crore in 2005-06 to ₹ 144.74 crore in 2007-08. The losses were incurred mostly in the manufacturing, promotional and welfare sectors. The enterprises in the financial sector and utility sectors were earning profits.

Table 23.2

Accumulated Profit and Loss of SLPEs

(₹ in lakh)

S. No.	*Particulars*	*2006-07*	*2005-06*
1	Financial	2750.33	2503.5
2	Manufacturing	-23789	-20914
3	Promotional	-450.94	-435.33
4	Utility	7400.91	7560.19
5	Welfare	-384.85	-286.59
	Total	-14474	-11572

Source: CAG (Commercial) India, 2007-08.

Top Five Profit-making and Loss-making Units

Tables 23.3 and 23.4 present the top five profit- and loss-making units in Puducherry. Puducherry Power Corporation Limited, Puducherry Industrial Promotion Development and Investment Corporation and Puducherry Distilleries Limited are ranked first, second and third respectively amongst the profit-making SLPEs.

Table 23.3

Top Five Profit-making Units (2006-07)

(*₹ in lakh)*

S. No.	*Name of the Enterprise*	*Amount*
1	Puducherry Power Corporation Limited	890.5
2	Puducherry Industrial Promotion Deve. Investment Corp.	472.82
3	Puducherry Distilleries Limited	405.02
4	Puducherry Agro Products, Food	40.39
5	Puducherry Agro Service & Industries	18.6

Source: CAG (Commercial) India, 2007-08.

Puducherry Textiles Corporation Limited, Swadeshi-Bharathee Textiles Mills Limited and Puducherry Adi-dravidar Development Corporation (PADC) are major loss-making units. PADC incurred loss owing to loopholes in the implementation of various schemes.

Table 23.4

Top Five Loss-making Units (2006-07)

(*₹ in lakh)*

S. No.	*Name of the Enterprise*	*Amount*
1	Puducherry Textiles Corporation Limited	2618.41
2	Swadeshi-Bharathee Textiles Mills Limited	563.23
3	Puducherry Adi-dravidar Development Corp.	98.26
4	Puducherry Road Transport Corp.	98.26
5	Puducherry Electronics Limited	2.88

Source: CAG (Commercial) India, 2007-08.

Budgetary Support

Table 23.5 shows the budgetary support to the SLPEs during the year 2006-07. The grants and subsidies given by the state and central governments constitute the major share in the budgetary support followed by the equity. The details regarding budgetary provision towards equity, loans and grants/subsidies for past two years are given in Table 23.5.

Table 23.5

Budgetary Support to SLPEs (2006-07)

(₹ in crore)

S. No.	*Particulars*	*2005-06*	*2006-07*
1	Equity	21.93	87.41
2	Loans	21.2	18.04
3	Grants/subsidies	1.13	4.94
4	Total	44.26	110.39

Source: CAG (Commercial) India, 2007-08.

The budgetary support to the SLPEs has been increasing over the years. The budgetary support increased from ₹ 44.26 crore in 2005-06 to ₹ 110.39 crore in 2006-07. There is a steep increase in the budgetary support as the government has increased its equity to the loss-making units to carry out day-to-day activities.

Performance

Of the 13 SLPEs functioning in the state, 5 enterprises are making profits and 5 enterprises are making losses. The SLPEs turnover to state GDP shows the extent of public enterprises activities in the state. Table 23.6 provides the details of SLPEs contribution to state GDP from 2005-06 to 2007-08.

Table 23.6

SLPEs Contribution to State GDP

(₹ in crore)

S. No.	*Particulars*	*2005-06*	*2006-07*	*2007-08*
1	Turnover	209.4	343.31	307.39
2	State GDP	6214	6401	7,103
3	Percentage of Turnover to State GDP	3.37	5.36	4.33

Source: CAG (Commercial) India, 2007-08.

The percentage of turnover to the state GDP increased by 2 per cent in 2006-07. There was an increase in the turnover of all the sectors which led to an increase in the contribution to the state GDP. The losses of SLPEs are mainly attributable to deficiencies in financial management, planning, implementation of project, running their operations and monitoring. The government has taken measures for the socioeconomic development of the territory by providing the requisite subsidies and schemes. The Puducherry Industrial Promotion Development and Investment Corporation promote investments in various sectors. The areas which are given prominence and have scope for development are tourism, information technology (IT), textiles and others.

24 Punjab

Introduction

Punjab is known for the entrepreneurial spirit and the state transforms every potential opportunity into a success story. Punjab was the first state in India to use agricultural technology and to start 'Green Revolution' in 1960s. With rich agricultural resources and favourable climate, the state continues to be one of the largest producers of food grains and cash crops in the country. The state produces 14 per cent of India's cotton, 20 per cent of India's wheat and 9 per cent of India's rice. On the economic front, the state is ranked 4th in terms of per capita income in the country. Its per capita income of ₹ 28,605 is well above the national average of just ₹ 6,929. The gross state domestic product (GSDP) registered 14 per cent growth during 2007-08 to 2008-09. The state is aiming growth in the fields of infrastructure development, industrial development, travel and tourism, biotechnology, information technology (IT) and IT enabled services (ITES), education and training, etc., with a well-defined and focused state policy and government support. The state has also attracted immense inflow of investments in the manufacturing sector including textiles, paper, paper products and pulp and chemicals.

Industrial Scenario

Punjab is essentially an agrarian economy with a lower industrial output as compared to other states of India. A prominent feature of the industrial scenario of the Punjab is its small-sized industrial units. State's industrial performance has been motivated by small-scale units. Small-scale industry dominates around 47 per cent of the production, 60 per cent of exports and 21 per cent investment of the industrial sector. Meanwhile, the manufacturing sector of the state has faced a huge inflow of investments. The excellent investment in the state was roughly US$ 19.4 billion as on June 1, 2008 (*Punjab Economic Survey*, Government of Punjab).

Overview of SLPEs

Punjab reflects a progressive economy with an average growth rate of 10 per cent per annum in the country. There were 29 working SLPEs in Punjab as on March 31, 2008. About 24 per cent of the enterprises were set up during the Tenth Plan period. Nearly 44.8 per cent of the enterprises are making profits and 41.4 per cent are incurring losses. The total investment was ₹ 14,045.04 crore consisting of paid-up capital and long-term loans. The capital employed increased by 11.04 per cent in 2007-08. The total number of employees declined from 0.91 lakh in 2006-07 to 0.87 lakh in 2007-08. There was a meager increase in the turnover by 1.75 per cent from ₹ 17,245.43 crore in 2006-07 to ₹ 17,552.45 crore in 2007-08. The SLPEs in Punjab incurred a loss of ₹ 1,859.97 crore in 2007-08. The details are given in Table 24.1.

Table 24.1

Overview of SLPEs in Punjab

(₹ in lakh)

Particulars	*2007-08*	*2006-07*	*2005-06*
Investment			
Paid-up Capital			
State Govt.	378957	366863	357844
Central Govt.	5420.35	9084.35	8988.35
Others	3558.99	3553.99	3556.43
Total	387937	379501	370389
Long-term Loan			
Government	266362	399664	402856
Others	750205	623051	534161
Total	1016567	1022715	937017
Total Investment	1404504	1402216	1307406
Capital Employed	1794741	1596623	1610748
Turnover	1755245	1724543	1476194
Net Profit/Loss	-185997	-11128	-383400
Accumulated Profit/Loss	-760601	-592001	-578041
No. of Employees	87131	91369	92169
Total Return on Capital Employed	-40368	127814	-254617
Percentage of Total Return on Capital Employed	127.09	530.5	649.58
Subsidies/Grants			
Central Govt.	0	671	1300
State Govt.	291849	149826	146933
Total	291849	150497	148233

Source: Comptroller and Auditor General (CAG) (Commercial) India, 2007-08.

Categorisation

The SLPEs are classified into five categories: financial, manufacturing, promotional, utility and welfare enterprises. The number of enterprises functioning under each category is shown in Figure 24.1. The promotional, utility and manufacturing enterprises are large in number. The growth in the number of SLPEs and the increasing number of profit-making units has increased the total investment level. The investment was ₹ 14,022.16 crore in 2005-06 which increased to ₹ 14,045.04 crore in 2007-08. The investments are financed through the budgetary support from the state and central governments and other financial institutions.

Figure 24.1

Category-wise SLPEs in Punjab

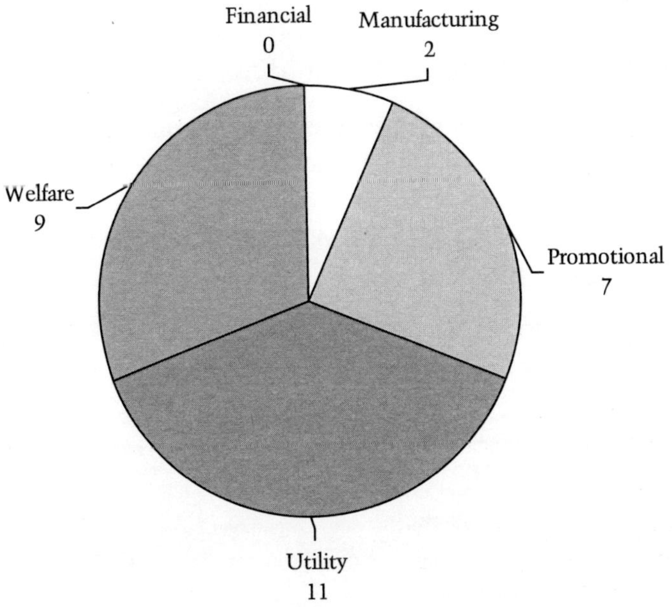

Source: CAG (Commercial) India, 2007-08.

Accumulated Profits and Losses

The accumulated losses of the SLPEs increased by 22.17 per cent i.e., from ₹ 5,920.01 crore in 2006-07 to ₹ 7,606.01 crore in 2007-08. The losses were incurred mostly in the utility and the promotional sectors. The enterprises in the manufacturing sector were earning profits.

Table 24.2

Accumulated Profit and Loss of SLPEs

(₹ in lakh)

S. No.	*Particulars*	*2007-08*	*2006-07*	*2005-06*
1	Financial	-27240	-24869.7	-22827.4
2	Manufacturing	-49799.4	-52353.1	-47640.6
3	Promotional	-48622.5	-43001.2	-36221
4	Utility	-634939	-471777	-471352
5	Welfare	0	0	0
	Total	-760601	-592001	-578041

Source: CAG (Commercial) India, 2007-08.

Top Five Profit-making and Loss-making Units

Tables 24.3 and 24.4 present the top five profit- and loss-making units in Punjab. Punjab Small Industries and Export Corporation, Punjab State Container and Warehousing Corporation and Punjab Information and Communication Technology Corporation are ranked first, second and third respectively amongst the profit-making SLPEs.

Table 24.3

Top Five Profit-making Units (2007-08)

(₹ in lakh)

S. No.	*Name of the Enterprise*	*Amount*
1	Punjab Small Industries and Export Corporation Ltd.	1741.36
2	Punjab State Container and Warehousing Corporation Ltd.	445.8
3	Punjab Information and Communication Technology Corporation Ltd.	433.45
4	Punjab Agro Power Corporation Ltd.	100.5
5	Punjab State Forest development Corporation Ltd.	91.67

Source: CAG (Commercial) India, 2007-08.

Punjab Electricity Board (PEB), Punjab State Industrial Development Corporation (PSIDC) and Punjab State Grains Procurement Corporation (PSGPC) are the major loss-making units. PEB incurred losses owing to the lack of efficiency in assessment of requirement and utilisation of material. PSIDC and PSGPC incurred loss due to the higher interest on outstanding balance and non-recovery of transportation charges.

Table 24.4

Top Five Loss-making Units (2007-08)

(₹ in lakh)

S. No.	*Name of the Enterprise*	*Amount*
1	Punjab Electricity Board	162638.6
2	Punjab State Industrial Development Corporation Ltd.	-8707.76
3	Punjab State Grains Procurement Corporation Ltd.	-7713.41
4	Punjab State Warehousing Corporation	-4649.03
5	Punjab Financial Corporation	-2313.43

Source: CAG (Commercial) India, 2007-08.

Budgetary Support

Table 24.5 shows the budgetary support to the SLPEs during the years 2006-2008. The grants and subsidies given by the state and central governments constitute the major share in the budgetary support followed by the equity.

Table 24.5

Budgetary Support to SLPEs (2006-08)

(₹ in crore)

S. No.	*Particulars*	*2005-06*	*2006-07*	*2007-08*
1	Equity	170.12	20.59	30.04
2	Loans	0	0	3.36
3	Grants/subsidies	1469.32	1498.26	2918.49
4	Total	1639.44	1518.85	2951.89

Source: CAG (Commercial) India, 2007-08.

The budgetary support to the SLPEs has been fluctuating over the years. The budgetary support declined from ₹ 1,639.44 crore in 2005-06 to ₹ 1,518.85 crore in 2006-07 by 7.94 per cent. It increased by 48.5 per cent in 2007-08. There is an increase in the budgetary support as the enterprises in the promotional and the utility sectors are in the initial stages and have not started operations.

Performance

Of the 29 SLPEs functioning in the state, more than 13 units are making profits, 2 enterprises are running on no-profit and no-loss basis and 12 enterprises are making losses. The SLPEs turnover to state GDP shows the extent of public enterprises activities in the state. Table 24.6 provides the details of SLPEs contribution to state GDP from 2005-06 to 2007-08.

Table 24.6

SLPEs Contribution to State GDP

(₹ in crore)

S. No.	*Particulars*	*2005-06*	*2006-07*	*2007-08*
1	Turnover	17552.45	17245.43	14761.94
2	State GDP	109735	123397	137486
3	Percentage of Turnover to State GDP	16.00	13.98	10.74

Source: CAG (Commercial) India, 2007-08.

The percentage of turnover to the state GDP has been declining steadily over the years. Though there is an increase in the turnover of the manufacturing and the utility sectors, their contribution to the state GDP declined owing to a decline in the turnover of the promotional sector. The losses of SLPEs are mainly attributable to deficiencies in financial management, planning, implementation of project, running their operations and monitoring. The state government brought about a number of changes in the policies of the government. The government started establishing SLPEs owing to the availability of resources in the state. They have initiated policies on public-private partnerships (PPP) in physical and social infrastructure and for engaging the non-governmental sector as development partners.

25 Rajasthan

Introduction

Rajasthan is emerging as one of the important states in India. The state is amongst the largest producers of edible oils and the second largest producer of oilseeds in India. Rajasthan is also the biggest wool-producing state in the country. The state is considered as a mining hub and has the second largest mineral reserves in India. The state's GDP grew at an impressive 12.85 per cent between 2002-03 and 2007-08. The gross state domestic product (GSDP) is recorded as ₹ 132,904 crore in 2008-09 by registering a growth rate of 5.48 per cent over 2007-08. In the past, agriculture was the major source of the GSDP and employment in the rural areas. However, in the recent years, the service sector is contributing largely to the state economy. Information technology (IT), IT enabled services (ITES) and business process outsourcing (BPO) are among the major sectors contributing to the state economy. The state government of Rajasthan is also reviewing the existing sector-specific policies of the state (particularly the ones for IT sector and mining sector), to provide better incentives and concessions to the industry, to enhance Rajasthan's competitive position *vis-à-vis* other business destinations within India. The state also aims to increase its national state domestic product (NSDP) by 5.5 times by 2025.

Overview of SLPEs

There were 28 working SLPEs in Rajasthan as on March 31, 2008. About 29 per cent of the enterprises were set up during the Tenth Plan period. Nearly 43 per cent of the enterprises are making profits and 14 per cent are incurring losses. The total investment was ₹ 21,960.69 crore consisting of paid-up capital and long-term loans. The capital employed increased by 20.96 per cent in 2007-08. The total number of employees increased by 27.16 per cent i.e., from 57,727 in 2006-07 to

79,252 in 2007-08. There was an increase in the turnover by 13.17 per cent i.e., from ₹ 14,445.07 crore in 2006-07 to ₹ 16,635.87 crore in 2007-08. The SLPEs in Rajasthan were earning a profit of ₹ 383.26 crore in 2007-08. The details are given in Table 25.1.

Table 25.1

Overview of SLPEs in Rajasthan

(₹ in lakh)

Particulars	*2007-08*	*2006-07*	*2005-06*
Investment			
Paid-up Capital			
State Government	610396.7	503300.7	381710.6
Central Government	2813.68	2813.68	2813.68
Others	4721.09	3758.48	2760.73
Total	617386.4	509872.8	452445
Long-term Loan			
Government	162355.5	113894.6	124922.2
Others	1416327	1023415	1046624
Total	1578683	1137310	1171547
Total Investment	2196069	1647183	1623992
Capital Employed	3268104	2583014	2248763
Turnover	1663587	1444507	1261680
Net Profit/Loss	38325.64	26877.6	21537.45
Accumulated Profit/Loss	20996.54	-1823.57	-14891.3
No. of Employees	79252	57727	58440
Total Return on Capital Employed	195777.7	160983.9	148598.9
Percentage of Total Return on Capital Employed	193.41	174.32	192.01
Subsidies/Grants			
Central Government	2343.58	29.07	1386.91
State Government	151631.6	125388.6	104399.3
Total	153975.2	125417.7	105786.2

Source: Comptroller and Auditor General (CAG) (Commercial) India, 2007-08.

Categorisation

The SLPEs are classified into five categories: financial, manufacturing, promotional, utility and welfare enterprises. The number of enterprises functioning under each category is shown in Figure 25.1. The utility enterprises constituted the largest number of SLPEs followed by the promotional and manufacturing enterprises. The increase in the number of SLPEs led to an increase in the total investment level. The investment was ₹ 16,474.83 crore in 2006-07 which increased to ₹ 21,960.69 crore in 2007-08 by 24.99 per cent. The investments are financed through the budgetary support from the state and central governments and other financial institutions.

Figure 25.1

Category-wise SLPEs in Rajasthan

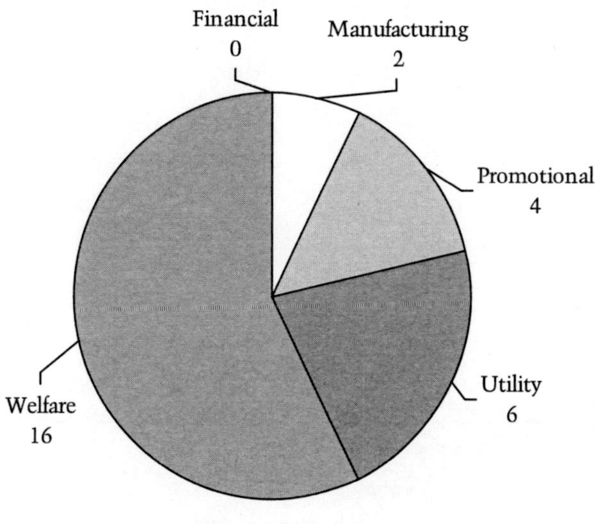

Source: CAG (Commercial) India, 2007-08.

Accumulated Profits and Losses

The accumulated losses of the SLPEs started declining after 2006-07. The SLPEs started earning profits from 2007-08 and the profits earned by these enterprise stood at ₹ 209.96 crore in 2007-08. The enterprises in the promotional and manufacturing sectors were earning profits, which led to decline in the accumulated losses.

Table 25.2

Accumulated Profit and Loss of SLPEs

(₹ in lakh)

S. No.	*Particulars*	*2007-08*	*2006-07*	*2005-06*
1	Financial	-5395.8	-5546.8	-6251.1
2	Manufacturing	46850.9	36137.2	25770.4
3	Promotional	17481.6	4576.36	-610.55
4	Utility	-37940.1	-36990.3	-33800.1
5	Welfare	0	0	0
	Total	20996.5	-1823.6	-14891

Source: CAG (Commercial) India, 2007-08.

Top Profit-making and Loss-making Units

Tables 25.3 and 25.4 present the top five profit- and loss-making units in Rajasthan. Rajasthan State Mines and Minerals Limited, Rajasthan State Industrial Development Corporation Limited and Rajasthan Renewable Energy Corporation Limited are ranked first, second and third respectively amongst the profit-making SLPEs.

Table 25.3

Top Five Profit-making Units (2007-08)

(₹ in lakh)

S. No.	*Name of the Enterprise*	*Amount*
1	Rajasthan State Mines and Minerals Limited	18344.54
2	Rajasthan State Industrial development Corporation Limited	18157.58
3	Rajasthan Renewable Energy Corporation Limited	1364.54
4	Rajasthan State Seeds Corporation Limited	814.05
5	Rajasthan State Warehousing Corporation Limited	625

Source: CAG (Commercial) India, 2007-08.

Rajasthan State Road Transport Corporation (RSRTC), Rajasthan State Handloom Development Corporation Limited (RSHDC) and Rajasthan Small Industries Corporation Limited (RSIC) are major loss-making units. RSRTC incurred losses due to the failure of the management to provide the basic amenities like drinking water, clean and hygiene environment to the commuters and the irregularities of the management. RSIC incurred losses owing to the mismanagement by the authorities in the administration of the activities.

Table 25.4

Top Four Loss-making Units (2007-08)

(₹ in lakh)

S. No.	Name of the Enterprise	Amount
1	Rajasthan State Road Transport Corporation	1914.05
2	Rajasthan State Handloom Development Corporation Ltd.	250.87
3	Rajasthan Small Industries Corporation Ltd.	51.25
4	Rajasthan Jal Vikas Nigam Ltd.	6.87

Source: CAG (Commercial) India, 2007-08.

Budgetary Support

Table 25.5 shows the budgetary support to the SLPEs during the years 2006-2008. The grants and subsidies given by the state and central governments constitute the major share in the budgetary support followed by the equity.

Table 25.5

Budgetary Support to SLPEs (2006-2008)

(₹ in crore)

S. No.	Particulars	2005-06	2006-07	2007-08
1	Equity	635.88	700.3	1065.71
2	Loans	176.96	151.76	668.44
3	Grants/subsidies	1043.99	1253.89	1516.92
4	Total	1856.83	2105.95	3251.07

Source: CAG (Commercial) India, 2007-08.

The budgetary support to the SLPEs has been increasing over the years. The budgetary support increased from ₹ 1,856.83 crore in 2005-06 to ₹ 3,251.07 crore in 2007-08 by 42.89 per cent. There is an increase in the budgetary support as the government has given subsidies to 10 SLPEs in the state mostly from the power sector.

Performance

Of the 28 SLPEs functioning in the state, 12 units are making profits and 8 are making losses. The enterprises in the power sector which were set up under the Agricultural and Rural Development Plan (ARDP) have not finalised their accounts. The SLPEs turnover to state GDP shows the extent of public enterprises activities in the state. Table 25.6 provides the detail of SLPEs contribution to state GDP from 2005-06 to 2007-08.

Table 25.6

SLPEs Contribution to State GDP

(₹ in crore)

S. No.	Particulars	2005-06	2006-07	2007-08
1	Turnover	11910	13729	15759
2	State GDP	128621	148849	169919
3	Percentage of Turnover to State GDP	9.26	9.22	9.27

Source: CAG (Commercial) India, 2007-08.

The percentage of turnover to the state GDP has been slightly increasing over the years. The increase in the turnover of the manufacturing, promotional and utility sectors led to an increase in their contribution to the state GDP, though there is a decline in the turnover of the financial sector. The losses of SLPEs are mainly attributable to deficiencies in financial management, planning, implementation of project, running their operations and monitoring. The government has taken various initiatives for achieving higher and sustainable economic growth and creates better employment opportunities. The sectors in which the state has natural and strategic advantages are given priority by providing support policies, institutional environment and better infrastructural facilities. The IT and ITES policy was launched in 2007, which aims at e-governance and capacity building within the government realm by promoting investment in IT and ITES sector was within the state and skill development through enhancement of employment opportunities. The e-governance started in Rajasthan is first of its kind in the country with 3 per cent budget allotment for all the departments. A new industrial and investment policy is being initiated for the provision of basic facilities for the development of industries in the state.

26 Sikkim

Introduction

The economy of Sikkim is largely agrarian in nature. The state is the largest producer of cardamom in India. The minerals mined in Sikkim are copper, dolomite, limestone, graphite, mica, iron and coal. The state has achieved a growth rate of 8.3 per cent in 2006-07. With regard to industrial development, number of small and medium units have been promoted in the state like the Sikkim Time Corporation (SITCO), Government Institute of Handicraft and Handloom, etc. The opening of the Nathu La Pass in July 2006 connecting Lhasa, Tibet, to India is expected to give a boost to the local economy. The pass, closed since the 1962 Sino-Indian War, was an offshoot of the ancient Silk Road, which was essential to the wool, fur and spice trade.

Overview of SLPEs

Sikkim is known as the "valley of rice" and is the only state with open border between India and China. There were 12 working SLPEs in Sikkim as on March 31, 2008. About 25 per cent of them were set up during the Fifth and Ninth Plan Periods. Nearly 25 per cent of the enterprises are making profits and 67 per cent are incurring losses. The total investment was ₹ 235.72 crore consisting of paid-up capital and long-term loans. The capital employed increased by 7.33 per cent in 2007-08. The total number of employees declined from 1,234 in 2006-07 to 1,135 in 2007-08. There was decline in the turnover in 2007-08. The losses of the SLPEs in Sikkim declined from ₹ 2.14 crore in 2006-07 to ₹ 0.41 crore in 2007-08. The details are given in Table 26.1.

Table 26.1

Overview of SLPEs in Sikkim

(₹ in lakh)

Particulars	*2007-08*	*2006-07*	*2005-06*
Investment			
Paid-up Capital			
State Govt.	8117.68	8117.68	8087.68
Central Govt.	1041.3	1041.3	1041.3
Others	1407.56	1407.56	1407.56
Total	10566.54	10566.54	10536.54
Long-term Loan			
Government	405.74	405.74	405.74
Others	12600.26	7834.12	6385.26
Total	13006	8239.86	6791
Total Investment	23572.54	18806.4	17327.54
Capital Employed	93712.03	86840.26	63349.37
Turnover	6768.49	6825.93	4843.09
Net Profit/Loss	-41.16	-213.75	-58.21
Accumulated Profit/Loss	-9483.69	-9663.28	-9759.4
No. of Employees	1135	1234	1272
Total Return on Capital Employed	715.79	541.67	-81.47
Percentage of Total Return on Capital Employed	34.97	28.99	30.2
Subsidies/Grants			
Central Govt.	0	0	0
State Govt.	0	0	0
Total	0	0	0

Source: Comptroller and Auditor General (CAG) (Commercial) India, 2007-08.

Categorisation

The SLPEs are classified into five categories: financial, manufacturing, promotional, utility and welfare enterprises. The number of enterprises functioning under each category is shown in Figure 26.1. The manufacturing enterprises constitute the largest number. The investment made in the power and the finance sector increased the investment in the SLPEs by 20.22 per cent. The investment was ₹ 188.06 crore in 2006-07 which increased to ₹ 235.72 crore in 2007-08. The investments are financed through the budgetary support from the state and central governments and other financial institutions.

Figure 26.1

Category-wise SLPEs in Sikkim

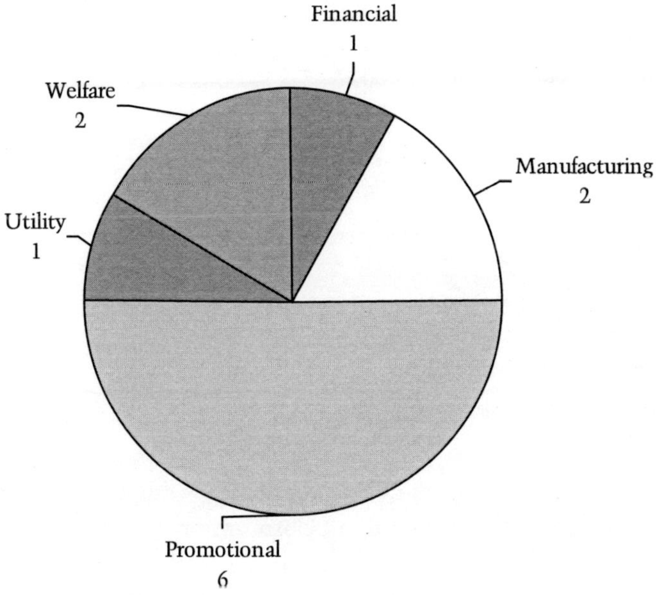

Source: CAG (Commercial) India, 2007-08.

Accumulated Profits and Losses

The accumulated losses of the SLPEs declined from ₹ 96.63 crore in 2006-07 to ₹ 94.84 crore in 2007-08 by 1.89 per cent. The losses in the financial and the manufacturing sector dropped, so there is a decline in the accumulated losses.

Table 26.2

Accumulated Profit and Loss of SLPEs

(₹ *in lakh*)

S. No.	*Particulars*	*2007-08*	*2006-07*	*2005-06*
1	Financial	-3756.8	-3907.2	-4099.3
2	Manufacturing	-5486.5	-5515.7	-5509.4
3	Promotional	545.48	545.48	545.48
4	Utility	-306.38	-306.38	-257.74
5	Welfare	-479.5	-479.5	-438.52
	Total	-9483.7	-9663.3	-9759.4

Source: CAG (Commercial) India, 2007-08.

Top Profit-making and Loss-making Units

Tables 26.3 and 26.4 present the top profit- and loss-making units in Sikkim. Sikkim Industrial Development and Investment Corporation, State Bank of Sikkim and State Trading Corporation of Sikkim are the major profit-making SLPEs.

Table 26.3

Top Profit-making Units (2007-08)

(₹ in lakh)

S. No.	*Name of the Enterprise*	*Amount*
1	Sikkim Industrial Deve. and Investment Corp.	150.44
2	State Bank of Sikkim	130.33
3	State Trading Corp. of Sikkim	112.67

Source: CAG (Commercial) India, 2007-08.

Sikkim Time Corporation Limited, Sikkim Mining Corporation (SMC) and Sikkim Tourism Development Corporation (STDC) are the major loss-making units. SMC incurred loss owing to the closure of production activities and low capacity utilisation. The under utilisation of resources, delay in the policy formulation and implementation paved for losses made by STDC.

Table 26.4

Top Five Loss-making Units (2007-08)

(₹ in lakh)

S. No.	*Name of the Enterprise*	*Amount*
1	Sikkim Time Corp. Limited	329.13
2	Sikkim Mining Corp.	217.49
3	Sikkim Tourism Development	42.43
4	Sikkim Jewels Limited	40.61
5	Sikkim Precision Industries Limited	35.8

Source: CAG (Commercial) India, 2007-08.

Budgetary Support

Table 26.5 shows the budgetary support to the SLPEs during the years 2006-2008. The equity made by the state and central governments has the major share in the budgetary support.

Table 26.5

Budgetary Support to SLPEs (2006-2008)

(₹ in crore)

S. No.	*Particulars*	*2005-06*	*2006-07*	*2007-08*
1	Equity	4.82	0.3	0
2	Loans	0	0	0
3	Grants/subsidies	0	0	0
4	Total	4.82	0.3	0

Source: CAG (Commercial) India, 2007-08.

Performance

Of the 12 SLPEs functioning in the state, 3 enterprises are making profits and 8 enterprises are making losses. The SLPEs turnover to state GDP shows the extent of public enterprises activities in the state. Table 26.6 provides the detail of SLPEs contribution to state GDP from 2005-06 to 2007-08.

Table 26.6

SLPEs Contribution to State GDP

(₹ in crore)

S. No.	*Particulars*	*2005-06*	*2006-07*	*2007-08*
1	Turnover	48.43	68.26	67.68
2	State GDP	1830	2038.54	2297.86
3	Percentage of Turnover to State GDP	2.65	3.35	2.95

Source: CAG (Commercial) India, 2007-08.

The percentage of turnover to the state GDP has been varying over the years. Though there is a meager increase in the turnover of the manufacturing and financial sectors, there contribution to the state GDP has been varying owing to sustainability in the turnover of the remaining sectors. The losses of SLPEs are mainly attributable to deficiencies in financial management, planning, implementation of project, running their operations and monitoring. The era of industrialisation in Sikkim began with the new industrial policy, fiscal incentives, subsidies and proactive policy of the government. The government has focused on chosen key industries based on their potentials for employment generation, relative comparative advantage and overall impact on the state economy. The agro-based industries are given priority based on proven potential in producing commercial crops and untapped potential in flora and fauna. The information technology (IT) sector, bio-technology, hydel power, food processing, handloom and handicrafts and other sectors are also given preference in the state.

27 Tamil Nadu

Introduction

Tamil Nadu is one of the leading producers of agricultural products in the country. The state also has a sound industrial base. According to the publications of the Tamil Nadu government, the gross state domestic product (GSDP) at current prices (base year 1999-2000) for the year 2008-09 was ₹ 339,212 crores. The per capita income at current prices is recorded at ₹ 51,097, which is steadily been above the national average. On the sectoral contribution front, service sector contributes about 45 per cent of the economic activity in the state, followed by manufacturing at 34 per cent and agriculture at 21 per cent. The government is the major investor in the state with 51 per cent of total investments, followed by private Indian investors at 29.9 per cent and foreign private investors at 14.9 per cent. The state has a network of about 113 industrial parks and estates offering developed plots with supporting infrastructure.

Manufacturing is the primary industrial activity in the state. Industries like textiles, engineering, plantations and fireworks are some of the major industries that are playing a dominant role in the development of the state. The global electrical equipment public sector company Bharat Heavy Electricals Limited (BHEL) has manufacturing plants at Tiruchirappalli and Ranipet. The Tamil Nadu state government owns the Tamil Nadu Newsprint and Papers (TNPL). The state is the leading producer of cement in India with plants in Tiruchirappalli, Karur, etc.

Overview of SLPEs

Tamil Nadu set up SLPEs to bring about a result-oriented cost benefit approach to development activities in the state. There were 56 working SLPEs in Tamil Nadu as on March 31, 2008. Large number of enterprises were set up during the Fifth Plan period. The total investment was

₹ 18,71,970 lakh consisting of paid-up capital and long-term loans in 2007-08 and the capital employed is increased by 6 per cent. The total number of employees was 2,55,316 which increased by 5.3 per cent in 2007-08. The turnover increased by 53.8 per cent with ₹ 21,13,211 lakh compared to 2006-07 and ₹ 32,49,443 lakh in 2007-08. The SLPEs in the state made a loss of ₹ 1,52,311 lakh in 2007-08. The details are given in Table 27.1.

Table 27.1

Overview of SLPEs in Tamil Nadu

(₹ in lakh)

Particulars	*2007-08*	*2006-07*	*2005-06*
Investment			
Paid-up Capital			
State Govt.	299067.3	227234.4	204730.3
Central Govt.	5033.02	5028.83	5028.83
Others	3155.34	3219.41	3269.11
Total	307255.7	235485.6	213028.3
Long-term Loan			
Government	41685.35	24411	23108.71
Others	1523029	1197715	1092936
Total	1564715	1222126	1116045
Total Investment	1871970	1457611	1329073
Capital Employed	1775844	1676072	1626938
Turnover	3249443	2113211	2468577
Net Profit/Loss	-152311	-149388	-149633
Accumulated Profit/Loss	-935394	-776602	-623771
No. of Employees	255316	242510	243910
Total Return on Capital Employed	-7527.83	-14213.2	-18551.4
Percentage of Total Return on Capital Employed	497.74	1371.32	423.92
Subsidies/Grants			
Central Govt.	61957.7	19211.3	21738.63
State Govt.	174617	180795	146501.2
Total	236574.7	200006.3	168239.9

Source: Comptroller and Auditor General (CAG) (Commercial) India, 2007-08.

Categorisation

The SLPEs are classified into five categories: financial, manufacturing, promotional, utility and welfare enterprise. The number of enterprises functioning under each category is shown in Figure 27.1. The manufacturing, promotional and utility enterprises constitute the largest number. The categorisation of SLPEs reveals that out of 56 enterprises, 22 were in the manufacturing sector, 13 each in promotional and utility sectors. The total investment in all the 56 enterprises grew by 28.4 per cent from ₹ 14,57,611.25 lakh in 2006-07 to ₹ 18,71,970.2 lakh in 2007-08. The investments are financed through the budgetary support from the state and central governments and other financial institutions.

Figure 27.1

Categorisation of SLPEs in Tamil Nadu

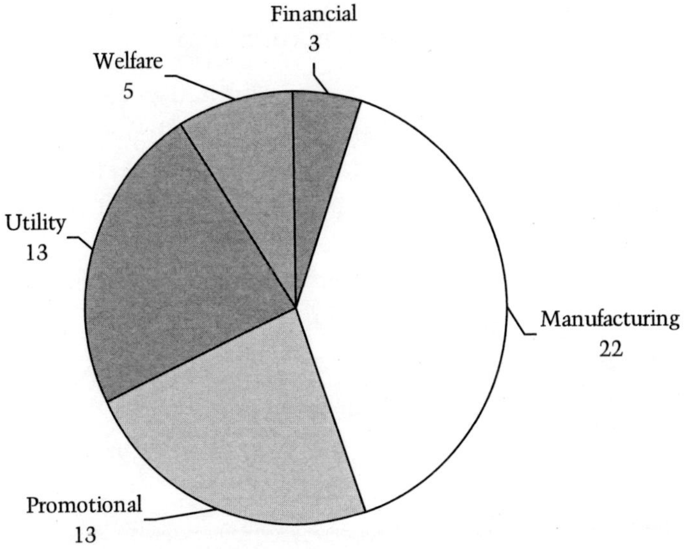

Source: CAG (Commercial) India, 2007-08.

Accumulated Profits and Losses

The accumulated losses of the SLPEs increased from ₹ 7,76,602 lakh in 2006-07 to ₹ 9,35,394 lakh in 2007-08. The enterprises in the financial, promotional and welfare sectors are the profit earners. Amongst the profit earners, the SLPEs in the financial sector top the list with an accumulated profit of ₹ 19,009 lakh in 2007-08. The losses were incurred mostly in the manufacturing and utility sectors (Table 27.2).

Table 27.2

Category-wise SLPEs Accumulated Profit and Loss

(₹ in lakh)

S. No.	*Category*	*2007-08*	*2006-07*	*2005-06*
1	Financial	19009	16395.1	13695.6
2	Manufacturing	-50443	-39829	-42121
3	Promotional	18451.3	12401.4	10667.3
4	Utility	-927781	-770115	-609067
5	Welfare	5370.18	4545.43	3053.54
	Total	-935394	-776602	-623771

Source: CAG (Commercial) India, 2007-08.

Top Five Profit-making and Loss-making Units

Tables 27.3 and 27.4 provide the information on top five profit-earning and loss-making enterprises. The State Industries Promotion Corporation of Tamil Nadu Limited (SIPCOT), Tamil Nadu Power Finance and Infrastructure Development Corporation Limited, and the Tamil Nadu Industrial Investment Corporation Limited (TIIC) are ranked first, second and third respectively amongst the profit-making SLPEs. Table 27.3 also reveals that the profit-making enterprises are centred in the promotional and finance sectors.

Table 27.3

Top Five Profit-making Units (2007-08)

(₹ in lakh)

S. No.	*Name of the Enterprise*	*Amount*
1	State Industries Promotion Corporation of Tamil Nadu Limited (SIPCOT)	6720.62
2	Tamil Nadu Power Finance and Infrastructure Development Corporation Limited	3132.76
3	Tamil Nadu Industrial Investment Corporation Limited (TIIC)	1945.57
4	Tamil Nadu Cements Corporation Limited	1539.14
5	Tamil Nadu Small Industries Corporation Limited (TANSI)	1173.29

Source: CAG (Commercial) India, 2007-08.

The SLPEs in the utility sector are the major loss-making enterprises. Table 27.4 indicates that Tamil Nadu Electricity Board, Tamil Nadu State

Transport Corporation (Madurai) Limited and Tamil Nadu State Transport Corporation (Coimbatore) Limited are the major loss-making enterprises.

Table 27.4

Top Five Loss-making Units (2007-08)

(₹ in lakh)

S. No.	*Name of the Enterprise*	*Amount*
1	Tamil Nadu Electricity Board	121894.00
2	Tamil Nadu State Transport Corporation (Madurai) Limited	10040.79
3	Tamil Nadu State Transport Corporation (Coimbatore) Limited	7535.52
4	Metropolitan Transport Corporation Limited	7186.30
5	State Express Transport Corporation Limited	5503.24

Source: CAG (Commercial) India, 2007-08.

Budgetary Support

Table 27.5 shows the budgetary support to the SLPEs during the years 2005-06 to 2007-08. The grants and subsidies given by the state and central governments constitute the major share in the budgetary support followed by the equity.

Table 27.5

Budgetary Support to SLPEs (2006-2008)

(₹ in crore)

S. No.	*Particulars*	*2005-06*	*2006-07*	*2007-08*
1	Equity	35.76	331.34	873.25
2	Loans	305.27	5.25	28.36
3	Grants/subsidies	2630.63	3817.87	3979.02
4	Total	2971.66	4154.46	4880.63

Source: CAG (Commercial) India, 2007-08.

The budgetary support to SLPEs is increasing over the years. The grants and subsidies from the state and central governments constitute the major part of budgetary support to the SLPEs. The government has adopted various administrative reforms, zero-base budgeting and rationalisation of subsidies, and debt management practices for streamlining and restructuring SLPEs. In 2007-08, the state government increased the share of grants/subsidies in the total budgetary support to a tune of 17.5 per cent.

Performance

Of the 56 SLPEs functioning in the state, 35 are profits-making enterprises and 18 enterprises are incurring losses. About 3 enterprises have not finalised their first accounts. SLPEs turnover to state GDP shows the extent of public enterprises activities in the state. Table 27.6 provides the detail of SLPEs contribution to state GDP from 2005-06 to 2007-08.

Table 27.6

SLPEs Contribution to State GDP

(₹ in crore)

S. No.	*Particulars*	*2007-08*	*2006-07*	*2005-06*
1	Turnover	32494.43	21132.11	24685.77
2	State GDP	279287	246266	223528
3	Percentage of Turnover to State GDP	11.6	8.6	11.0

Source: CAG (Commercial) India, 2007-08.

The percentage of turnover to the state GDP is increasing steadily over the years. This is due to the increase in turnover of the financial and promotional enterprises. In 2007-08, due to an increase in the turnover in the financial, promotional and welfare enterprise, the contribution of SLPEs to GDP has increased drastically. The Government of Tamil Nadu identified the problems that are related to performance evaluation and monitoring of SLPEs on a continued basis, such are: absence of audit, lack of professional management, etc. Therefore, for an effective manpower planning and to generate adequate surplus over the capital invested, the government is setting up committees and commissions for streamlining and restructuring SLPEs.

28 Tripura

Introduction

Tripura is one of the seven states in the North Eastern part of India. The economy of Tripura is agrarian. More than 50 per cent of its population depends on agriculture for livelihood, and contribution of agriculture & allied activities to the gross state domestic product (GSDP) is about 23 per cent. The GSDP at constant prices increased from ₹ 4,866.73 crore in 1999-2000 to ₹ 8,349.58 crore in 2007-08. Low availability of infrastructure, communication bottlenecks and inadequate exploitation of resources have made the process of economic development extremely difficult in this backward state. But, the state has put efforts for ensuring sustainable economic growth by augmenting better fiscal consolidation and economic development. The per capita income of the state rose from ₹ 14,119 in 1999-2000 to ₹ 33,283 in 2007-08 with the new base of 1999-2000. Most of the parts in the state are in rural areas; therefore, the state government also is working on the policies for the upliftment of rural poor as well as improvement in the quality of life of the economically weaker sections.

Overview of SLPEs

There were 10 working SLPEs in Tripura as on March 31, 2008. About 30 per cent of the enterprises were set up during the Fifth Plan period. Nearly 20 per cent of the enterprises are making profits and 80 per cent are incurring losses. The total investment was ₹ 488.02 crore consisting of paid-up capital and long-term loans. The capital employed increased by 97.11 per cent in 2007-08 over the previous year. The total number of employees increased from 2,885 in 2006-07 to 6,587 in 2007-08. There is an increase in the turnover by 80.78 per cent with ₹ 48.07 crore in 2006-07 to ₹ 250.07 crore in 2007-08. The losses are declined by 71.82 per cent i.e., from ₹ 16.33 crore in 2006-07 to ₹ 9.50 crore in 2007-08. The details are given in Table 28.1.

Table 28.1

Overview of SLPEs in Tripura

(₹ in lakh)

Particulars	*2007-08*	*2006-07*	*2005-06*
Investment			
Paid-up Capital			
State Govt.	45842.08	33132.14	29509.73
Central Govt.	471.28	471.02	471.02
Others	167.5	167.5	167.5
Total	46480.86	33770.65	30148.24
Long-term Loan			
Government	1905.69	392.69	392.69
Others	415.65	395.36	415.77
Total	2321.34	788.05	808.46
Total Investment	48802.2	34558.7	30956.7
Capital Employed	78983.55	2280.64	2468.24
Turnover	25007.37	4806.87	5250.7
Net Profit/Loss	-950.48	-1633.08	-1911.27
Accumulated Profit/Loss	-21039.7	-19811.9	-19652.7
No. of Employees	6587	2885	3360
Total Return on Capital Employed	-324.23	-1068.68	-1347.65
Percentage of Total Return on Capital Employed	32.71	38.06	14.8
Subsidies/Grants			
Central Govt.	0.13	0.15	0.2
State Govt.	50	45	0
Total	50.13	45.15	0.2

Source: Comptroller and Auditor General (CAG) (Commercial) India, 2007-08.

Categorisation

The SLPEs are classified into five categories: financial, manufacturing, promotional, utility and welfare enterprises. The number of enterprises functioning under each category is shown in Figure 28.1. The promotional and manufacturing enterprises constitute the largest number. There are no enterprises in the financial and the welfare sectors. The investment made in the SLPEs in the power, industry and transport sectors increased the investment by 29.19 per cent. The investment was ₹ 345.59 crore in 2006-07 which increased to ₹ 488.02 crore in 2007-08. The investments are financed through the budgetary support from the state and central governments and other financial institutions.

Figure 28.1

Category-wise SLPEs in Tripura

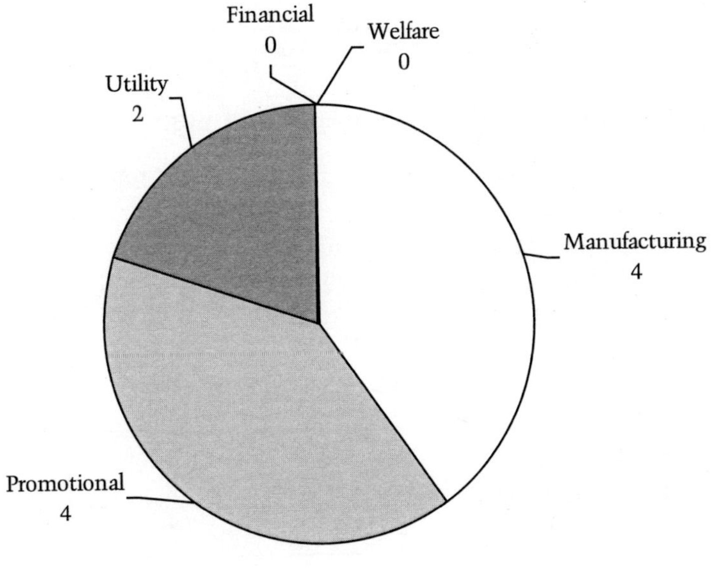

Source: CAG (Commercial) India, 2007-08.

Accumulated Profits and Losses

The accumulated losses of the SLPES increased from ₹ 198.12 crore in 2006-07 to ₹ 210.40 crore in 2007-08. The losses were incurred in almost all the sectors and heavy losses were incurred by the enterprises in the promotional sector.

Table 28.2

Accumulated Profit and Loss of SLPEs

(₹ *in lakh)*

S. No.	*Particulars*	*2007-08*	*2006-07*	*2005-06*
1	Financial	0	0	0
2	Manufacturing	-7781	-7694.9	-7275.1
3	Promotional	-819.84	-437.96	-698.53
4	Utility	-12439	-11679	-11679
5	Welfare	0	0	0
	Total	-21040	-19812	-19653

Source: CAG (Commercial) India, 2007-08.

Top Profit-making and Loss-making Units

Tables 28.3 and 28.4 present the information on top profit- and loss-making units in Tripura. Tripura State Electricity Corporation and Tripura Rehabilitation Plantation Corporation are the only two profit-making enterprises in Tripura.

Table 28.3

Top Profit-making Units (2007-08)

(₹ *in lakh)*

S. No.	*Name of the Enterprise*	*Amount*
1	Tripura State Electricity Corp.	881.12
2	Tripura Rehabilitation Plantation Corp.	290.06

Source: CAG (Commercial) India, 2007-08.

Tripura Road Transport Corporation (TRTC), Tripura Forest Development and Plantation Corporation (TFDPC) and Tripura Handloom & Handicraft Development Corporation are the major loss-making enterprises. TRTC incurred losses owing to the inefficiency of the management in the operation of services which increased the expenses than the revenue. TFDPC incurred losses due to the irregularities of the management in the maintenance of the manpower, financial aspects, capacity utilisation and inventory.

Table 28.4

Top Five Loss-making Units (2007-08)

(₹ in lakh)

S. No.	Name of the Enterprise	Amount
1	Tripura Road Transport Corp.	1640.99
2	Tripura Forest Development and Plantation Corp.	144.6
3	Tripura Handloom & Handicraft Deve. Corp.	124.12
4	Tripura Small Industries Deve. Corp.	80.25
5	Tripura Jute Mills Limited	62.86

Source: CAG (Commercial) India, 2007-08.

Budgetary Support

Table 28.5 shows the budgetary support to the SLPEs during the years 2006-2008. The equity given by the state and central governments constitutes the major share in the budgetary support followed by the grants and subsidies.

Table 28.5

Budgetary Support to SLPEs (2006-2008)

(₹ in crore)

S. No.	Particulars	2005-06	2006-07	2007-08
1	Equity	23.41	36.22	29.07
2	Loans	0	11.04	4.78
3	Grants/subsidies	0	45	50
4	Total	23.41	92.26	83.85

Source: CAG (Commercial) India, 2007-08.

The budgetary support to the SLPEs has been fluctuating over the years. The budgetary support increased from ₹ 23.41 crore in 2005-06 to ₹ 92.26 crore in 2006-07. There was a decline by 10.02 per cent in 2007-08. There is an increase in the budgetary support as the government supported the electricity corporation in 2006-07.

Performance

Of the 10 SLPEs functioning in the state, 2 units are making profits and 8 enterprises are making losses. The SLPEs turnover to state GDP shows the extent of public enterprises activities in the state. Table 28.6 provides the detail of SLPEs contribution to state GDP from 2005-06 to 2007-08.

Table 28.6

SLPEs Contribution to State GDP

(₹ in crore)

S. No.	*Particulars*	*2005-06*	*2006-07*	*2007-08*
1	Turnover	52.51	48.07	250.07
2	State GDP	7296.61	7888.98	8521.68
3	Percentage of Turnover to State GDP	0.72	0.61	2.93

Source: CAG (Commercial) India, 2007-08.

The percentage of turnover to the state GDP increased from 0.61 per cent in 2006-07 to 2.93 per cent in 2007-08. The increase in the turnover of the manufacturing and the utility sectors has increased their contribution to the state GDP, though there is a decline in the turnover of the promotional sector. The losses of SLPEs are mainly attributable to deficiencies in financial management, planning, implementation of project, running their operations and monitoring.

The North East Industrial and Investment Promotion Policy (NEIIP) declared by the Government of India (GoI) for the north east region provides a number of incentives for the development of the industrial sector. The Tripura Industrial Investment Promotion Incentives Scheme 2007 is another policy of the government. It identifies the core sectors that will act as growth engines, build the human capital, formulate a detailed implementation plan and articulate the communication strategy to convey to potential investors. The development-oriented outlook of the government is matched with a business and investor friendly policy and operative environment is nurturing in the prompt development of the state.

29 Uttar Pradesh

Introduction

Uttar Pradesh (UP) state with a population of over 190 million is located in the northern part of India. The state is considered as most populous state in India, as well as the world's most populous sub-national area. UP is the second largest state-economy in the country with a contribution of 8.17 per cent to India's total GDP and between 2004-05 and 2008-09, the state registered an economic growth of 6.29 per cent. In India, UP has the largest number of small and medium enterprises and the cities like Kanpur, NOIDA, Lucknow, Meerut, Mirzapur, Moradabad, Aligarh, Agra, etc., are emerging as the important industrial hubs. Over the years, the state has observed an all-round growth in industry and infrastructure development. This short paper provides an analysis of the performance of existing SLPEs in UP by focusing on various issues like objectives behind setting up of SLPEs, categorisation, accumulated profits and losses, overview of top profit- and loss-making units, budgetary support to SLPEs and their overall performance. Finally, the paper will also focus on the governmental reforms and measures to strengthen the overall base of these enterprises in the state.

Overview of SLPEs

There were 55 working SLPEs in UP as on March 31, 2008, as per the Comptroller and Auditor General (CAG) (Commercial), 2007-08, Government of India (GoI). About 21 were set up during the Fifth Five Year Plan period (Figure 29.1) and majority of the SLPEs are small- to medium-sized enterprises. On the objectives front, the Government of UP set up these enterprises to accelerate the pace of economic development in the state. The other basic objectives are: (i) to achieve rapid industrialisation in the state, (ii) to reduce the regional imbalances with the development of industrial infrastructure and (iii) exploration of available natural resources.

Figure 29.1

Plan-wise Growth of SLPEs in Uttar Pradesh

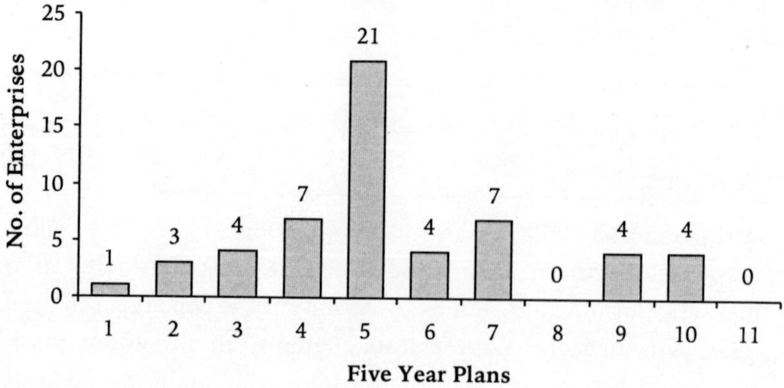

Source: CAG (Commercial), GoI.

Investment

The total investment was ₹ 28,39,942 lakh consisting of paid-up capital and long-term loans in 2007-08 and the capital employed increased by 6.5 per cent in 2007-08 over the previous year. The total number of employees in the SLPEs was 1,30,077, which has registered a minimal growth of 2 per cent in 2007-08. The turnover also increased by 40 per cent from ₹ 19,99,914.34 lakh in 2006-07 to ₹ 28,00,707.04 lakh in 2007-08 (Table 29.1). It is also evident from the table that the increase in the investment, human resources, turnover, etc., brought down the losses from ₹ 49,996.5 lakh in 2006-07 to ₹ 2,32,888 lakh in 2007-08.

Categorisation

The SLPEs are classified into five categories: financial, manufacturing, promotional, utility and welfare enterprises. The number of enterprises functioning under each category is shown in Figure 29.2. The utility and promotional enterprises constitute the largest number followed by enterprises in the manufacturing and welfare sectors. The categorisation of SLPEs reveals that out of 55 enterprises, 14 were in the utility sector, 12 in promotional, 8 each in manufacturing and welfare sectors, and 6 in financial sector. The total investment in all the 55 enterprises grew by only

1.4 per cent from ₹ 28,00,900.24 lakh in 2006-07 to ₹ 28,39,941.95 lakh in 2007-08. The increase in this investment during 2007-08 was mainly due to infusion of capital by the state government in manufacturing and welfare sectors. The investments are financed through the budgetary support from the state and central governments and other financial institutions.

Table 29.1

Overview of SLPEs in Uttar Pradesh

(₹ in lakh)

Particulars	*2007-08*	*2006-07*	*2005-06*
Investment			
Paid-up Capital			
State Government	1709162	1701792	1659459
Central Government	16805.84	16805.84	16019.2
Others	210967.5	213967.5	213960.4
Total	1936935	1932565	1889439
Long-term Loan			
Government	137081.6	119665.2	104453.6
Others	765925.3	748669.9	706390.1
Total	903006.9	868335	811203.7
Total Investment	2839942	2800900	2700643
Capital Employed	1728758	1622566	1978805
Turnover	2800707	1999914	1864238
Net Profit/Loss	-232888	-49996.5	-157362
Accumulated Profit/Loss	-1488102	-1002589	-1021884
No. of Employees	130077	128089	130233
Total Return on Capital Employed	-118258	50358.23	-44941.7
Percentage of Total Return on Capital Employed	1000.23	1061.27	1351.09
Subsidies/Grants			
Central Government	725.35	0	8655.54
State Government	32236.62	14975.54	48408.85
Total	32961.97	14975.54	57064.39

Source: CAG (Commercial) India.

Figure 29.2

Categorisation of SLPEs in Uttar Pradesh

(in numbers)

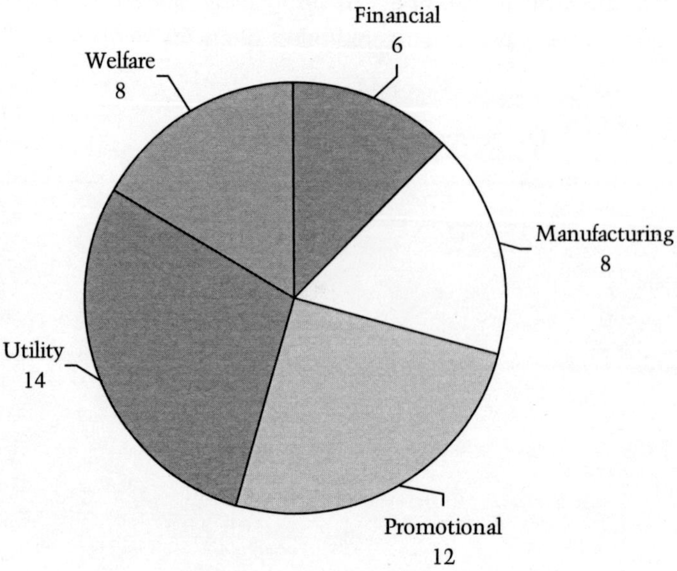

Source: CAG (Commercial) India.

Accumulated Profits and Losses

The accumulated losses of the SLPEs increased from ₹ 10,02,588.92 lakh in 2006-07 to ₹ 14,88,102.2 lakh in 2007-08. The enterprises in promotional and welfare sectors have earned profits to some extent, but the major enterprises in the manufacturing and utility sectors incurred losses (Table 29.2). It has also been observed that all the state electricity boards in western, eastern and central UP are major loss-making enterprises.

Table 29.2

Category-wise SLPEs Accumulated Profit and Loss

(₹ in lakh)

S. No.	Category	2007-08	2006-07	2005-06
1	Financial	-82894.27	-89538.69	-89653.04
2	Manufacturing	-215452.33	-199230.19	-129048.46
3	Promotional	23183.45	8132.79	-10478.66
4	Utility	-1217638.89	-726203.16	-796004.19
5	Welfare	4699.84	4250.33	3300.83
	Total	-1488102.2	-1002588.92	-1021883.52

Source: CAG (Commercial) India.

Top Five Profit-making and Loss-making Enterprises

Tables 29.3 and 29.4 provide information on top five profit- and loss-making enterprises in UP. The enterprises in the promotional and welfare sectors have performed reasonably well; however, the SLPEs in vital segments of infrastructure such as power and other utility enterprises lagged in their performance. The Uttar Pradesh Avas Evam Vikas Parishad, Uttar Pradesh Rajkiya Nirman Nigam Limited and Uttar Pradesh Financial Corporations are ranked first, second and third respectively amongst the profit-making SLPEs. Table 29.3 also indicates that the profit-making enterprises are from the promotional and utility sectors.

Table 29.3

Top Five Profit-making Units (2007-08)

(₹ in lakh)

S. No.	Name of the Enterprise	Amount
1	Uttar Pradesh Avas Evam Vikas Parishad	17858.18
2	Uttar Pradesh Rajkiya Nirman Nigam Limited	7840.07
3	Uttar Pradesh Financial Corporation	6010.07
4	Uttar Pradesh State Industrial Development Corporation Limited	4554.19
5	Uttar Pradesh State Road Transport Corporation	4003.02

Source: CAG (Commercial) India.

The SLPEs in the utility sector are the major loss-making enterprises, especially, the electricity boards in the state are the major loss-incurring units. Table 29.4 indicates that Dakshinanchal Vidyut Vitaran Nigam Limited, Purvanchal Vidyut Vitaran Nigam Limited and Madhyanchal Vidyut Vitaran Nigam Limited are the major loss-making enterprises.

Table 29.4

Top Five Loss-making Units (2007-08)

(₹ in lakh)

S. No.	*Name of the Enterprise*	*Amount*
1	Dakshinanchal Vidyut Vitaran Nigam Limited	59144.06
2	Purvanchal Vidyut Vitaran Nigam Limited	40122.4
3	Madhyanchal Vidyut Vitaran Nigam Limited	38573.67
4	Paschimanchal Vidyut Vitaran Nigam Limited	34961.34
5	Uttar Pradesh Rajya Vidyut Utpadan Nigam Limited	27314.54

Source: CAG (Commercial) India.

The Tables 29.3 and 29.4 indicates that a good performance in manufacturing and financial sectors is needed for rapid growth. Therefore, the state government must concentrate on the development of manufacturing and infrastructure sectors to revitalise the enterprises in other sectors.

Budgetary Support

The performance of the SLPEs does improve when the full reform package is put in place. For example, the government's budgetary support in the form of grants and subsidies, borrowings from banks, etc., has yielded little increase in performance and accountability. Table 29.5 shows the budgetary support to the SLPEs during the year 2005-06 to 2007-08. The grants and subsidies given by the state and central governments constitute the major share in the budgetary support followed by the equity and loans. Table 29.5 also indicates that SLPEs in UP are overdependent on the state government for their operations.

Table 29.5

Budgetary Support to SLPEs (2006-2008)

(₹ in crore)

S. No.	*Particulars*	*2005-06*	*2006-07*	*2007-08*
1	Equity	1478.15	2697.93	3249.73
2	Loans	371.62	263.13	369.51
3	Grants/subsidies	2432.35	2966.29	3402.6
4	Total	4282.12	5927.35	7021.84

Source: CAG (Commercial) India.

The budgetary support to SLPEs is increasing over the years. The grants and subsidies from the state and central governments constitute the major part of budgetary support to the SLPEs followed by the equity. In 2007-08, the state government increased the share of grants/subsidies in the total budgetary support to a tune of 14.7 per cent. The state government is making industrial policies in keeping view the balanced regional development and employment generation.

Figure 29.3

Trends in Budgetary Support

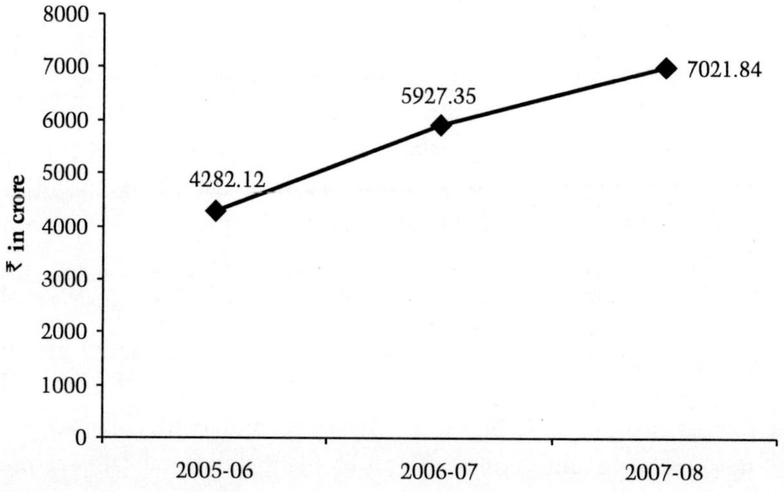

Source: CAG (Commercial) India.

Performance

Of the 48 SLPEs functioning in the state, many are making profits. The SLPEs turnover to state GDP shows the extent of public enterprises activities in the state. Table 29.6 provides the detail of SLPEs contribution to state GDP from 2006-07 to 2007-08.

Table 29.6

SLPEs Contribution to State GDP

(₹ *in crore)*

S. No.	*Particulars*	*2007-08*	*2006-07*
1	Turnover	28007.07	19999.14
2	State GDP	280086	254533
3	Percentage of Turnover to State GDP	9.99	7.86

Source: CAG (Commercial) India.

It can be seen from the table that the percentage of SLPEs turnover to the state GDP has increased from 7.86 per cent in 2006-07 to 10 per cent in 2007-08. According to the Planning Commission, GoI, the enterprises in UP have vast potential but they are growing at a slower rate. This is due to overall declining turnover in general and turnover of promotional enterprises in particular, which also constitute 25 per cent of the total SLPEs in the state. According to the CAG reports and Planning Commission sources, the reasons for the decline and losses that are incurred by these SLPEs are primarily due to the obsolete technology and plant and machinery, recurrent labour problems, lack of trained personnel, adequate procedural checks and labour problems, which are resulting in low-capacity utilisation of plants and low productivity.

Government Reforms and Initiatives

The above discussion indicates that the SLPEs in UP are over-dependent on the state government for their operations. The SLPEs are not competitive primarily due to the using of outdated technology, plants and machinery. In this context, it can be highlighted that UP was one of the first states in the country to attempt comprehensive reforms in the working of SLPEs. The state's Industrial Policy of 1992 highlighted the privatisation of all SLPEs in the state. However, the government's process of privatisation has not been successful due to several reasons. The possible reasons are: lack of clear and well-defined goals; lack of an organised approach; lack of commitment; lack of political will to implement the process of privatisation; lack of appropriate organisational structure; and also lack of technical expertise in the areas of valuation, legal procedures, business, etc.

Conclusion

The SLPEs play a crucial role in the sustainability of fiscal health of the state economy, but majority of the SLPEs are small to medium enterprises which have become unviable in the current competitive environment. Therefore, the state government needs to take initiatives in terms of reforms and measures which are important for the development and better performance of these enterprises in the state. As a part of its initiatives and to enable the SLPEs to sustain in the competitive environment, the government has adopted tools like restructuring, divestment, privatisation and closure of activities in such a way so as to take advantage of the economies of scale and to create viable entities. The government also planning for the revamping of the utilities sector, by providing greater investment support as well as inviting the private sector for participation to deliver quality and efficient services at reasonable rates.

30 Uttarakhand

Introduction

Uttarakhand was formed on the November 9, 2000, as the 27th state of India. Within a short span of its existence, Uttarakhand emerged as a significant destination for investments in manufacturing sector, tourism and infrastructure. The state is laying emphasis on stimulating all three sectors (i.e., agriculture, industry and services) to their fullest potential. The state is rich in mineral deposits like limestone, marble, rock phosphate, dolomite, magnesite, copper, gypsum, etc. There are 1,802 heavy and medium industries with an investment of ₹ 20,000 crore and employs 5 lakh persons. The number of small-scale industries is 25,294 which provide employment to 63,599 persons. Most of the industries are forest based. There are around 54,047 handicraft units. The state is blessed with rare bio-diversity, with 175 rare species of aromatic and medicinal plants. The climatic condition makes it amenable to a variety of commercial opportunities in horticulture, floriculture and agriculture. It has a vast tourism potential in adventure, leisure and eco-tourism with many glaciers, rivers, dense forests and snow-clad mountain peaks. There is abundant availability of quality human resources as the literacy rate is higher than the national average. The Government of Uttarakhand has undertaken several policy measures and incentives in order to encourage inflow of investment into the various sectors of its economy.

Overview of SLPEs

There were 18 working SLPEs in Uttarakhand as on March 31, 2008. About 28 per cent of them were set up during the Tenth Plan period. Nearly 22 per cent of the enterprises are making profits and 66 per cent are incurring losses. The total investment was ₹ 3,360.65 crore consisting of paid-up capital and long-term loans. The capital employed increased by 27.6 per cent in 2007-08. The total number of employees increased from 7,308 in 2006-07 to 21,120 in 2007-08. There is an increase in the turnover by 7.6 per cent from ₹ 1,271.28 crore in 2006-07 to ₹ 1,372.82 crore in 2007-08. The SLPEs in Uttarakhand incurred a loss of ₹ 142.25 crore in 2007-08. The details are given in Table 30.1.

Table 30.1

Overview of SLPEs in Uttarakhand

(₹ in lakh)

Particulars	*2007-08*	*2006-07*	*2005-06*
Investment			
Paid-up Capital			
State Govt.	98745.72	73393.39	54872.49
Central Govt.	1263.14	1263.14	339.14
Others	876.57	2051.5	301.57
Total	100885.4	76708.03	55513.2
Long-term Loan			
Government	56330.65	42783.16	35550.39
Others	178849	151879.2	127598.5
Total	235179.6	194662.3	163148.9
Total Investment	336065	271370	218662
Capital Employed	272780.8	198444.6	188662.1
Turnover	137582	127128	119802.8
Net Profit/Loss	-14225	-7654.45	-6601.74
Accumulated Profit/Loss	-28576.5	-17237.7	-15060.6
No. of Employees	21120	7308	20778
Total Return on Capital Employed	-13982.8	22594.85	12004.4
Percentage of Total Return on Capital Employed	117.74	100.61	71.97
Subsidies/Grants			
Central Govt.	1730.88	700	1751.65
State Govt.	2868.86	1667.55	6264.57
Total	4599.74	2367.55	8016.22

Source: Comptroller and Auditor General (CAG) (Commercial) India, 2007-08.

Categorisation

The SLPEs are classified into five categories: financial, manufacturing, promotional, utility and welfare enterprises. The number of enterprises functioning under each category is shown in Figure 30.1. The manufacturing and utility enterprises constitute the largest number. The increase in the number of enterprises led to an increase in the total investment level. The investment was ₹ 2,713.7 crore in 2006-07 which increased to ₹ 3,360.65 crore in 2007-08. The investments are financed through the budgetary support from the state and central governments and other financial institutions.

Figure 30.1

Category-wise SLPEs in Uttarakhand

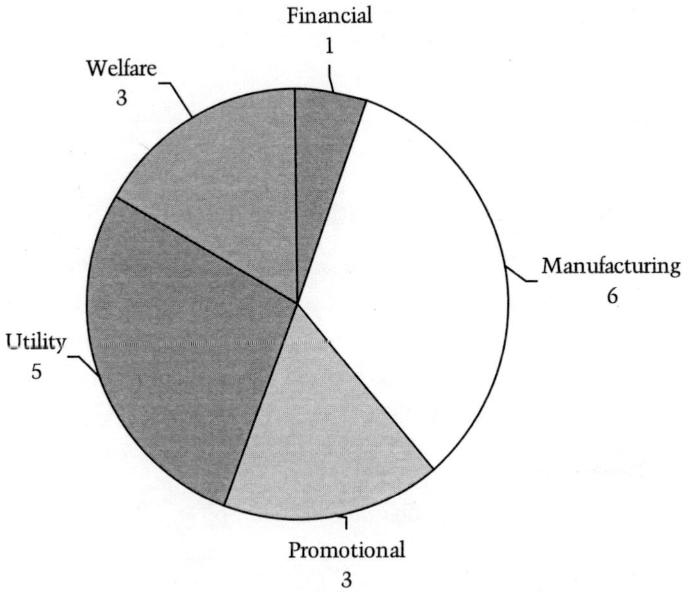

Source: CAG (Commercial) India, 2007-08.

Accumulated Profits and Losses

The accumulated losses of the SLPEs increased from ₹ 172.38 crore in 2006-07 to ₹ 285.77 crore in 2007-08, i.e., an increase of 39.7 per cent. The losses were incurred mostly in the utility and manufacturing sectors. Though enterprises in the financial and the promotional sectors were earning profits, still there is an increase in the accumulated losses (Table 30.2).

Table 30.2

Accumulated Profit and Loss of SLPEs

(₹ *in lakh)*

S.No.	*Particulars*	*2007-08*	*2006-07*	*2005-06*
1	Financial	6277.69	2083.3	8.32
2	Manufacturing	-7563.3	-6040.6	-5663.2
3	Promotional	61.48	-165.49	-95.56
4	Utility	-27366	-13128	-9386.7
5	Welfare	13.15	13.15	76.58
	Total	-28577	-17238	-15061

Source: CAG (Commercial) India, 2007-08.

Top Profit-making and Loss-making Units

Tables 30.3 and 30.4 provide information on top four profit- and loss-making units in Uttarakhand. State Industrial Development Corporation of Uttaranchal, Uttaranchal Jal Vidyut Nigam and Uttarakhand Purv Sainik Kalyan Udham Limited are ranked first, second and third respectively amongst the profit-making SLPEs.

Table 30.3

Top Four Profit-making Units (2007-08)

(₹ *in lakh)*

S. No.	*Name of the Enterprise*	*Amount*
1	State Industrial Development Corporation of Uttaranchal	4184.59
2	Uttaranchal Jal Vidyut Nigam Limited	1472.16
3	Uttarakhand Purv Sainik Kalyan Udham Limited	226.97
4	Uttaranchal Bahudeshia Vitta Evam Vikas Nigam Limited	62.44

Source: CAG (Commercial) India, 2007-08.

Uttarakhand Power Corporation Limited, Uttarakhand Parivahan Nigam and Kichha Sugar Company Limited are the major loss-making units. The power corporation was running in loss due to the delay in the completion of projects and excess in expenditure. Uttarakhand Parivahan Nigam incurred losses owing to lack of coordination between the departments.

Table 30.4

Top Four Loss-making Units (2007-08)

(₹ in lakh)

S. No.	*Name of the Enterprise*	*Amount*
1	Uttarakhand Power Corporation Limited	16828.2
2	Uttarakhand Parivahan Nigam	1511.05
3	Kichha Sugar Company Limited	970.54
4	Doiwala Sugar Company Limited	541.83

Source: CAG (Commercial) India, 2007-08.

Performance

Of the 18 SLPEs functioning in the state, 4 enterprises are making profits and 12 enterprises are making losses. The losses of SLPEs are mainly attributable to deficiencies in financial management, planning, implementation of project, running their operations and monitoring. The state government has taken innumerable measures for the development of these enterprises as well as the economy of the state. A comprehensive Industrial Incentive Scheme 2008 was declared for the promotion of industries in the hilly and remote areas. Under the scheme, infrastructure development, subsidy on capital investment and interest payment, etc., were provided. The government announced a new policy for the promotion of small hydroelectric projects including schemes for renewable sources of energy. Based on the guidelines of the National Agriculture Development Scheme, more provisions are made in agriculture & allied sectors.

The state government is providing assistance in establishing small- and medium-sized agro parks, food parks, etc., which in turn are expected to provide common infrastructure facilities for storage, processing, grading and marketing. Four agri export zones (AEZs) are declared under the AEZ scheme of the Government of India (GoI) for *leechi*, horticulture, herbs, medicinal plants and *basmati* rice. Uttarakhand is included in difficult area category by the Ministry of Food Processing Industry (MFPI) and hence units being set up in Uttarakhand will be eligible for higher incentives under the scheme of MFPI. The government is also providing matching subsidy for projects under various schemes of Agricultural and Processed Food Products Export Development Authority (APEDA), National Horticulture Board (NHB), Ministry of Food Processing Industry (MFPI) and the Natural Medicinal Plant Board (NMPB) subject to a maximum limit of ₹ 20 lakh.

31 West Bengal

Introduction

The economy of the West Bengal is the third largest in India and the state has been recording an impressive and sustained rate of growth over the years. The state has contributed significantly for the development of the national economy. Some of the most vital areas that contributed to the economic development of the state as well as the national economy include food processing, information technology (IT) and information technology enabled services (ITES), leather products, petroleum and petrochemicals, steel and others. The sectors like chemical products, breweries, coal, drugs and pharmaceuticals, electrical and electronics, engineering goods, gems and jewellery, iron and steel, jute products, leather and leather products, locomotives, paper, plastics, software and InfoTech, tea, textiles, and vegetable oils have demonstrated their proven capabilities.

West Bengal is the third largest contributor to India's GDP (about 7.7% of total GDP). The gross state domestic product (GSDP) of West Bengal was ₹ 23,680,620 lakh in 2008-09, registered a growth rate of 6.34 per cent over the previous year 2007-08. The compound annual growth rate (CAGR) from the period 2001-02 to 2008-09 was calculated to be about 7 per cent, which is a great achievement for the state.

Industrial Scenario

The state is well known for its position among one of the leading industrialised states of India. There are up to 10,000 registered units in the state. In order to provide all kinds of assistance to the investors, the state government has opened up "Shilpa Bandhu", a single window agency. There are numerous steel plants in the state apart from the alloy steel plant at Durgapur. The centre has established a number of industries in the areas of tea, sugar, chemicals and fertilisers. The natural resources like tea and jute made West Bengal a major centre for the jute and tea industries not only in the country but also in the world.

Overview of SLPEs

There were 69 working SLPEs in West Bengal as on March 31, 2008. About 60 per cent of them were set up during 1969-1989 Plan periods. Nearly 38 per cent of the enterprises are making profits and 49 per cent are incurring losses. The total investment was ₹ 33,631.67 crore consisting of paid-up capital and long-term loans. The capital employed decreased by 14.36 per cent in 2007-08 over the previous year. The total number of employees declined from 74,790 in 2006-07 to 55,293 in 2007-08 by 35.26 per cent. There was a decline in the turnover by 89.70 per cent i.e., from ₹ 12,494.88 crore in 2006-07 to ₹ 6,586.56 crore in 2007-08. The loss of the SLPEs in West Bengal was ₹ 2.17 crore in 2007-08. The details are given in Table 31.1.

Table 31.1

Overview of SLPEs in West Bengal

(₹ in lakh)

Particulars	*2007-08*	*2006-07*
Investment		
Paid-up Capital		
State Govt.	857635.3	626662.1
Central Govt.	8099.63	8074.63
Others	4260.36	3923.74
Total	869995.2	638660.4
Long-term Loan	0	0
Government	964823	1330405
Others	1528346	1483252
Total	2493172	2813657
Total Investment	3363167	3452318
Capital Employed	2241452	2563319
Turnover	658656.2	1249488
Net Profit/Loss	-217.42	7629.63
Accumulated Profit/Loss	-370332	-946084
No. of Employees	55293	74790
Total Return on Capital Employed	153606.2	203269.5
Percentage of Total Return on Capital Employed	582.5	611.16
Subsidies/Grants	0	0
Central Govt.	8457.04	6209.34
State Govt.	34791.3	137561.2
Total	43414.68	143770.6

Source: Comptroller and Auditor General (CAG) (Commercial) India, 2007-08.

Categorisation

The SLPEs are classified into five categories: financial, manufacturing, promotional, utility and welfare enterprises. The number of enterprises functioning under each category is shown in Figure 31.1. The promotional and manufacturing enterprises constitute the largest number. Over the years, the number of profit-making enterprises is on increase, which led to decrease in the investment level in these enterprises. The total investment was ₹ 34,523.18 crore in 2006-07 which declined to ₹ 33,631.67 crore in 2007-08. The investments are financed through the budgetary support from the state and central governments and other financial institutions.

Figure 31.1

Category-wise SLPEs in West Bengal

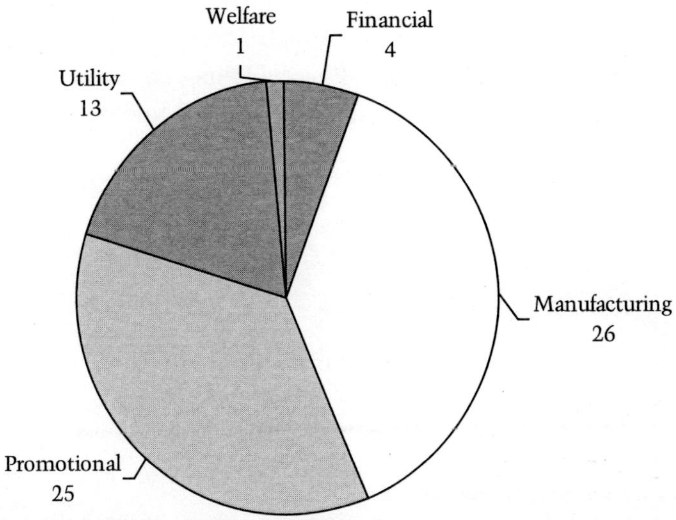

Source: CAG (Commercial) India, 2007-08.

Accumulated Profits and Losses

The accumulated losses of the SLPEs declined from ₹ 9,460.84 crore in 2006-07 to ₹ 3,703.32 crore in 2007-08. The losses declined mostly in the utility sector. The enterprises in the financial, welfare and utility sectors were earning profits, so there is a decline in the accumulated losses.

Table 31.2

Accumulated Profit and Loss of SLPEs

(₹ *in lakh)*

S. No.	*Particulars*	*2007-08*	*2006-07*
1	Financial	43159.9	27159.3
2	Manufacturing	-197926	-200945
3	Promotional	-30055	-29523
4	Utility	-186155	-743369
5	Welfare	643.82	594.13
	Total	-370332	-946084

Source: CAG (Commercial) India, 2007-08.

Top Five Profit-making and Loss-making Units

Tables 31.3 and 31.4 present the top five profit- and loss-making units in West Bengal. West Bengal Infrastructure Development Finance Corporation Limited, The Durgapur Projects Limited and The West Bengal Power Development Corporation Limited are ranked first, second and third respectively among the profit-making SLPEs.

Table 31.3

Top Five Profit-making Units (2007-08)

(₹ *in lakh)*

S. No.	*Name of the Enterprise*	*Amount*
1	West Bengal Infrastructure Deve. Finance Corp. Ltd.	17015.46
2	The Durgapur Projects Ltd.	8970.91
3	The West Bengal Power Development Corp. Ltd.	5809.24
4	West Bengal Housing Infrastructure Deve. Corp. Ltd.	1224.54
5	West Bengal Forest Development Corp. Ltd.	1060.5

Source: CAG (Commercial) India, 2007-08.

Calcutta State Transport Corporation (CSTC), Calcutta Tramways Company Limited (CTCL) and the Kalyani Spinning Mills (KSM) Limited are the major loss-making enterprises. The CSTC incurred losses due to the negligence of the management in the financial and the operations performance of the enterprises, which resulted decline in revenue and increased the cost of production. CTCL incurred losses owing to the lack of maintenance, modernisation, unreliable services and other drawbacks.

Table 31.4

Top Five Loss-making Units (2007-08)

(₹ in lakh)

S. No.	Name of the Enterprise	Amount
1	Calcutta State Transport Corporation	4700.17
2	The Calcutta Tramways Company Ltd.	4220.49
3	The Kalyani Spinning Mills Ltd.	4216.25
4	West Bengal Rural Energy Deve. Corp. Ltd.	3875.13
5	Greater Calcutta Gas Supply Corporation Ltd.	2544.2

Source: CAG (Commercial) India, 2007-08.

Budgetary Support

Table 31.5 shows the budgetary support to the SLPEs during the years 2006-2008. The equity given by the state and central governments constitutes the major share in the budgetary support followed by the loans.

Table 31.5

Budgetary Support to SLPEs (2006-2008)

(₹ in crore)

S. No.	Particulars	2005-06	2006-07	2007-08
1	Equity	181.91	725.96	1552.37
2	Loans	908.78	1254.9	907.82
3	Grants/subsidies	990.12	380.85	348.96
4	Total	2080.81	2361.71	2809.15

Source: CAG (Commercial) India, 2007-08.

The budgetary support to the SLPEs increased over the years. The budgetary support increased from ₹ 2,080.81 crore in 2005-06 to ₹ 2,361.71 crore in 2006-07. The budgetary support increased by 16 per cent in 2007-08. There is a steep increase in the budgetary support as the government has raised its equity and loans to the enterprises. The government invested in the form of equity and loans to around 27 SLPEs in the state to carry out day-to-day activities as well as to meet their wage bills.

Government Initiatives and Performance

Of the 69 SLPEs functioning in the state, 26 enterprises are making profits and 34 enterprises are making losses. The remaining 9 enterprises have not finalised their accounts. There is an increase in the turnover of the manufacturing and the welfare sectors. There is a decline in the turnover of the utility sector by 57 per cent in 2007-08. The losses of SLPEs are mainly attributable to deficiencies in financial management, planning, implementation of project, running their operations and monitoring. The Public Sector Enterprises Restructuring Programme was initiated in 2003 with the support of the Department for International Development (DFID) which was divided into two phases. Under the first phase (2003-2007), 19 SLPEs were closed, 4 restructured, 4 were disinvested and another 4 are under the restructuring process. The second phase (2008-2011) will cover mainly the SLPEs in the power and transport sectors and 23 SLPEs in other sectors.

The Early Retirement Scheme was introduced under the first phase which was opted by 6,000 employees who were covered under health insurance. Nearly 3,000 persons completed training as per the Social Safety Net Programme (SSNP) and 35 per cent were redeployed. The government has taken innumerable measures for the rapid industrial development by providing better infrastructural facilities. The government is emphasising on setting up of industries in the backward areas, industrial growth zones and special industrial parks. The food processing, bio-technology, rubber, polymer, gems and jewellery and fertiliser industries are given prominence in the state. The government is providing incentives for the private and joint sector for the upgradation and development of industries.

Annexures

Table A-1

Overview of SLPEs in India, 2007-08

Particulars	*Total Investment (in lakh)*	*Capital Employed (in lakh)*	*Turnover (in lakh)*	*Net Profit/Loss (in lakh)*
Andhra Pradesh	312155.47	3299853.25	3692254.47	35781.4
Arunachal Pradesh	1020.35	5003.48	571.55	-477.27
Assam	279350.69	256446.66	203855.97	-25745.93
Bihar	797490.96	335598.76	158826.29	-90791.8
Chhatisgarh	315177.73	229639.04	449372.52	30652.9
Delhi	1368018.24	228834.96	301971.45	-114691.53
Goa	46124.43	56319.5	34958.78	3242.91
Gujrat	4650681.3	5864148.35	3469648.18	157189.19
Haryana	1744965.74	1466800.31	-48624.49	-240503.48
Himachal Pradesh	383746.03	352015.59	351283.17	-7146.24
Jammu & Kashmir	473440.04	359592.09	20266.99	-127415.18
Jharkhand	367328.87	498902.8	36490.13	-12139.54
Karnataka	4781328.57	5159088.11	2821805.05	99602.06
Kerala	724985.892	1323272.75	1030267.29	20135.84
Madhya Pradesh	1471107.4	1230938.12	1280073.27	-166865.29
Maharashtra	2829741.42	2999259.62	3433669.52	-66638.22
Manipur	4349.64	2628.11	674.99	80.2
Meghalaya	137240.83	93222.76	36547.49	-1076.76
Mizoram	9295.58	5973.59	179.19	-534.29
Nagaland	65.19	34.63	3.7	-1.33
Orissa	802180.19	937945	725007.35	127943.8
Punjab	1404504	1794741.14	1755245.29	-185996.74
Rajasthan	2281140.5	2897982.76	1576781.02	38074.77
Sikkim	23572.54	93712.03	6768.49	-41.16
West Bengal	1056856.37	130799.92	17105.21	43159.94
Tamil Nadu	1871970.2	1775843.76	3249442.52	-152310.94
Tripura	48802.2	78983.55	25007.37	-950.48
Uttarakhand	300306.86	275718.47	141850.46	14435.75
Uttar Pradesh	2839941.95	1728757.91	2800707.04	-232888.36
India	31326889.18	33482057.02	27572010.26	-855915.78

Source: Comptroller and Auditor General (CAG) (Commercial) India (2007-08).

Table A-2

Overview of SLPEs in India, 2007-08

Particulars	*Accumulated Profit/Loss (in lakh)*	*No. of Employees (in nos.)*	*Total Return on Capital Employed (in lakh)*	*Percentage of Total Return on Capital Employed (in %)*	*Subsidies/ Grants (in lakh)*
Andhra Pradesh	-276920.76	262054	208708.61	6.32	556657.73
Arunachal Pradesh	-287.36	550	-477.27	0	20
Assam	-101892.66	38778	-15066.17	88.41	31782.49
Bihar	-277875.51	22326	224.3	138.52	2300
Chhatisgarh	72851.53	19677	52273.43	618.38	194690.7
Delhi	-1085179.19	33777	15508.4	134.37	10184.17
Goa	-17385.39	3242	8749.86	19.5	8516.32
Gujrat	191625.97	58633	313011.07	295.56	340364.11
Haryana	38757	33510	124.16	0	269681.94
Himachal	-100261.58	16661	13810.2	85.71	8101.73
Jammu & Kashmir	29977	189661	74.43	0	7952.96
Jharkhand	-26545.4	9042	23672.81	673.53	127258
Karnataka	214831.38	168811	250962.97	787.96	257031.12
Kerala	-113345.05	86305	109082.79	-12.98	30886.22
Madhya Pradesh	603246.31	35675	-44452.47	2.44	132726.11
Maharashtra	-455613.66	218389	160086.95	5.34	50091.5
Manipur	46.79	224	172.12	62.7	0
Meghalaya	-52412.69	5313	2731.01	14.72	3713.78
Mizoram	-3330.21	266	-319.93	0	317.71
Nagaland	-12.25	226	1.33	203	9.8
Orissa	25753.45	27508	175114.6	663.43	40825.95
Punjab	-760600.94	87131	-40367.66	127.09	291849.41
Rajasthan	24887.4	91173	175417.66	188.95	153661.4
Sikkim	-9483.69	1135	715.79	34.97	0
West Bengal	274	121548	18.43	0	291849.41
Tamil Nadu	-935393.69	255316	-7527.83	497.74	236574.68
Tripura	-21039.73	6587	-324.23	32.71	50.13
Uttarakhand	20114.17	0	-14193.58	0	4599.74
Uttar Pradesh	-1488102.2	130077	-118257.64	1000.23	32961.97
India	-4503316.96	1923598	1269474.14	5668.6	3084659.08

Source: CAG (Commercial) India (2007-08).

Bibliography

Atmanand (1997). *Productivity and Management of State Level Public Enterprises in India.* India: Mittal Publications.

Basu, Prahlad K. (2008). "Reinventing Public Enterprises and their Management as the Engine of Development and Growth", in *Public Enterprises: Unresolved Challenges and New Opportunities*. New York: United Nations.

IPE (2009). *IPE Database on State Level Public Enterprises*. Hyderabad: Institute of Public Enterprise.

Maheshwari, B.L. (1981). "State Level Public Enterprises: Issues of Autonomy and Performance", *Economic and Political Weekly* 16(48): 165-71.

Mathew, P.M. (1990). "State Sector Enterprises in Kerala", *Economic and Political Weekly* 25(24/25): 1349-51.

Mendon, D.K. (ed.) (1964). *Industrial Mysore 1964*. Mumbai: Tainudi Publication.

Menon, Parvathi (2003). "Karnataka's Agenda", *Frontline* 20(1): 18-31, January.

Mishra, R.K. (2006). "Privatisation of State Level Public Enterprises: A Macro Analysis", in R.K. Mishra and Ch. Lakshmi Kumari (eds.), *State Level Public Enterprises: Past and Present*. New Delhi: Anmol Publications.

Mishra, R.K. and Ch. Lakshmi Kumari (2006). *State Level Public Enterprise: Past and Present.* New Delhi, India: Anmol Publications.

Planning Commission (2007). *Eleventh Five Year Plan 2007-12: Volume III*. New Delhi: Planning Commission, Government of India.

Rajeev, Meenakshi (2004). "Reforms in State Public Enterprises in Karnataka: A Review", *Working Paper 148.* Bangalore: Institute for Social and Economic Change.

Sankar, T.L., R.K. Mishra and R. Nandagopal (1990). "Can State Level Public Enterprises in India Earn a Rate of Return?", *Economic and Political Weekly* 25(47): 169-74.

———. (1991). "Working of State-Level Manufacturing Public Enterprises: Promise and Performance", *Economic and Political Weekly* 26(21): 42-6.

Sankar, T.L., R. Nandagopal and R.K. Mishra (1989). "State Level Public Enterprises in India: An Overview", *Economic and Political Weekly* 24(8): 33-40.

Website:

Department of Public Enterprises. *http://dpe.nic.in/*

State Development Reports. Available at *http://planningcommission.nic.in/plans/sdrbody.html*